D#: 197311

GOD AND
THE POETS

GOD AND THE POETS

The Gifford Lectures, 1983

BY

DAVID DAICHES

CLARENDON PRESS · OXFORD

1984

Oxford University Press, Walton Street, Oxford OX2 6DP
London New York Toronto
Delhi Bombay Calcutta Madras Karachi
Kuala Lumpur Singapore Hong Kong Tokyo
Nairobi Dar es Salaam Cape Town
Melbourne Auckland
and associated companies in
Beirut Berlin Ibadan Mexico City Nicosia

Oxford is a trade mark of Oxford University Press

Published in the United States
by Oxford University Press, New York

British Library Cataloguing in Publication Data
Daiches, David
God and the poets.
1. Poetry—History and criticism   2. God
in literature   3. Christian poetry—History
and criticism
I. Title
809.1'9382   PN1083.G62
ISBN 0-19-812825-8

Set by DMB (Typesetting), Oxford
and printed in Great Britain
at the University Press, Oxford

PREFACE

When I was honoured with an invitation from Edinburgh University to give the Gifford Lectures for 1983, I was sent an extract from the Deed of Foundation by Lord Gifford (who died in 1887) and was thus for the first time given an opportunity to learn what the Gifford Lectures were really supposed to be about. The lectures, said Lord Gifford, were to be for 'promoting, advancing, teaching, and diffusing the study of Natural Theology in the widest sense of that term, in other words, the Knowledge of God, the Infinite, the All, the First and Only Cause, the One and Sole Substance, the Sole Being, the Sole Reality, and the Sole Existence, the Knowledge of His Nature and Attributes, the Knowledge of the Relations which men and the whole Universe bear to Him, the Knowledge of the Nature and Foundation of Ethics or Morals, and of all Obligations and Duties thence arising'. The Deed of Foundation went on to say: 'The lecturers appointed shall be subject to no test of any kind, and shall not be required to take any oath, or to emit or subscribe any declaration of belief, or to make any promise of any kind; they may be of any denomination whatever or of no denomination at all; they may be of any religion or way of thinking, or, as is sometimes said, they may be of no religion, or they may be so-called sceptics or agnostics or freethinkers, provided only that the "patrons" will use diligence to secure that they be able reverent men, true thinkers, sincere lovers of and earnest inquirers after truth.'

On receiving this brief I decided not to enquire too closely into my fitness to meet Lord Gifford's criteria, and I turned my mind to the question of how I, with my particular interests and knowledge, could best carry out his intentions. I was of course aware that many distinguished Gifford Lecturers had interpreted the brief with extreme latitude, and I could not in fact recollect a single one who had treated specifically the subject of natural theology, which I take to mean the examination of the proofs of God's existence and the clues to his nature provided by the natural world. Indeed, it might be said that in Edinburgh, where I delivered the lectures, natural theology in that sense had been given the *coup de grâce* by David Hume's *Dialogues on Natural Religion*. I studied Hume's *Dialogues* with Professor Kemp Smith in the second ordinary philosophy class of Edinburgh University in 1932-3, when Kemp Smith was in the middle of editing them, and knowledgeable readers of my third chapter may be able to detect traces of this. But I am a literary critic and a literary historian, not a philosopher, and I did not feel it appropriate for me to provide in these lectures a philosophical criticism of natural theology in any of its branches. After considerable reflection I decided that if I discussed the way God emerged in a number of different poets from biblical times to the present I could bring in natural theology very precisely in considering the way certain poets saw God in Nature, but I could also range further afield and discuss not only devotional and other kinds of religious poetry but also poetry in which God is significant by his presence in oblique or indirect ways or even by his absence.

The problem of what poets to choose solved itself quite easily. I had to begin with the Book of Job, the classic dramatic poem of theodicy, and as I am lucky enough to have been brought up with a knowledge of biblical Hebrew from earliest childhood (my father having been a Hebrew scholar who had written a Hebrew grammar) I thought it especially appropriate that I should devote my first lecture to talking about Job with special reference to the Hebrew text. Milton's *Paradise Lost* was another obvious choice. I have been much involved with Milton in my years as a university teacher of English literature (in fact ever since that great Edinburgh Professor of English, H.J.C. Grierson, lectured to us on him) and here was a splendid opportunity to pull my thoughts together on the subject of Milton, God, and man. I also felt that it would be appropriate for me to discuss some medieval Hebrew poetry involving attitudes to God, if only because this was not a field hitherto touched by any Gifford Lecturer. I could not leave out Dante, and mention of Dante gives me an opportunity of paying tribute to another influential teacher of Edinburgh University in my undergraduate days, the man who first introduced me to Dante in Italian. This was John Purves, who during the years when I studied for an Honours English degree at Edinburgh conducted, as Lecturer in Italian (there was no Chair in those days), a class in Italian language for English students, in the belief that every serious student of English literature should know Italian, and followed this with a class in Dante and one in later Italian poetry. Some half-dozen students of English literature took advantage of these classes, of whom I was sensible enough to be one; they gave me a foundation on which to build.

The other poets I chose seemed appropriate in different ways. I thought it right that in the year when Edinburgh University was celebrating the 400th anniversary of its founding I should devote some attention to Scottish poets, and as it happened James Thomson (both James Thomsons indeed), Burns, and James Hogg illustrated with great clarity different aspects of my theme, while the twentieth-century modern Scottish poets, Edwin Muir and Hugh MacDiarmid, were obvious choices if I were to explore certain kinds of visionary poetry in modern Scotland. As both these poets were my friends, I found it especially satisfying to pay tribute to their work in this way.

The lectures are presented here exactly as they were delivered. I have not tried to alter the tone of the speaking voice, or to exclude the sense of personal contact with an audience. I have done so partly because several people who heard the lectures have urged that I should, and partly because I myself prefer to keep the sound of the spoken voice in my writing. If the result is random touches of impressionism and the lack of interruption of the text by detailed bibliographical references, that, too, is part of my intention. These lectures are presented as reflections rather than excavations.

Edinburgh   DAVID DAICHES
July 1983

ACKNOWLEDGEMENTS

Quotations of poems and of extracts of poems by Hugh Mac-Diarmid, Edwin Muir, and Wallace Stevens are used by permission as indicated below:

Hugh MacDiarmid. Reprinted by permission of the executors of the MacDiarmid estate.

Edwin Muir. Reprinted by permission of Faber and Faber Ltd. from *The Collected Poems of Edwin Muir*, and by permission of Oxford University Press, Inc., New York, from *Collected Poems* by Edwin Muir, copyright © 1960 by Willa Muir.

Wallace Stevens. Reprinted by permission of Faber and Faber Ltd. from *The Collected Poems of Wallace Stevens*, and by permission of Alfred A. Knopf, Inc. from *The Collected Poems of Wallace Stevens*.

CONTENTS

1   THE BOOK OF JOB:
GOD UNDER ATTACK

The only completed successful epic poem in the English language is Milton's *Paradise Lost*. It differs from all the other great epics of the Western world by having a precise theological aim: to justify the ways of God to men. Milton is here using the word 'justify' in the third definition of the word given in the *Oxford English Dictionary*: 'to show . . . to be just or in the right.' That God, who is by definition just and right as well as omnipotent, should require justification by a human poet seems somewhat extraordinary. To justify the ways of men to God might seem a reasonable undertaking, but to justify the ways of God to men implies that there is prima facie evidence that God deals unjustly with men and that God is in need of a defence. Further, Milton sees that defence as especially needed by religious people, by committed Christians indeed, that 'fit audience though few' to whom his poem is addressed. It seems therefore that he considered the account of God's dealings with men as revealed in the Old and New Testaments to be in itself an inadequate explanation of the inconsistencies between the concept of an all-good and all-powerful God and the facts of human experience. Milton went further than that. In his posthumously published Latin work on Christian doctrine he stated boldly that the facts of human experience 'have compelled all nations to believe, either that God, or that some evil power whose name was unknown, presided over the affairs of the world'.[1] He considered the view that evil ruled the world to be 'as unmeet as it is incredible', yet he conceded that it was warranted by simple observation of what happens to men in the world.

The dilemma is of course an ancient one: how to reconcile human suffering, especially the suffering of the righteous, with the existence of an omnipotent God of justice and love. This question of theodicy, the vindication of God's justice, is quite

---

[1] *The Christian Doctrine*, Book I, Chapter II: the translation here and in other quotations from this work is that of Bishop Sumner, London, 1825.

separate from the question of God's existence, which Milton took for granted just as the authors of the Bible took it for granted. In the Psalms there is never any question of God's existence, apart from the remark at the beginning of Psalm 53: 'The fool hath said in his heart, there is no God.' There is no argument; the atheist is simply a fool. (The Hebrew word used here, *naval*, can really mean either.) But there is much anguish over God's dealings with men, over the sufferings of the virtuous and the prosperity of the wicked. While many of the Psalms assure us that the righteous shall prosper and the wicked shall be destroyed—the very first Psalm is an eloquent statement of this position—there are as many that ask the question put most directly in Psalm 94: 'Lord, how long shall the wicked triumph?' There is the cry for help in Psalm 12: 'Help, Lord; for the godly man ceaseth; for the faithful fail among the children of men.' There is the bitter question of Psalm 22: 'My God, my God, why hast thou forsaken me?' Every kind of variation is played on the theme of the good man left to misery and suffering and the wicked man prospering. 'The wicked walk on every side, when the vilest men are exalted' is the desperate conclusion of Psalm 12. Side by side with these protests we find great outbursts of confidence that the Lord will in the end reward the good and punish the bad, most strongly of all in Psalm 37, which goes so far as to make a statement, said to derive from experience but which in fact seems to run counter to what we experience in the real world: 'I have been young, and now am old; yet have I not seen the righteous forsaken, nor his seed begging bread.' If Milton could have accepted this, he would not have felt the need to write *Paradise Lost*.

Milton's justification of God was, at least on the surface, based on his explanation of the fact that God endowed the first man with free will and that punishment of him and his descendants for the abuse of that free will was perfectly just, while the Christian scheme of redemption, that allowed a tiny minority of the world's inhabitants throughout history to gain salvation through acceptance of Christ's sacrifice, was a mitigation of strict justice by love. What Milton really made of this argument in *Paradise Lost* is a topic I wish to return to later. At this stage I am concerned with the general problem of theodicy as it impinged on poets who accepted without question the existence of an omnipotent God. The Psalms mingle praise of God, anguished questioning of his justice, and confidence that all will be well in the end. The praise and the confidence represented what might be called the orthodox position. The implications of this position could be disturbing. If God did really punish the wicked and reward the virtuous, then it would seem that misfortune was evidence of prior wickedness, and happiness and prosperity a sign of virtue. The Mosaic injunctions as formulated in Chapter 28 of Deuteronomy make it clear that obedience to God's law will bring happiness and prosperity and disobedience will bring misfortune and suffering. The Hebrew prophets saw the sufferings of their people, especially their conquest and exile, as punishment for wrongdoing. Now it is one thing to say that society as a whole will suffer in the long run if its members persistently practise injustice, but it is quite another to see individual, personal fortune as the direct consequence of the individual's degree of virtue, so that the virtuous prosper and the wicked do not. As I have noted, experience contradicts this and has been acknowledged to contradict this from ancient times. This has not prevented religious leaders from proclaiming this doctrine. It was precisely because they did so that people were lead to reflect on the relation between doctrine and experience and the problems of theodicy that they raised. It was the poets who first raised the question, which was simply this: We do not dispute God's existence or his power; but what about his justice? This was the question posed by the greatest of all the poets of theodicy, the author of that remarkable dramatic poem we call the Book of Job.

The Book of Job uses an old folk-tale for its beginning and its ending. The folk-tale is of a good and prosperous man who was tried by every kind of misfortune and affliction but who in spite of everything bore all misfortunes patiently and without losing faith in God until he was rewarded by a restoration of all he had lost and increased happiness and prosperity. The first and last chapter of the existing Book of Job tell this story, and there is evidence that it is considerably older than the main part of the book, not only from the style and language, which belongs to simple folk-history, but also from the phrase 'the patience of Job' which antedates the book as we have it and refers to the simple tale of trust and patience rewarded. Between the opening and closing brackets, that derive from the old folk-tale, a great poet has inserted a dramatic poem of extraordinary richness and vitality, powerful in imagery, often difficult in language, bold in thought, that confronts the question of the justice of God's dealings with men. Job here is not the patient Job of the folk-tale. Far from it: he is angry to the point of blasphemy and keeps demanding an explanation from God.

The opening chapter introduces us to Job as a virtuous, God-fearing man who is also rich and highly esteemed. He is not an Israelite, but located in the land of Uz, which cannot be definitely identified. The scene changes to God reviewing his angels, among whom is the Satan (note the definite article: Satan is not yet a proper name, nor does it refer to the Devil: the Satan was an angel, the accuser, the prosecuting counsel among the angels whose task was to find out and report on evil acts in the world). God boasts about the exemplary virtue of his servant Job, and the Satan replies that it is easy to be virtuous when everything goes well: change his good fortune to misery and see what happens. God gives the Satan permission to do this. Job loses all his possessions and his children, but he does not lose his trust in God. Then, at a further assembly in Heaven, the Satan points out that Job has not been afflicted in his physical person, and God gives him permission to afflict Job in this way, so long as his life is spared. So Job is afflicted with sore boils and is both unsightly and in agony. This virtuous man has now lost all his possessions, his children, and his physical well-being: he is disgusting to look at. His impatient wife tells him to curse God and die, but Job replies: 'Shall we receive good at the hand of God and not receive evil?', and repudiates the advice. He sits on an ashpit outside his house and mourns in silence. Three friends then come to visit him, and respect his grief by waiting in silence for seven days and nights. At the end of that period Job begins to speak. And with the lyric lamentation that bursts from his lips we enter into the real, poetical Book of Job.

The compact energy of Job's lyric cry is difficult to render in English. According to the Authorized Version, the lament begins:

Let the day perish wherein I was born
And the night in which it was said, There is a man child conceived.

That is twenty-two words to eight of the original Hebrew, which moreover contains a pun, on the words יֹאבַד ('let it perish') and אִוָּלֵד ('I was born'). Something of the forceful brevity of the original is suggested by Marvin Pope's[2] rendering:

> Damn the day I was born,
> The night that said, 'A boy is begot.'

He regrets having been born, and wishes that at least he had died at birth. In the grave there is release from suffering (Job knows nothing of an afterlife) and true equality: there kings and princes lie at rest with their humble subjects.

> There the wicked cease from troubling,
> And there the weary are at rest.

At this stage Job is not arguing; he is lamenting. He yearns for death, which comes not, and seeks after it more than for hidden treasure. His way is hidden: God has fenced him in. The lament ends with a sentence that is not adequately rendered by the King James translators:

$$\text{לֹא שָׁלַוְתִּי וְלֹא שָׁקַטְתִּי}$$
$$\text{וְלֹא־נַחְתִּי וַיָּבֹא רֹגֶז.}$$

Eight powerful and incisive Hebrew words, which can perhaps be rendered:

> I have no rest, no peace;
> What has come is agony.

Job is not yet directly arraigning God's justice: he is expressing his total disillusion with life and his wish for death. His complaint is answered by Eliphaz, the first of the three friends. Like his two colleagues, he speaks for the orthodox view that God punishes the wicked and rewards the virtuous here on earth. At first he tries to reassure Job that if he is really virtuous, things are bound to turn out all right for him:

> Is not your fear of God your confidence,
> Your hope your upright conduct?

---

[2] *The Anchor Bible: Job*. Introduction, Translation, and Notes by Marvin H. Pope, New York, 1965.

> Remember, pray, whoever perished being innocent,
> Or where were the upright cut off?

Well, Job was innocent and upright, and he has, in a sense, 'perished' and been 'cut off'. Eliphaz seems to realize that this *argumentum ad hominem* won't work, so he turns to generalities before introducing a new note. In the sight of God, *nobody*, not even the angels, can be truly virtuous. This thought is expressed as a strange, visionary insight, that came to him in the dead of night, when a spirit seemed to pass before him, so that his bones shook and his hair stood on end, and a voice proclaimed

> Shall mortal man be more just than God?
> Shall a man be more pure than his maker?
>
> Behold, he put no trust in his servants:
> And his angels he charged with folly.
>
> How much more them that dwell in houses of clay,
> Whose foundation is in the dust,
> Who are crushed before the moth.

The *frisson* that accompanies this vision and this mystical utterance cannot alter the fact that it does not help Job. If all the creatures created by God are imperfect in his sight, that might well be a reflection on God's handiwork. The point is, by what guilt of their own did they become imperfect? (Milton faces, albeit briefly, the question of hereditary guilt, when he has Adam admit that his progeny will be justly held guilty because of his offence, but such a thought is far from the author of the Book of Job.) Eliphaz does not himself seem to be sure of the implications of his vision for Job's case, for he leaves this point abruptly and goes on to cite a number of proverbial sayings about God frustrating the wicked and saving the virtuous poor from the hand of the mighty. Again, this does not seem to be relevant to Job's case. He then moves on to a quite new point, which would be relevant to Job's case if Job accepted it.

> Behold, happy is the man whom God correcteth;
> Therefore despise not the chastening of the Almighty.

The implications of this are not pursued, however, and Eliphaz goes on to cite in traditional form cases of the goodness and care of God. Here the rendering in the Authorized Version conveys the feel of the original very well:

He shall deliver thee in six troubles,
Yea in seven shall no evil touch thee.

In famine he shall redeem thee from death,
And in war from the power of the sword. . . .

At destruction and famine thou shalt laugh,
Neither shalt thou be afraid of the beasts of the earth. . . .

Thou shalt know also that thy seed shall be great,
And thy offspring as the grass of the earth.

Thou shalt come to thy grave in a full age,
Like as a shock of corn cometh in in his season.

'You are going to be all right, Job' is what these concluding
sentences of Eliphaz's speech amount to. But Job is in no mood
to be comforted by traditional proverbs. In his reply he ignores
Eliphaz's arguments and continues his lament. He says that
God has grievously persecuted him and again says that he
wishes for death. As for his friend's words, they are like the
wadis of Syria and Palestine, rushing torrents in the rainy season but dry and desolate in the summer when the traveller
needs them. Nothing that has been said is of any help to him in
his misery. He pleads with God to remember that his life is but
a breath and that it is time God let him go. Only in death will
he escape from God's watchful persecution. Here Job embarks
on a daring parody of the Psalmist's view of God's watchful
care for man. He is now directly arraigning God.

> Am I a sea, or a sea-monster,
> That thou settest a watch over me?

In Psalm 8 the author takes pride and comfort in the fact that
God is mindful of man:

> When I consider thy heavens, the work of thy fingers,
> The moon and the stars which thou hast ordained,
>
> What is man, that thou art mindful of him?
> And the son of man that thou visitest him?
>
> For thou hast made him a little lower than the angels,
> And hast crowned him with glory and honour.

This is directly parodied by Job:

> What is man, that thou shouldst magnify him,
> And that thou shouldst set thy heart upon him?

And that thou shouldst visit him every morining,
And try him every moment?

Will you never look away from me,
Nor let me alone till I swallow down my spittle?

This is being hounded by a Hound of Heaven indeed.

Even if he has sinned, Job goes on—and it is made clear later that if he has, God has not told him what he is charged with—how can that affect God: 'What difference does it make to you, man watcher?' That terrible phrase נֹצֵר הָאָדָם, 'man watcher', spat out in fury, completes the reversal of the Psalmist's view.

This second speech of Job modulates at its conclusion into a minor key. If he has committed some sin of which he is unaware, why will not God forgive him and let him die in peace? The last line, וְשִׁחֲרְתַּנִי וְאֵינֶנִּי —'you would look for me then and I wouldn't be there'—has a curious note of self-pity, as though he is saying, 'You'll be sorry then, God.' It always reminds me of that passage in Joyce's *Portrait of the Artist as a Young Man* when the young Stephen, lying sick in the school sick-bay, contemplates his own death and funeral and thinks how sorry the school bully will be *then*.

The second of the three visitors, Bildad, then answers Job. He begins with less courtesy than Eliphaz had shown, being clearly shocked by Job's attitude as revealed in his second speech. But all he has to say is to repeat the traditional view that God punishes sinners and rewards the virtuous. He has not the slightest doubt that a simple law of retribution prevails. If you were pure and upright, he tells Job, you would not be suffering now. For that, he says, is the view of all former generations. Can we know better than our ancestors? With considerable poetic liveliness he plays variations on the theme of God's retributive justice, concluding with words reminiscent of one of the moods of the Psalms:

Behold, God will not cast away a perfect man,
Neither will he help the evil-doers;

Till he fill thy mouth with laughing,
And thy lips with rejoicing.

They that hate thee shall be clothed with shame,
And the dwelling-place of the wicked shall come to nought.

Bildad has not yet reached the position where he says that Job must have been an evil-doer or he would not be suffering as he is—that is to come later. True, he begins by saying that if he had been virtuous he would not be suffering now, but he seems to backtrack in his conclusion, when he reassures Job that if he has been virtuous all will eventually be well with him. He does not quite see which horn of the dilemma to come to rest on.

In his reply Job totally ignores Bildad's arguments. His object is to draw up an indictment of the way God administers human affairs. He does not need to be persuaded of God's power, of which Eliphaz had painted a vivid picture. He can describe that as eloquently as anyone:

> Who removeth the mountains and they know it not,
> Who overturneth them in his anger.
>
> Who shaketh the earth out of her place,
> And the pillars thereof tremble.
>
> Who commandeth the sun, and it riseth not,
> And sealeth up the stars.
>
> Who alone spreadeth out the heavens,
> And treadeth upon the waves of the sea.
>
> Who maketh the Bear, Orion and the Pleiades,
> And the chambers of the south.
>
> Who doeth great things past finding out,
> Yea, marvellous things without number.

He is a powerful God, and also a hidden God, a *deus absconditus*; אֵל מִסְתַּתֵּר as the Deutero-Isaiah called him:

> Lo, he goeth by me, and I see him not;
> He passeth on also, but I perceive him not.

No one can call God to account.

> Who will say unto him: 'What doest thou?'

How can he argue before God, who could break him with a tempest and would not suffer him to take his breath? Then come the crux of Job's case:

> If it is a matter of strength, yes, he is mighty.
> But if it is a matter of justice, who could arraign him?

אִם לְכֹחַ אַמִּיץ הִנֵּה

3. וְאִם לְמִשְׁפָּט מִי יוֹעִידֵנוּ

God, supreme in power, is subject to no court; no one can
make a legal plea before him. Further, God can force the innocent to confess guilt:

> Even though I be righteous, mine own mouth shall condemn me;
> Though I be innocent, he shall prove me perverse.

> I am innocent: I care not for myself;
> I despise my life.

> It is all one: therefore I say,
> He destroys the innocent and the wicked.

> If the scourge slay suddenly,
> He will laugh at the calamity of the innocent.

> The earth is given into the hand of the wicked;
> He covereth the faces of the judges thereof.
> If not he—then who?

אִם־לֹא אֵפוֹ מִי־הוּא·

God is responsible. Job does not take a Manichaean position,
but accepts the traditional view that God is the creator of *everything*, including evil. The Deutero-Isaiah had made this point
quite explicitly:

> I form the light, and create darkness.
> I make peace, and create evil.
> I the Lord do all these things.

It is not Satan, the Prince of Darkness, who creates evil. God is
all-powerful and is the creator of everything that exists. But
Isaiah did not draw Job's conclusions, which is that if God did
it all, he is responsible, he is to blame.

Job now goes further. One cannot get justice from God
because there is no one above him to act as arbitrator between
him and his suffering creature. I am found guilty already, he
says: 'why then do I labour in vain?' He makes the point quite
precisely in an incisive sentence לֹא יֵשׁ בֵּינֵינוּ מוֹכִיחַ there is
between us no *mochiaḥ*, no umpire, who can listen impartially to
both points of view. The urgency and the passion rise as Job now

---

3 Accepting Pope's emendation of יוֹעִידֵנִי to יוֹעִידֵנוּ

pleads with God to let him approach him and plead his cause.

> Let him take his rod away from me
> And let not his fear terrify me:
> Then would I speak and not fear him.

Let God stop exercising power and exercise justice. Let him at least tell Job what the case against him is. 'Make me know wherefore thou contendest with me.' He goes on to ask God if he knows what it is like to be a man.

> Hast thou eyes of flesh,
> Or seest thou as man seeth?
>
> Are thy days as the days of man,
> Are thy years as man's days,
>
> That thou inquirest after mine iniquity
> And searchest after my sin,
>
> Although thou knowest that I am not guilty
> And there is no escape out of thy hand?

After all, he goes on in a moving passage expressing the mystery of conception and uterine growth, it was God who made him:

> Remember, I beseech thee, that thou hast made me as the clay;
> And wilt thou bring me into dust again?
>
> Hast thou not poured me out as milk,
> And curdled me like cheese?
>
> Thou hast clothed me with skin and flesh
> And knit me with bones and sinews.

Yet all the time, Job continues, God was hiding his dark intention of ultimately reducing him to misery, regardless of whether he were wicked or virtuous. What then was the use of his having been born?

> Wherefore then hast thou brought me forth out of the womb?
> Would that I had died, and no eye had seen me!
>
> I should have been as though I had not been
> And been carried from womb to grave.
>
> Are not my days few? Let me be,
> Turn away from me so that I may have a little comfort
>
> Before I go, never to return,
> To a land of darkness and gloom,

> A land of thick darkness, like darkness itself,
> Of utter gloom without order
> Where the light is as darkness.

The third visitor, Zophar, now enters the argument. He denounces Job's insistence on his guiltlessness as arrogant boasting. God knows what he is doing and can spy iniquity when men think he does not see. If Job repents of the evil he *must* have done, then all will be well with him. At this point Zophar falls into the standard poetic description of the security and hope of the virtuous and the plight of the wicked. Job's reply shows his exasperation. It begins with bitter irony:

> No doubt but ye are the people,
> And wisdom shall die with you.

He knows the truth as well as they, and the truth is that he has become a laughing-stock to his neighbours. Those who are comfortable are not concerned with the misfortunes of others.

> The tents of robbers prosper
> And they that provoke God are secure.

The very beasts of the field and birds of the air know this. They know that it is God who has done all this:

> Who knoweth not in all these
> That the hand of the Lord hath wrought this?

This again is a bitter parody of a common thought in earlier biblical literature. But it is not wonders that the hand of the Lord hath wrought so far as Job is concerned: it is injustice. God's power is in fact destructive:

> Behold he destroyeth, and it cannot be built again;
> He shutteth up a man, and there can be no opening.

> Behold, he withholdeth the waters, and they dry up;
> Also he sendeth them out, and they overturn the earth.

> With him are strength and victory,
> The deceived and the deceiver are both his.

> He leadeth counsellors away stripped
> And of judges he maketh fools.

Job goes on to list God's activities in loosening and binding kings, in stripping priests and taking away the reason of elders, in making nations great and then destroying them, in making imbeciles of wise men and leaders, in short of playing havoc with human order so that men grope in darkness without light and stagger like drunkards. He does not need to be told about God's activities by his friends.

Then comes a remarkable turn in Job's argument, when he makes a point he reiterates in subsequent chapters of the book:

> Notwithstanding I would speak to the Almighty,
> And I desire to reason with God.

This is to emerge as a central demand of Job's. He wants a chance to put his case before God. Even if God destroys him, he will persist in this demand. He is determined to put his case *against* God *to* God. He cries:

> Yes, he may slay me: I have no hope:
> But I will argue my case to his face!

(This is the famous passage that has been traditionally rendered: 'Though he slay me, yet will I trust in him: but I will maintain mine own ways before him.' The Hebrew word for 'not' and the Hebrew word for 'to him' sound the same but are spelled differently. The text has the word, *lo*, spelled *lamed aleph*, meaning 'not', but the Masoretes, the Jewish scribes who edited and vocalized the Hebrew text of the Bible, put in the margin that though the text read *lo* meaning 'not' it should be read as though it were *lo* spelled *lamed vav* meaning 'to him' or 'in him', thus avoiding what seemed to them a blasphemous implication. Generations of readers have as a consequence taken this sentence as a ringing declaration of faith in the midst of despair. Unfortunately, as all scholars agree, the meaning of the Hebrew *lo ayachel* is certainly 'I have no hope' or something like that and cannot mean 'I will trust in him'. Job is saying that even though God pursues him to death, he will insist on his right to confront him and present his case.)

Job goes on to appeal to God to hear him. He has, he says, prepared his case and he knows that he would be acquitted if given a chance to present it. The language here is the language of the lawcourts. It has been suggested that Job's question 'Who is he that will contend with me?' is the opening formula of a plaintiff in a lawcourt. Certainly the Hebrew word trans-

lated as 'contend' has the connotation of 'dispute' in the legal
sense, and the noun from the same root can mean both a quar-
rel and a lawsuit.

After the recital of this legal formula, Job appeals to God:

> Withdraw thy hand far from me,
> And let not thy terror make me afraid.
>
> Then call thou, and I will answer,
> And let me speak and answer thou me.
>
> How many are mine iniquities and sins?
> Let me know my transgression and my sin.

As he makes even clearer later, Job feels that if he is being punished for something he has done, he has the right to know what
he is accused of. To be found guilty and punished before the
case has even come to court and without the accused having
any idea of what he is charged with is not in accordance with
justice, still less so when, as in this case, the accuser, the judge,
and the punisher are the same individual.

Job then breaks into an elegiac lyric:

> Man that is born of a woman
> Is of few days, and full of trouble.

Man's life passes like a shadow. (One is reminded of Pindar's
description of human life as σκιᾶς ὄναρ, the dream of a
shadow). If a tree is cut down it will sprout again, but 'man
lieth down and riseth not'. The thought strikes him that *if* there
were a life after death there might be an opportunity then for
a dialogue with God:

> If a man die, may he live again?
> All my weary days I would wait
> Till my relief should come.
>
> Thou wouldst call and I would answer thee
> Thou wouldst care for the work of thy hands.
>
> But as things are, thou numberest my steps,
> Thou dost not even wait for my sin.

This moving expression of a *rapprochement* with God after death
represents a momentary hope, which soon fades. For Job there
is no recompense for the sorrows of this world in the next. This
speech of Job's ends with his relapsing into total pessimism,
and on this note the first cycle of speeches concludes.

The second cycle begins with Eliphaz elaborating once again
the traditional view. No man is perfect, therefore no man has a
right to complain if suffering comes upon him. As for the sinner, even when he seems to be at peace and happy he is inwardly
troubled. Eliphaz ends by giving an eloquent description of the
ultimate fate of the wicked. It is interesting that in presenting
the traditional morality against which the Book of Job is a pro-
test the author puts passionate and persuasive poetry into the
mouths of Job's friends. They are not made to seem feeble or
stupid, any more than Milton's fallen angels are made to seem
feeble or stupid when he presents them debating. This helps to
give the book great dramatic power. The positions put forward
by Job's friends are deeply felt and often expressed with moving
conviction. But they never really meet the points that Job
makes. 'Sorry comforters are ye all' says Job to the three of
them after Eliphaz has concluded his second speech.

After dismissing his friends' 'windy words' and remarking
that he could speak like that too if their positions were reversed,
Job turns again to God, charging him with having betrayed
and broken him even though he is innocent. He cries out:

> O earth, cover not thou my blood,
> And let my cry have no resting-place.

But then his note changes quite remarkably. He turns from
God the arbitrary wielder of power to God the dispenser of
justice. Surely there is somebody on high who will bear witness
on his behalf:

> Even now, behold, my witness is in heaven
> And he that testifieth for me is on high.

The single word here rendered as 'he that testifieth for me' is
an Aramaic word, *sahed*, meaning 'witness', which is also the
meaning of the noun in the previous line. Marvin Pope renders
it 'guarantor' and comments: 'Many exegetes take the heavenly witness here to be God himself, the God of justice and
steadfast love, to whom Job appeals against the God of wrath.
. . . In this context, however, the heavenly witness, guarantor,
friend can scarcely be God who is already Accuser, Judge, and
Executioner.' This view seems to be borne out by the verses
that immediately follow:

> Are my friends my intercessors?
> It is to God that my mine eye poureth out tears,
>
> That he would set a judge between a man and God
> As a man does for his neighbour.

But the Hebrew text here has clearly suffered damage and the precise meaning cannot be certain. It seems fairly clear that although the thought starts off as meaning something like 'Rather God than *these* friends, in spite of everything', it moves on to suggest the need for a judge (just as he had earlier asked for an umpire) between man and God, a third party who would arbitrate between them. Always hovering in the background, however, is the thought that the powerful God who is responsible for Job's suffering is also the God of justice and of love and there must be some way of appealing from one to the other. It is as though Job cannot reconcile himself to a view of God as simply hostile. He does not pursue this line any further at this stage, but returns to elegy:

> For the few years pass,
> And I go the way of no return.
>
> My spirit is broken, my days are spent:
> It is the grave for me.

This speech of Job's ends in total gloom:

> Where then is my hope?
> My hope, who can see it?
>
> It goes down with me to Sheol,
> Together we shall descend to the dust.

The movement to and fro between indignation and elegy, between defiance and self-pity, and more fundamentally between despair and hope, is part of the fabric of the poetry of Job's speeches. When we think of his passionate cry, 'O earth cover not thou my blood', we may be reminded of the last great cry of Prometheus at the end of Aeschylus' play *Prometheus Bound*, ἐσορᾷς μ' ὡς ἔκδικα πάσχω—'You see me, how I suffer injustice.' But the situation there is really very different from that in Job. Prometheus is being punished by Zeus for something that he did, and although Prometheus does not consider his action in bringing fire down to man as a crime, Zeus does, and Prometheus knows that Zeus does. Further, Zeus is shown clearly as a tyrant, and there is the suggestion in the play that the time will eventually come when he will modify his position and learn to abate his tyranny. Aeschylus' play is not an enquiry into the bases of Zeus' activity. The Book of Job *is* an enquiry into the bases of God's activity. It is an enquiry forced on Job by his own experience and is conducted not so much by an amassing of evidence as by the fluctuations of feeling.

Bildad now replies again to Job, evincing no sympathy whatever for his plight nor understanding of his arguments. He is outraged by Job's attitude, and having expressed his outrage he goes on to repeat the old argument. If Job suffers, he must have erred: the wicked always meet an appropriate fate. He describes the fate of the wicked at some length, with the implication that what has happened to Job shows him to have been wicked. Job then rounds on him and asks how long will he torment him with words. He is *not* guilty and is not being punished for wickedness. He can get no answer from God. אֲשַׁוַּע וְאֵין מִשְׁפָּט —'I cry out, but there is no justice.' God has destroyed him absolutely. His kinsfolk and friends have failed him, his servants have abandoned him, his wife finds him loathsome, even street urchins despise him. And those whom he loved have turned against him. In desperation he turns from crying to God to crying to his three friends.

> Have pity on me, have pity on me, O ye my friends,
> For the hand of God hath touched me.
>
> Why do ye persecute me like God
> And are not satisfied with my flesh?

He wishes that his words were written down and permanently graven in rock. He does not say why, but the implication is that he wishes his case to be on permanent record. But the thought turns at once into something different and surprising:

> But as for me, I know that my vindicator liveth
> And that he will at last arise upon earth.

The traditional translation here of course is the famous 'I know that my Redeemer liveth', which has all sorts of theological implications read into it. But the Hebrew word גֹּאֵל, *goel*, means

.a vindicator; it is used in Deuteronomy and 2 Samuel to denote
the nearest kinsman whose duty it was to exact vengeance in a
blood feud. By extension, God came later to be called '*goel
Yisrael*', generally rendered Redeemer of Israel, but it seems
clear that it is the original basic meaning that is intended here.
The real question concerns the identity of the vindicator in
whom, in an unexpected surge of confidence, Job affirms his
belief. Is he saying, 'I know that eventually someone will arise
to defend me against the injustices from which I suffer at God's
hand', or is he saying in what Robert Gordis in his edition of
the book[4] calls 'a moment of mystical ecstasy' that God himself
will in the end vindicate him? Scholars differ, as they differ too
on the interpretation of the difficult and evidently textually
corrupt passage that follows. The Authorized Version renders it

> And though after my skin worms destroy this body,
> Yet in my flesh shall I see God.

The New English Bible takes whole passage in a legal sense and
translates:

> But in my heart I know that my vindicator lives
> and that he will rise at last to speak in court;
> and I shall discern my witness standing at my side
> and see my defending counsel, even God himself . . . .

This reading is based on emendations of a partly unintelligible
text. Marvin Pope renders:

> Even after my skin is flayed
> Without my flesh I shall see God

Robert Gordis renders:

> Deep in my skin this has been marked,
> and in my very flesh do I see God.

It is a pity that at such a critical moment in the expression of
Job's changing attitudes the text is so obscure. But there seems
little doubt that Job is expressing confidence in his vindication,
and whether we interpret the *goel* to be God or to be some other
vindicator, in the end he will have a satisfactory face-to-face
resolution of the matter with God. Goridis's rendering of what

---

[4] *The Book of God and Man: A Study of Job*, by Robert Gordis, Chicago and London,
1965, p. 87.

he considers a transitory moment of mystical vision in the present tense ('and in my very flesh do I see God') is in conformity with his view that this is a fleeting moment of ecstasy that Job cannot sustain. One cannot be certain of this. It does however seem to be a moment of visionary confidence in the ultimate happy ending, and it is true it is not sustained.

Zophar now answers with a speech that is an impressive weaving together of thoughts found in the Psalms and elsewhere in biblical literature of the shortness of the triumph of the wicked and their eventual condign punishment. Even if the sinner is not immediately punished he will be inwardly miserable as he awaits his inevitable doom. It is a picture presented with passionate eloquence, but of course it is of no help to Job. Job's reply simply denies outright the truth of Zophar's statements. The wicked prosper; they do not suffer; look around and you will see.

> How oft is the lamp of the wicked put out?
> That their calamity cometh upon them?
> That God distributeth pains in his anger?

The wicked die unpunished, at ease and quiet. There is no correlation between what happens to a man and his degree of virtue. The good and evil in the end lie down alike in the dust and the worms get them both. His friends can ask rhetorically where one can find the flourishing houses of the wicked. Just ask any traveller, says Job: you cannot deny their evidence. Why then do you indulge in all this vain talk?

At this point in the Book of Job as we have it a third cycle of speeches commences, which has suffered a great deal of dislocation so that editors have had to reassign passages to different speakers. But some points emerge clearly. Eliphaz now says that he is convinced that Job must have committed grave misdeeds and in fact goes on to catalogue them. He *must* have done these evil things—he has oppressed the poor, refused food and drink to the hungrey, sent widows and orphans away empty-handed. God has seen all this and has punished him. Then, in what is almost a parody of the great Old Testament prophets' pleas to the people of Israel to repent of their sins and return to the Lord, he goes on to beseech Job to return to the Almighty and put away his unrighteousness. If he does so, all will be well with him. Job's reply again presents his complaint that he is given no opportunity of presenting his case before God. His search for a confrontation with God gets steadily more passionate:

> Oh that I knew where I might find him,
> That I might come even to his seat!

But wherever he may go, he cannot see him. God remains in darkness. On earth the rich oppress the poor and a great cry rises up from the oppressed, but God seems to think nothing wrong. Murderers, thieves, and adulturers flourish. In the end, all die. There follows a fine poetic evocation of God's power as evinced in nature that seems to belong to Bildad although in the text as we have it it is attributed to Job, another account of the doom of the wicked that seems to belong to Zophar, the splendid poem on Wisdom, an independent poem that has got into the Book of Job either by deliberate insertion or in some other way, and a speech of Job full of nostalgia for the days of his prosperity and happiness. Finally, Job delivers his last great speech of self-vindication, consisting of a series of what are known as 'oaths of clearance'. He swears that he has not committed any of the crimes he lists. This speech has been called Job's 'Code of a Man of Honour'. He has always dealt generously and properly with women, he has dealt fairly with servants, he has been considerate towards the poor and helped the widow and the orphan, for he has always been aware of the basic equality of all human beings. He has never been proud or complacent with respect to his wealth. He has never acted deceitfully. He has been generous to his enemies and has never turned away a stranger from his door. He concludes:

> Oh that I had one to hear me!
> Behold my signature, let the Almighty answer me,
> And let my adversary write a document.

The last line means 'let the prosecutor draw up his indictment'. The traditional rendering, 'Oh that mine adversary had written a book', obscures the legal implication of the wish. The word rendered 'adversary' is אִישׁ רִיבִי —'the man of my dispute', 'the man of my law-case', his opponent or prosecutor in a court of law. It is Job's final demand for a confrontation with God.

At this point in the text as we have it there come the speeches of Elihu, a newcomer to the scene. Almost all scholars see this as a later interpolation, and I am sure that it is. It certainly interferes with the tremendous dramatic impact of the theophany, which should surely follow immediately on Job's ending his speeches. 'The words of Job are ended', is how he concludes his last speech. Then suddenly (if we omit the Elihu interpolation) Job gets, in a quite unexpected way, the confrontation with God that he has been demanding. It is overwhelming. In an outburst of spectacular cosmic poetry the voice of God hammers home the point that the goings-on in the universe are far beyond the wit of man to comprehend; that nature was not created for man and has its otherness and its mysteries that man can never penetrate; and it is against this background of miracle and mystery which dwarfs man that the problems of human suffering must be set. The Authorized Version communicates the power and the poetry of the divine declaration, although sometimes we may prefer a more pithy statement, such as Pope's 'Tell me, if you know so much' for the Authorized Version's 'Declare, if thou hast understanding'. But here is how it begins:

Then the Lord answered Job out of the whirlwind, and said,

Who is this that darkneth counsel
By words without knowledge?

Gird up now thy loins like a man;
For I will demand of thee, and answer thou me.

Where was thou when I laid the foundations of the earth?
Declare, if thou hast understanding.

Who hath laid the measures thereof, if thou knowest?
Or who hath stretched the line upon it?

Whereupon are the foundations thereof fastened?
Or who laid the corner-stone thereof?

When the morning stars sang together,
And all the sons of God shouted for joy?

Or who shut up the sea with doors,
When it broke forth, as if it had issued out of the womb?

When I made the cloud the garment thereof,
And thick darkness and swaddling-band for it,

> And brake up for it my decreed place,
> And set bars and doors,
>
> And said, Hitherto shalt thou come, but no further;
> And here shall thy proud waves be stayed?
>
> Hast thou commanded the morning since thy days,
> And caused the dayspring to know his place;
>
> That it might take hold of the ends of the earth,
> That the wicked might be shaken out of it?

The divine voice goes on and on, insisting again and again on the mysterious dimensions of the universe.

> Hast thou perceived the breadth of the earth?
> Declare, if thou knowest it all.

The nature of light, the coming of rain, desert and blossoming ground—these and other natural mysteries are presented in a series of what almost might be called bullying rhetorical questions:

> Hath the rain a father?
> Or who hath begotten the drops of dew?
>
> Out of whose womb came the ice?
> And the hoar-frost of heaven, who hath gendered it? . . .
>
> Canst thou bind the chains of the Pleiades,
> Or loose the bands of Orion?
>
> Canst thou bring forth Mazzaroth in his season?
> Or canst thou guide Arcturus with his sons?
>
> Knowst thou the ordinances of heaven?
> Canst thou set the dominion thereof in the earth?

The voice goes on to ask whether Job understands how lions hunt, how lion cubs get their food, how the raven is provided for, at what time wild goats bear their young. The natural world is full of wonders which have nothing to do with man. It is in this context that we get the famous description of the war-horse:

> Hast thou given the horse strength?
> Hast thou clothed his neck with thunder? . . .
>
> He paweth in the valley, and rejoiceth in his strength:
> He goeth on to meet the armed men.

> He mocketh at fear, and is not affrighted;
> Neither turneth he back from the sword . . .

> He swalloweth the ground with fierceness and rage:
> Neither believeth he that it is the sound of the trumpet.

> He saith among the trumpets, Ha, ha;
> And he smelleth the battle afar off,
> The thunder of the captains, and the shouting.

This is Job's answer from God.

> Moreover the Lord answered Job, and said,

> Shall he that contendeth with the Almighty instruct him?
> He that reproveth God, let him answer it.

Job is hammered into submission. He replies (and I am modifying the Authorized Version here):

> Behold, I am of small account; how can I answer thee?
> I lay my hand upon my mouth.

> Once have I spoken, but I will not answer again;
> Yea, twice, but I will proceed no further.

God, however, brushes aside Job's submissive reply and goes on to bombard him further with rhetorical questions illustrating God's power and the unfathomable mysteries of the universe he created. But also for the first time there is something that sounds very like an implicit admission that evil exists in the world and God has not been able to conquer it fully. After throwing at Job the questions

> Wilt thou also make void my judgement?
> Wilt thou condemn me, that thou mayst be justified?

> Hast thou an arm like God?
> Or canst thou thunder with a voice like him?

God goes on to ask Job if he, Job, can cope with the problem of putting the wicked in his place. If Job can do that

> Then will I also confess unto thee
> That thine own right hand can save thee.

It is almost as though God is saying that He, God, finds the problem of evil intractable, and that if Job can solve it, he can take over. But the thought is not lingered over, for the voice goes on immediately to one of the most powerful and memorable of all the descriptions in these divine speeches, the account of behemoth (which some commentators take to be the hippopotamus and others to be a purely mythical monster) and leviathan (sometimes held to denote the crocodile but more likely also a mythical monster). The pictures given here of wondrous beasts leading their own strange lives with their enormous size and total imperviousness to any human attempt to control them once more stress that the universe was not created for man, that there are elements in it far from his concerns, his power, and his comprehension. The poetic imagery in these passages is positively startling, and the range of vocabulary remarkable.

Job's questions concern the relation between power and justice. They are not directly answered by the divine voice. Ethical questions are answered by—almost, one might say, are subsumed in—natural description. What emerges is that the only real answer to Job's question is that there is no answer. The universe is more complicated than man can ever hope to understand, so he had better refrain from discussing the principles on which it is run. The position taken up here is totally opposed to the Wordsworthian view of Nature, that has had so much influence on the British imagination. The mind of man and principles of Nature are not intimately fitted to each other, as Wordsworth believed. There are no moral principles to be deduced from Nature, and no comfort to be derived from it, apart from the dubious comfort of realizing its mysterious otherness. This sense of the otherness of the natural world appears intermittently in later European literature; it is given splendid expression in Hugh MacDiarmid's *On a Raised Beach*; but it can hardly be said to play a central part in the European literary imagination.

At the end of God's second speech Job submits. He has had his confrontation and there is no more to say. But then comes the surprise. The divine voice turns to Eliphaz. 'My wrath is kindled against thee and against thy two friends: for ye have not spoken of me the thing that is right, as my servant Job hath.' The repetition of pious platitudes about the wicked being punished and the righteous rewarded, and the inference that porsperity indicates virtue and suffering indicates sin are offensive to God. Job may have been rash and arrogant to challenge

God to an explanation, but at least in doing so he showed his awareness of the mysteries and paradoxes of God's creation. God's reply emphasizes the mystery and the paradox. Man must recognize them, but he must accept that he cannot fathom them. The solution to Job's problem, in fact, is subsumed in *wonder*.

There are some apparent contradictions in all this. God simultaneously reproves Job for speaking in ignorance and says that he is right in what he says about God. The Hebrew word here rendered as 'right' is *nechonah*, correct. Is the implication that it is correct to challenge neat traditional views about God's ways even though the challenger is bound to be ignorant of what really lies behind those ways? Perhaps so. But it is interesting that this coda, which follows God's speeches and Job's submission, is in prose, not poetry, and precedes the prose folk-tale conclusion in which Job is restored to more than his former good fortune.

The real theodicy is in the words of the divine voice. But is it really a justification of the ways of God to men? Nothing is said about God's justice. The problem remains insoluble. Certainly Milton, who knew and admired the Book of Job and regarded it as a 'brief epic', cannot have regarded it as a satisfactory justification of the ways of God to men. His own justification was intended to be wholly rational. The paradox of having a rational theodicy presented by means of an epic poem is something I shall look at in my second lecture.

2 *PARADISE LOST:* GOD DEFENDED

At the beginning of *Paradise Lost*, in announcing his theme, Milton invokes the 'Heav'nly Muse', the Muse that inspired Moses on Mount Horeb and Mount Sinai so that he was able to write the Pentateuch, which included the story of the Creation and the Fall of man. Milton is going to go further: he is pursuing 'things unattempted yet in Prose or Rhyme', which means that he is attempting something more than the biblical story as told in Genesis and more than other poets achieved in their creation poems, such as Joshua Sylvester's *Divine Weeks and Works*, a version of the epic poem on the Creation by the French Pro-testant poet Guillaume de Salluste Seigneur du Bartas (though *Paradise Lost* shows some local influence of Sylvester's poem). Milton also appeals to the spirit of God that brooded over the waters in the primal act of creation: he is actually comparing himself not only to Moses writing the Pentateuch but to God creating the universe. At the beginning of Book III, before moving the scene to Heaven and introducing God as a speaker, he makes a further appeal for divine inspiration and again com-pares his poetic task to the original divine creation of the uni-verse out of the void.

Familiarity, if not with *Paradise Lost* at least with the fact of its three-hundred-year existence as a classic of our literature, may have dulled our sense of the audacity of Milton's aim. He seeks divine inspiration to speak for God—not as the Hebrew prophets did, by saying 'Thus saith the Lord' and then introducing God's words as mediated through the prophet, but directly, by putting long speeches into God's mouth in the course of an account of what actually occurred in Heaven. Of course Milton knew that he was *inventing* God's speeches and he knew too that he was rendering divine matters in the only way intelligible to limited mortal faculties. At the same time he believed that God really had made man in his image and that, as the Bible makes clear, God is capable of grief and anger and regret and can be in need of rest and refreshment. In his book *Christian Doctrine* he cites biblical evidence for this, and asks: 'Why should we hesitate to conceive of God according to what he has not hesitated to declare explicitly respecting himself?' So he felt that in some sense God's behaviour in Heaven as he rendered it in his epic gave a real impression of what actually occurred, and it was because he wanted his imagination to apprehend it accurately that he sought divine inspiration. He must have believed that he got it.

God's voice in *Paradise Lost* is very different from God's voice in Job. It is not the voice of mysterious power proclaiming the inconceivable wonders of creation and its indifference to the needs of individual man. It is the voice of what might be called defensive rationality. God knows that he has a case to answer and he tries to answer it by irrefutable logic. It is exactly the same logic that Milton used in his *Christian Doctrine*. A major part of Milton's and God's case is that God created man with free will, and that by the abuse of free will man rendered himself justly liable to punishment. God's foreknowledge that man would act in this way does not absolve man, for foreknowledge is not compulsion:

God of his wisdom determined to create men and angels reasonable beings, and therefore free agents; at the same time he foresaw which way the bias of their will would incline, in the exercise of their own uncontrolled liberty. What then? Shall we say that this foresight or foreknowledge on the part of God imposed on them the necessity of acting in any definite way? No more than if the future event had been foreseen by any human being. For what any human being has foreseen as certain to happen, will not less certainly happen than what God himself has predicted. Thus Elisha foresaw how much evil Hazael would bring upon the children of Israel in the course of a few years, 2 Kings viii. 12. Yet no one would affirm that the evil took place necessarily on account of the foreknowledge of Elisha; for had he never foreknown it, the event would have occurred with equal certainty, through the free will of the agent. So neither does anything happen because God has foreseen it; but he is acquainted with their natural causes, which, in pursuance of his own decree, are left at liberty to exert their legitimate influence . . . .[1]

Milton sums up his long discussion of this matter by concluding: 'we must hold that God foreknows all future events, but that he has not decreed them absolutely: lest all sin should

---

[1] Book I, Ch. III.

be imputed to the Deity, and evil spirits and wicked men should be exempted from blame.' Adam's fall, he says, 'was certain, but not necessary, since it proceeded from his own free will, which is incompatible with necessity'. I do not propose here to enter into the morass of argument about free will and determinism, except to say that it *is* a morass and that Milton's argument slides over some central points. You cannot compare, for example, human foreknowledge that somebody will act in character with God's foreknowledge, if only for the reason that God created the persons involved and men did not. Elisha had not created Hazael, and could know what he would do without feeling responsible. But man was God's creation, and the workman is responsible for his workmanship. I shall return to Milton's position on this question, but first I want to quote the self-justifying words Milton put into God's mouth in Book III of *Paradise Lost*. He is addressing the Son, and is telling him that Satan, the fallen angel, is on his way to the newly created world to tempt man with lies so that he will disobey God's command:

> And now
> Through all restraint broke loose he wings his way
> Not far off Heav'n, in the Precincts of light,
> Directly towards the new created World,
> And Man there plac't, with purpose to assay
> If him by force he can destroy, or worse,
> By some false guile pervert; and shall pervert;
> For man will hark'n to his glozing lies,
> And easily transgress the sole Command,
> Sole pledge of his obedience: So will fall
> Hee and his faithless Progenie: whose fault?
> Whose but his own? ingrate, he had of mee
> All he could have; I made him just and right,
> Sufficient to have stood, though free to fall.
> Such I created all th' Ethereal Powers
> And Spirits, both them who stood and them who faild;
> Freely they stood who stood, and fell who fell.
> Not free, what proof could they have givn sincere
> Of true allegiance, constant Faith or Love,
> Where only what they needs must do, appeard,
> Not what they would? what praise could they receive?
> What pleasure I from such obedience paid,

When Will and Reason (Reason also is choice)
Useless and vain, of freedom both despoild,
Made passive both, had servd necessitie,
Not mee. They therefore as to right belongd,
So were created, nor can justly accuse
Thir maker, or thir making, or thir Fate;
As if Predestination over-ruled
Thir will, dispos'd by absolute Decree
Or high foreknowledge; they themselves decreed
Thir own revolt, not I: if I foreknew,
Foreknowledge had no influence on their fault,
Which had no less prov'd certain unforeknown.

The Son intervenes, and pleads that man should not be totally
lost as a consequence of the foreseen disobedience. God agrees:

All hast thou spok'n as my thoughts are, all
As my Eternal purpose hath decreed:
Man shall not quite be lost, but sav'd who will,
Yet not of will in him, but grace in me
Freely vouchsaft; once more I will renew
His lapsed powers, though forfeit and enthrall'd
By sin to foul exorbitant desires;
Upheld by me, yet once more he shall stand
On even ground against his mortal foe,
By me upheld, that he may know how frail
His fall'n condition is, and to me ow
All his deliv'rance, and to none but me.
Some I have chosen of peculiar grace
Elect above the rest; so is my will:
The rest shall hear me call and oft be warnd
Thir sinful state, and to appease betimes
Th' incensed Deitie while offerd grace
Invites . . . .

God goes on to say that prayer, repentance, and obedience will
always help man to gain God's ear, and that he will place in
man 'My Umpire *Conscience*' who, if hearkened to, will help
man to achieve grace. (How this is related to the elected few,
chosen by God simply because it is his will and not through any
merit of theirs, is not made clear.) He adds that only the
hardened sinners are to be totally excluded from God's mercy.
(But it is clear from Michael's history of the world as told in
brief to Adam after the Fall, in Books XI and XII, that the

hardened sinners will be the large majority of men throughout all human history.)

God then goes on to say that because of Adam's foreseen (but not necessary) disobedience, 'he with his whole posterity must die', and he continues

> Dye hee or Justice must; unless for him
> Some other able, and as willing, pay
> The rigid satisfaction, death for death.

The Son offers to give his life for man, and so leave open a way of grace for that tiny minority of Adam's descendants who will behave so as to deserve it.

This gives the core of Milton's justification of the ways of God to men. Men suffer deservedly for their abuse of free will in Adam's original disobedience, and divine love mitigated the punishment, at least for those in the proper state of mind to take advantage of Christ's sacrifice. But there is something odd going on here. When God says that man must die, or else Justice must, unless someone else is willing to 'pay / The rigid satisfaction, death for death', is he really saying that Justice demands that if a crime has been committed *someone*—it does not really matter who, so long as it is someone—must die? Is this really the Christian view of the Atonement? It is as though a judge, after a man has been found guilty, addresses the court and says that the condemned man must be executed unless some innocent member of the public would offer to be executed instead, in which case justice would be done equally well. And what is the Justice that must die unless the offender or else some innocent bystander be put to death? Is it something above God, constraining him? In putting the matter the way he does, Milton seems to show a certain fundamental lack of sympathy with the Christian doctrine of vicarious atonement. Yet it does give him an opportunity of giving fine poetic expression to the claims of love, by the difference in tone and cadence and the throb of compassion that runs through the words of the Son as compared with those of God the Father.

Having disposed, in words spoken by God himself, of the free-will and foreknowledge argument, Milton is left with one major problem. Given that it was just to punish Adam and Eve for their disobedience, why should all their posterity be held guilty too? Why should the first sin taint all mankind? Interestingly Milton, except for the remark about Justice already quoted, does not attempt to have God defend this. It is Adam who defends it. Yet it is hardly a defence, more a statement, an acceptance. This is what Adam says after the Fall:

> Ah, why should all mankind
> For one mans fault thus guiltless be condemn'd,
> If guiltless? But from mee what can proceed,
> But all corrupt, both Mind and Will deprav'd,
> Not to do onely, but to will the same
> With me? how can they then acquitted stand
> In sight of God? Him after all Disputes
> Forc't I absolve . . . .

This is a curiously perfunctory argument, if indeed argument it is. Because of Adam's disobedience, all his descendants *must* be depraved in mind and will. The nature of this necessity remains obscure. But there is also the further point about the nature of guilt, which Milton nowhere takes up. One might concede that men are all born corrupt; but if that is how they are born, how can they be held *responsible* for their corruption, be considered guilty, and be punished for it? Of course there is a whole library of theological debate about this, and in Edinburgh of all places a reminder of this is hardly needed.

It is Milton's fault that at certain points in *Paradise Lost* the reader is forced into speculation along such lines as these. For he, either through God or through Adam, presents a case in a highly rational manner, so that it is open to rational objection if we do not agree. Sometimes Milton gives away a whole section of his logical edifice, as when he reveals that Christ 'our second *Adam*' is an improved model of man whose will was created stronger than Adam's was. Early in *Paradise Regained* God tells his angels that Satan will now be faced with a much more formidable opponent than Adam:

> He now shall know I can produce a man
> Of female Seed, far abler to resist
> All his sollicitations . . . .

The extraordinary suggestion here is that Christ is Man Mark II, superior in will-power to Adam, who was Man Mark I. One might be tempted to ask why Adam could not have been created with a stronger will—still free, but stronger. But really the whole question is otiose. Milton presents an omnipotent, omniscient, all-foreknowing creator. We see him and his supporters struggling with opponents, and eventually winning, but at a terrible cost—the ruin of his Brave New World. He created man in order to raise up a new species who would eventually rise to take the place of the fallen angels. But he knew before he created man that man would fall and the kind of world he envisaged would be destroyed by Satan. The whole concept of planning, purposing, struggling, regretting, persuading, taking precautions against disaster, and so on, makes no sense in presenting the behaviour of an omnipotent, omniscient, foreknowing creator. The epic is not an appropriate form for a poem about God's relations with men, for the epic demands struggle and intermittent dubiety about the outcome and above all a sense of the limitations even of its greatest heroes. Further, the justification of the ways of God to men in terms of arguments put mostly into God's mouth is simply not persuasive, raising as many questions as it answers. Milton must have known this, at some deep level, for his poem is very much more than a series of rather dubious arguments employed defensively by God. It is much more than a straightforward justification of the ways of God to men by means of a versification of select passages of *Christian Doctrine*. This constitutes a very small part of the epic, and far from the most memorable. Something else is going on. In terms of the movement of the poetry, its interwoven patterns, its recurring imagery, its use of post-lapsarian references to illustrate and illuminate Milton's dream of an ideal pre-lapsarian world and to suggest at the same time the inadequacies of that world, a whole set of suggestions are built up that constitute what might almost be called a counter-poem, another kind of justification of the ways of God to men, another way of looking at the paradoxes and ambiguities of the human condition than that provided by simple argument about man's deserving his fate because of Adam's wilful disobedience. It is in the way he presents in his poetry the biblical story of our first parents that he manages to produce something much more moving and convincing than any prose paraphrase of the action or the speeches could suggest.

Early in Book III, immediately after his second appeal for divine inspiration, Milton refers to his own blindness, expressing the hope that he may, like the blind poets and prophets of antiquity, be granted a compensating interior illumination

> as the wakeful Bird
> Sings darkling, and in shadiest Covert hid
> Tunes her nocturnal Note.

This image from the post-lapsarian world, of the nightingale singing in the dark, is an image of comfort and serenity. That Nature was cursed after the Fall, that the eternal spring and the peaceful coexistence of all animal life were then lost as part of the resulting punitive distortion of the whole natural world—and these are points made explicit later in *Paradise Lost* when Milton discusses the consequences of Eve's and Adam's eating of the forbidden apple—seems here to be forgotten. Milton goes on:

> Thus with the Year
> Seasons return, but not to me returns
> Day, or the sweet approach of Ev'n or Morn,
> Or sight of vernal bloom, or Summers Rose,
> Or flocks, or heards, or human face divine;
> But cloud in stead, and ever-during dark
> Surrounds me, from the chearful ways of men
> Cut off, and for the Book of knowledge fair
> Presented with a Universal blanc
> Of Natures works to mee expung'd and ras'd,
> And wisdom at one entrance quite shut out.

The changing seasons are here represented as a blessing, whereas theologically, as it were, they are later represented as a curse. In Book X Milton gives a vivid description of the consequences of the Fall in terms of the bringing in of alternating seasons, with 'decrepit winter' being called in from the north and 'solstitial summer's heat' from the south, with changes in weather being inaugurated with 'noxious efficacy' and the angels turning the poles 'twice ten degrees and more from the Sun's Axle'

> to bring in change
> Of Seasons to each Clime; else had the Spring
> Perpetual smil'd on Earth with vernant Flow'rs,
> Equal in Days and Nights . . . .

This is all part of the punishment, visited on all mankind for
the whole of history, for the eating of the fatal apple. I see that
in a youthful marginal note at this point in *Paradise Lost* I have
pencilled the query: 'Was this really necessary?' In the passage
in Book III Milton seems to be saying that it was necessary if
man was to be enabled to get those special kinds of satisfactions
that changing seasons bring—a blessing disguised as a curse.
At the end of Book XI the archangel Michael tells Adam that
after the flood God set his rainbow in the sky as a pledge that

> Day and Night,
> Seed time and Harvest, Heat and hoary Frost
> Shall hold thir course,

and he is here echoing the moving words of Genesis: 'While
the earth remaineth, seed-time and harvest, and cold and heat
and summer and winter, and day and night shall not cease.'
This is a promise of comfort, of reassurance. Seasonal change
is guaranteed for the life of the earth.

> Sing a song of seasons!
> Something bright in all!
> Flowers in the summer,
> Fires in the Fall!

That is the concluding stanza of Robert Louis Stevenson's little
poem 'Autumn Fires', from *A Child's Garden of Verses*, and it
may seem a long way from Milton. But is it really? Stevenson
had his own Presbyterian heritage to reconcile with his actual
experience, and the reconciliation of inherited theological belief
with personal experience is what provides the poetic tension in
an extraordinary variety of works that include the Book of Job,
Paradise Lost, and Dante's *Divine Comedy*.

Life in the Garden of Eden was static, perpetual Spring, with
fruit and flower on the tree simultaneously. This changelessness
gave way to change after the Fall, and change can be both a
curse and a blessing.

Behold this compost! behold it well!
Perhaps every mite has once formed part of a sick
    person—yet behold!
The grass of spring covers the prairies,
The bean bursts noiselessly through the mould in the garden,
The delicate spear of the onion pierces upward,
The apple-buds cluster together on the apple-branches,
The resurrection of the wheat appears with pale visage
    out of the graves . . . .[2]

That is how Walt Whitman expressed his sense of the blessing
inherent in change, however threatening change might sometimes appear. And it *is* threatening. Whitman wrote in the
same poem:

Now I am terrified at the Earth, it is that calm and patient,
It grows such sweet things out of such corruptions,
It turns harmless and stainless on its axis, with such
    endless successions of diseas'd corpses,
It distils such exquisite winds out of such infused fetor,
It renews such unwitting looks, its prodigal, annual,
    sumptuous crops,
It gives such divine materials to men, and accepts such
    leavings from them at last.

Time both threatens and consoles: this is the theme of
Shakespeare's last plays, especially *The Winter's Tale*, where
'great creating Nature' eventually heals the wounds that occur
in time and links the generations. It is the theme of Keats's
great odes, where after brooding over the intractable problems
posed by time and change, and especially by the transience of
beauty, in 'Ode on a Grecian Urn' and 'Ode to a Nightingale',
the poet at last, in his 'Autumn' ode, finds comfort in the *movement* of the seasons, each with its appropriate blessings. After
images of ripening, swelling, and maturing we move to images
of harvesting and repletion, to conclude with images of fulfilment, achievement, and preparation for new cyclical movement:

Where are the songs of Spring? Ay, where are they?
    Think not of them, thou hast thy music too,—
While barrèd clouds bloom the soft-dying day
    And touch the stubble-plains with rosy hue . . . .

2 "This Compost", a poem in *Autumn Rivulets. The Poetry and Prose of Walt Whitman*,
ed. Louis Untermeyer, New York, 1949, p. 349.

The beauty of the harvested fields is a beauty appropriate to
the season, to this moment of time. Even the 'wailful choir' of
'the small gnats' pleases, because seasonable and therefore
satisfying. The last four lines of the poem remind us of time
moving—the spring lambs are now full grown—and the mention of the red-breast brings thoughts of winter, of which the
red-breast in the snow has long been a symbolic figure. The
poem ends with the swallows gathering for migration in face of
the coming winter:

> And full-grown lambs loud bleat from hilly bourn;
> Hedge-crickets sing; and now with treble soft
> The red-breast whistles from a garden croft;
> And gathering swallows twitter in the skies.

The seasons are moving in accordance with the great primal
laws of Nature (imposed first as a curse, on the strict
theological view) and God's promise to Noah, and we take a
deep satisfaction—sad-sweet perhaps, but deep none the
less—in the process. Looked at in this way, time and change
are no longer a threat. The seasons *depend* on change, and if we
can take pleasure in what is seasonal we have found a way of
taking pleasure in change. So we come back to Book III of
Paradise Lost where Milton mourns his loss of sight for depriving
him of the satisfaction of observing nature in its seasonal
changes. If seasonal change were really the curse Milton
declares it to be in Book X, then he should take satisfaction in
having it obscured from his view. But here it is the very loss of
perpetual spring that satisfies the movement from 'vernal
bloom' to 'Summer's Rose'. Further, in the same passage
Milton mourns his inability to see flocks and herds, and this
suggests pastoral activity, men looking after animals that he
keeps for food—again, a curse resulting from the Fall, for pre-
lapsarian Adam and Eve were vegetarian and only after their
disobedience did nature become 'red in tooth and claw', in
Tennyson's famous phrase. Yet pastoral activity and the contemplation of it are pleasing; in Milton's mind it was associated
both with poetry, in the long tradition of pastoral from
Theocritus, and loving care of men (as in 'the Lord is my
shepherd'), as well as with satisfying agricultural labour.

Again, labour was a curse resulting from the Fall. 'In the sweat of thy face shalt thou eat bread', God says to man in Genesis, particularizing a central part of his punishment. But throughout the whole body of Milton's poetry we find again and again images of agricultural labour as symbols of satisfaction. Indeed, Milton has great difficulty in *Paradise Lost* in providing Adam and Eve with something to do, and he is clearly dissatisfied with their sole work of trimming a changeless garden. One can hear Milton himself speaking when in Book X Adam comments on the curse of work imposed on him and his descendants:

> On mee the Curse aslope
> Glanc'd on the ground, with labour I must earne
> My bread; what harm? Idleness had been worse.

Yet this is not offered explicitly as a justification of God's ways. God intended it as a curse most certainly, and the bleak picture of human history presented by Michael to Adam after the Fall makes it clear that, in terms of the surface argumentation of the poem, the consequences of the Fall were all utterly bad for man at least as they affected his ordinary human life on earth. The notion that the curse of work was a disguised blessing emerges obliquely and forms part of what I have called the counter-poem.

It is not only the sight of seasonal change and of flocks and herds that Milton tells us he misses as a result of his blindness: most of all it is the 'human face divine'. The oxymoron here is striking. The word 'face' is wedged between two adjectives that say opposite things, 'human' and 'divine'. This is a favourite word-order of Milton's, and its rhetorical significance is of considerable importance in establishing the total cumulative effect of *Paradise Lost*. But the point here is that in spite of all the horrors of human life as depicted later in the poem, despite Milton's disillusion with human purposive activity that led him towards the end of Book XII to advise the giving up of all hope for reform or improvement and concentrate on the 'paradise within', the human face is also divine and not to be able to contemplate it is a cause for sadness. He also laments that his blindness has cut him off from 'the cheerful ways of men'. It is hard to reconcile this phrase with the picture of human history given in the last two books:

> so shall the World go on,
> To good malignant, to bad men benign,
> Under her own weight groaning, till the day
> Appear of respiration to the just,
> And vengeance to the wicked . . . .

There is no hope in ordinary human affairs until the Last
Judgement. Should not Milton then have rejoiced at being cut
off from the ways of men and forced to dwell in the 'paradise
within'? One could say, of course, that Book III was written
earlier than Books XI and XII and that Milton's attitude
became embittered after the Restoration and the loss of all his
political and religious hopes for his country. But Milton was
too great an artist to allow obvious inconsistencies to remain in
his poem, which we know he thought about in detail after he
had completed it, for he changed the structure from ten to
twelve books in the second edition. There is something more
here than a simple change of mind.

Let me take up one more point from that passage in Book III
that I quoted earlier. His blindness has cut him off not only
from watching the changing seasons, pastoral and agricultural
labour, 'the human face divine', and 'the chearful ways of
men': he is

> for the Book of knowledge fair
> Presented with a Universal blanc
> Of Natures works to mee expung'd and ras'd,
> And wisdom at one entrance quite shut out.

He is deprived of the knowledge and the wisdom that could
have been obtained by visual observation of the natural world.
But Eve fell through her quest for knowledge. She and Adam
should have been content to contemplate unchanging nature
in seasonless Eden, with the limited knowledge that could
bring. That accursed nature after the Fall should bring both
knowledge and wisdom to him who contemplates it seems
inconsistent with Milton's whole account of the Fall and its
consequences. Inconsistency is not, however, the charge that I
want to bring against Milton. What is involved is something
more like subtlety, ambiguity, multiple suggestiveness. This
emerges not only from the fairly obvious contrast between the
explicit statements in Book III that I have been discussing and

passages in later books: it is part of the texture of the whole story as Milton presents it.

Let us consider, for example, how Eve comes to fall—for she, of course, was the one who fell first and Adam fell out of love for her and the desire to share her fate. Unknown to her, Satan had squatted by her ear in the form of a toad while she slept and given her nightmarish thoughts. She tells her bad dream to Adam, quite unaware of course of its origin, and he comforts her, reassuring her that

> Evil into the mind of God or Man
> May come and go, so unapprov'd, and leave
> No spot or blame behind.

But it does, apparently, leave something behind. For, under the unconscious influence of Satan's night-time presence, she suggests to Adam later in the morning that it would be a good idea if they worked for a while in different parts of the garden.

> Let us divide our labours, thou where choice
> Leads thee, or where most needs, whether to wind
> The Woodbine round this Arbour, or direct
> The clasping Ivy where to climb, while I
> In yonder Spring of Roses intermixt
> With Myrtle, find what to redress till Noon:
> For while so near each other thus all day
> Our task we choose, what wonder if so near
> Looks intervene and smiles, or object new
> Casual discourse draw on, which intermits
> Our day's work brought to little, though begun
> Early, and th' hour of Supper comes unearn'd.

The somewhat meaningless gardening she describes is nevertheless regarded as labour in a purely post-lapsarian sense; for the notion that one must earn one's supper by work was part of the curse imposed after the Fall. There is no suggestion that it is a satanic thought that one should earn one's supper. It emerges naturally from the context of Eve's thought as a proper argument, and Adam, though he resists Eve's desire to work separately, does not question this particular notion. He replies to Eve in tones of sweet loving reasonableness and she answers him in turn, steadily maintaining her point, but still (for they are both as yet unfallen) in cadences of

great sweetness. In the end Adam reluctantly grants her re-
quest to work for a while apart:

> Go; for thy stay, not free, absents thee more;
> Go in thy native innocence, relie
> On what thou hast of vertue, summon all,
> For God towards thee hath done his part, do thine.

He knows, for Raphael had told him, that she is at risk from
Satan (whom God, incidentally, had *allowed* out of Hell and
permitted to come to the Garden of Eden to tempt Eve). Eve
knows too. Both are confident that they know what virtue is
and could not be led astray.

Milton's picture of Eve, sweetly obstinate, leaving her husband to work in another part of the garden is presented with
great human feeling. He lingers over this last moment when
unfallen man and woman are together, and as Eve softly
withdraws her hand from Adam's he draws on all the resources
of classical precedent to emphasize her grace and beauty: she is
compared to a wood nymph, to Diana, to Prosperine, among
others, in soaring and sonorous verse. As she departs, Adam
repeats his urging that she should come back soon:

> Oft he to her his charge of quick returne
> Repeated, shee to him as oft engag'd
> To be return'd by Noon amid the Bowre,
> And all things in best order to invite
> Noontide repast, or Afternoons repose.

She will be back for lunch, in fact. But she never came back:
the Eve who returned, having already eaten the fatal apple
instead of lunching with Adam in the bower, was not the same
person:

> O much deceav'd, much failing, hapless *Eve*,
> Of thy presum'd return! event perverse!
> Thou never from that hour in Paradise
> Founst either sweet repast or sound repose.

It was all part of Satan's plan—to remove Eve from Adam so
that he could tempt her when alone into eating the forbidden
apple. He appears to her as a serpent, not slithering on the
ground which snakes were condemned to do after the Fall, but
prancing playfully and showing off his 'turret Crest, and sleek

enamel'd Neck'. Eve of course does not know that this is not a
genuine snake. Not having yet eaten of the tree of knowledge of
good and evil, she is unaware of the nature of evil. This is a
beautiful and courteous snake that she has met, and she
innocently admires him. Satan, in the form of the snake, also
admires Eve: he is struck by her loveliness. His feelings are
described by Milton in a significant simile:

> As one who long in populous City pent,
> Where Houses thick and Sewers annoy the Aire,
> Forth issuing on a Summers Morn to breathe
> Among the pleasant Villages and Farmes
> Adjoynd, from each thing met conceaves delight,
> The smell of Grain, or tedded Grass, or Kine,
> Or Dairie, each rural sight, each rural sound;
> If chance with Nymphlike step fair Virgin pass,
> What pleasing seemd, for her now pleases more,
> She most, and in her look summs all Delight.

This little glimpse of post-lapsarian country life, 'among the
pleasant Villages and Farms', comes with a curious sense of
refreshment into the poem. It is presented as something deeply
satisfying. So at the very moment when the Enemy of Mankind
is about to seduce Eve into that fateful disobedience to the
divine command we have for a moment a breath of fresh
country air blowing through the poem, coming from life as it is
known long after the Fall. And it is associated with *Satan's*
feeling.

The serpent addresses Eve, who is struck with wonder that a
serpent can talk. When she expresses her surprise—it is an
innocent surprise, as Milton makes absolutely clear—he explains
to her, with many a flattering compliment, that he gained the
power of human speech by eating the fruit of one of the trees in
the garden. Eve is impressed, and asks him what that tree was
and where it is. He offers to lead her to it.

> So glister'd the dire Snake, and into fraud
> Led *Eve* our credulous Mother, to the Tree
> Of prohibition, root of all our woe . . . .

In Book III of *Paradise Lost*, when Satan is trying to find the way
to the newly created world in order to destroy Adam and Eve
by inducing them to eat the forbidden apple, he disguises

himself as a cherub and as such enquires the way from the archangel Uriel. Uriel, thinking that he is addresing a real cherub, tells him the way. Milton explains why Uriel, mighty archangel though he is, is unable to detect that it is really Satan to whom he is giving this dangerous information:

> For neither Man nor Angel can discern
> Hypocrisie, the onely evil that walks
> Invisible, except to God alone,
> By his permissive will, through Heav'n and Earth . . . .

Uriel is not held guilty for his inability to penetrate Satan's disguise. So clearly Eve cannot be faulted for innocently assuming that the snake was what he claimed to be and that the powers of speech and reason really were, as he said, conferred on him by his eating the fruit. Nevertheless, when she sees that the tree to which he has led her is the one forbidden by God, she at once tells him that their journey has been in vain, since that is the one tree whose fruit she and Adam are forbidden to eat. When the disguised Satan laughs incredulously at his news, Eve, 'yet sinless' as Milton insists, repeats that it is the one tree of all in the garden of which they must not eat. Satan now realizes that he has his work cut out to break down Eve's resistance. He draws on all the resources of rhetoric:

> As when of old som Orator renound
> In *Athens* or free *Rome*, where Eloquence
> Flourishd, since mute, to some great cause addrest,
> Stood in himself collected, while each part,
> Motion, each act won audience ere the tongue,
> Sometimes in highth began, as no delay
> Of Preface brooking through his Zeal of Right;
> So standing, moving, or to highth upgrown
> The Tempter all impassiond thus began.

Innocent Eve, credulous because innocent, is about to be subjected to the most artful oratory ever known in history. As I have noted, she cannot be held guilty for not having been able to penetrate Satan's disguise. God himself, 'by his permissive will', Milton tells us, allows hypocrisy to go undetected. (*Why* God should allow this remains unexplained.) She is credulous, Milton tells us, but credulity is part of her innocence. She could only have been suspicious of the snake if she had already eaten of the tree of knowledge of good and evil. So the paradox is that she could only have been in a position to resist Satan's temptation if she had already fallen.

This raises the whole question of the relation between innocence and ignorance. Eve fell because of her innocence and credulity. She was fooled. But in order not to have been fooled she would have to have lost her innocence. True, Milton points out later in the poem that both Adam and Eve *ought* to have known that to eat of the prohibited tree was wrong under any circumstances, since God himself had forbidden them to do it. But if what Satan, in the form of a persuasive and beautiful snake, said was true, that threw a whole new light both on God's position and on Eve's. And Eve *could not know that it was untrue*, or even suspect that it might not be true, in her innocent state. Is it morally culpable to be unsuspicious?

The implication seems to be—and this is borne out by hosts of suggestions built up by patterns of imagery in the poem— that a knowledge of evil is necessary if any meaningful virtue is to be achieved. Milton had made this point years before in his *Areopagitica*. 'I cannot praise a fugitive and cloistr'd vertue, unexercis'd and unbreath'd, that never sallies out and sees her adversary, but slinks out of the race, where that immortall garland is to be run for, not without dust and heat.' He pleaded for liberty of the press because 'the knowledge and survey of vice is in this world so necessary to the constituting of human vertue, and the scanning of error to the conformation of truth'. Now it may be argued that this is true only in a fallen world. But the scene of Eve's temptation makes it clear that in an unfallen world ignorance of evil can lead to being fooled by evil. So there is really no way out of the paradox. In any case, for Milton a life of effortless virtue in a seasonless and workless Paradise was, as Socrates said of the unexamined life, ἀνεξέταστος βίος, no life for a human being, οὐ βιωτὸς ἀνθρώπῳ.

In Aldous Huxley's *Brave New World* the Savage rejects the world of effortless adjustment and universal happiness as in some profound sense unsatisfying to the human spirit. There can be nothing noble and fine and heroic, he argues with the world leader Mustapha Mond, without a struggle for an ideal, and that posits the existence of God. The conversation continues:

'My dear young friend,' said Mustapha Mond, 'civilisation has absolutely no need of nobility or heroism . . . . In a properly organized society like ours, nobody has any opportunities for being noble or heroic. . . . Where there are wars, where there are divided allegiances, where there are temptations to be resisted, objects of love to be fought for or defended—there, obviously, nobility and heroism have some sense. But there aren't any wars nowadays. The greatest care is taken to prevent you from loving anyone too much. There's no such thing as a divided allegiance; you're so conditioned that you can't help doing what you ought to do. And what you ought to do is on the whole so pleasant, so many of the natural impulses are allowed free play, that really there aren't any temptations to resist.'

The Savage replies that struggle is necessary, tears are necessary, risk is necessary, and further all this nourishes great art. Mustapha Mond answers that in the new society art is unnecessary. Once a month everyone takes a drug which floods the whole system with adrenalin, 'the complete physiological equivalent of fear and rage' and people get 'all the tonic effects of murdering Desdemona and being murdered by Othello, without any of the inconveniences'. The Savage says that he *wants* the inconveniences.

'We don't,' said the Controller. 'We prefer to do things comfortably.'
'But I don't want comfort. I want God, I want poetry, I want real danger, I want freedom, I want goodness, I want sin.'
'In fact,' said Mustapha Mond, 'you're claiming the right to be unhappy.'
'All right then,' said the Savage defiantly. 'I'm claiming the right to be unhappy.'
'Not to mention the right to grow old and ugly and impotent; the right to have syphilis and cancer; the right to have too little to eat; the right to be lousy; the right to live in constant apprehension of what may happen tomorrow; the right to catch typhoid; the right to be tortured by unspeakable pains of every kind.'
There was a long silence.
'I claim them all,' said the Savage at last. Mustapha Mond shrugged his shoulders. 'You're welcome,' he said.

Mustapha Mond's picture of the ills that afflict mankind out-

side his perfectly adjusted state is reminiscent of the vivid list of
diseases and afflictions that Adam is shown by Michael in Book
XI of *Paradise Lost* as representing the fate of his descendants.
On what some philosophers have called the conative theory of
virtue nothing of merit can be achieved without struggle
against obstacles. That is what the Savage believes in *Brave New
World* and it is what Milton argued in *Areopagitica*. The implication is clearly there in his account of Eve's temptation. On
this reading, the Fall was necessary to make true virtue possible. So God knew what he was doing after all in arranging the
temptation.

After Eve has succumbed to the serpent's temptation (having
been persuaded by words which, as Milton expressly and
significantly tells us, were 'impregn'd / With Reason, to her
seeming, and with Truth') she returns to Adam and in tones of
drunken gaiety babbles to him about the marvellous fruit she
has just tasted. She begins by apologizing for being late and
goes on, in a rush of words, to praise the tree and explain that
what they had been told about it was all wrong. Adam, aghast,
lets drop from his slack hand the garland of roses he had been
weaving for Eve—in a fine touch they are suddenly described
as 'faded roses', the first sign of post-lapsarian decay—and
then addresses Eve in tones of love and grief. He realizes that,
having committed the forbidden act, she is now doomed to
death. He goes on:

>   som cursed fraud
> Of Enemie hath beguil'd thee, yet unknown,
> And mee with thee hath ruind, for with thee
> Certain my resolution is to Die;
> How can I live without thee, how forgoe
> Thy sweet Converse and Love so dearly joyn'd,
> To live again in these wild Woods forlorn?
> Should God create another *Eve*, and I
> Another Rib afford, yet loss of thee
> Would never from my heart; no, no, I feel
> The Link of Nature draw me: Flesh of Flesh,
> Bone of my Bone thou art, and from thy State
> Mine never shall be parted, bliss or woe.

In proper theological terms, the duty of someone who loves
another who has sinned is to intercede for her while he himself

is yet sinless, not to join her in the sin. But in terms of human
experience Adam's response seems worthy of our admiration.
Or is it? Is it perhaps a kind of selfishness? He cannot bear to
live without Eve, he loves her so, and therefore he is determined to join in whatever fate God visits on her. But then there is
an element of selfishness in all love. A hurt to a loved one hurts
the lover, and it can be difficult to determine the degree of
disinterestedness with which a lover seeks to prevent hurt coming to the loved one or decides to share that hurt as the only
way of remaining together with her. Milton is here suggesting
some of the paradoxes and ambiguities of love. Adam is being
both noble and self-interested, both self-sacrificing and self-
indulgent, both selflessly and selfishly loving.

Eve sinned out of innocent credulity, genuinely believing in
the reason and truth of the serpent's words. Adam sinned
knowing exactly what he was doing—

> Against his better knowledge, not deceav'd
> But fondly overcome with Femal charm.

'Fondly overcome with Femal charm' sounds an unexpectedly
priggish note, as though Milton were trying to stifle some of the
suggestions he had already set going. This is part of the overt
justification of the ways of God to men. Adam was to be justly
punished, for he sinned wilfully. Had he not been warned by
Raphael that 'in loving thou dost well, in Passion not'? But it is
not blind passion that motivates Adam here: it is a calm and
reasoned acceptance of the implications of his deep love for
Eve. If Eve's eating the apple brought out some of the deep
human problems involved in the relation between ignorance
and innocence and suggested the necessity of the Fall so that
evil could be properly known and struggled against, Adam's
eating it brought out some of the complexities of love and of the
relation between the selfless and the selfish aspects of loving
acts.

The immediate consequences of both Eve and Adam eating
the apple are described by Milton as a loss of innocence in
sexual relations, so that they become both enjoyable and bitter,
and a loss of the sweetly loving reasonableness that showed in
their pre-lapsarian discourse. Now 'high Passions, Anger,
Hate, / Mistrust, Suspicion, Discord' begin to shake their

minds. But this does not last indefinitely. One of the finest things in the whole of *Paradise Lost* is Milton's charting of the couple's recovery. It is begun by Eve, who after a bitter speech of recrimination by Adam, replies in a speech (beginning 'Forsake me not thus, *Adam*', Book X, lines 914 ff.) which in its beautiful modulations of tone, its simple humility, its gentle appeal for support and understanding, its quiet and undramatic self-reproach, represents something quite new in the verse of *Paradise Lost*. This is post-lapsarian goodness, not the ideal paradisial goodness of pre-lapsarian behaviour, which Milton had expressed earlier with great eloquence, but a movingly chastened goodness which we can recognize as accessible and relevant to the human condition as we know it. If *this* is one of the consequences of the Fall, then they cannot be all bad, the implication seems to be.

Of course the orthodox view of the consequences of the Fall involved the *felix culpa*, the theory that the Fall made possible the manifestation of divine love in the Christian scheme of redemption. Milton refers to this, once very cursorily in his opening statement of theme, and once when he has Michael tell briefly about the sacrifice of Christ. But it plays no prominent part in the poem. God is not justified in *Paradise Lost* by a demonstration of the remarkable consequences of Christ's love. He is ostensibly justified by a quasi-rational demonstration that all human suffering represents a just consequence of the misuse of free will by Adam and Eve, though these sufferings can be compensated in some way and for a small minority by Christ's sacrifice. He is indirectly justified by the pattern of suggestions built up by what I have called the counter-poem.

Christ is not the hero of *Paradise Lost*, neither is God. In a sense, Adam and Eve represent the Troy over which God and Satan fight. Satan wins, but his victory, though real enough, is fraught with disastrous consequences to himself and his companions. The real winner, though, is post-lapsarian man: the true twin heroes of the epic, whether Milton consciously intended this or not, are Adam and Eve. Eve is tricked by plausible villainy into the original sin; Adam joins her in that sin out of desire to share her fate because of his love for her; both deteriorate in character after the Fall, then rally, and at last, having been presented with a grim picture of the future of their descendants, face the post-lapsarian world with hope and dignity. They leave Paradise, now made terrible by armed cherubim, and slowly, hand in hand, leave their forfeited garden for the real world.

>   for now too high
> Th' Archangel stood, and from the other Hill
> To thir fixt Station, all in bright array
> The Cherubim descended; on the ground
> Gliding metereous, as Ev'ning Mist
> Ris'n from a river o'er the marish glides,
> And gathers ground fast at the Labourers heel
> Homeward returning. High in Front advanc't,
> The brandisht Sword of God before them blaz'd
> Fierce as a Comet; with which torrid heat,
> And vapour as the *Lybian* Air adust,
> Began to parch that temperate Clime; whereat
> In either hand the hastning Angel caught
> Our lingring Parents, and to th' Eastern Gate
> Led them direct, and down the Cliff as fast
> To the subjected Plaine; then disappeer'd.
> They looking back, all th' Eastern side beheld
> Of Paradise, so late thir happie seat,
> Wav'd over by that flaming Brand, the Gate
> With dreadful Faces throng'd and fierie Armes:
> Som natural tears they drop'd, but wip'd them soon;
> The World was all before them, where to choose
> Thir place of rest, and Providence thir guide:
> They hand in hand with wandring steps and slow,
> Through *Eden* took thir solitarie way.

The image of the labourer returning home looks forward to the ideal of satisfying rest after work in the post-lapsarian world which, as we have seen, plays so important a part in the imagery of Milton's poetry. The couple descend from Eden to 'the subjected Plain'—'subjected' in the Latin meaning of 'lying below' but also suggesting its English meaning of 'conquered': they were setting out to subdue the world of fallen nature by agricultural activity (the labourer referred to a few lines before is clearly an agricultural labourer). Paradise is now uninhabited and indeed uninhabitable, 'with dreadful Faces throng'd'. Man's destiny lies in a more chequered world. It is

also a world of challenge. 'The World was all before them.'
They go to it hand in hand, yet their way is 'solitarie' for there
can be loneliness in the midst of love and the many paradoxes
that involve human relations in a fallen world are here summed
up in the two expressions 'hand in hand' and 'solitarie'. Such
is the mixed texture of our experience; such are the difficulties,
contradictions, challenges, and rewards that await purposive
man in the world. It is not the effortless peace of the Garden of
Eden. It is something more interesting and more testing. And
ultimately, to Milton, so the poetry if not the argument tells us,
it is more satisfying. Good comes out of evil not in the theological way of the *felix culpa*, the 'fortunate fall', but more obliquely
in the emergence of a world that in spite of everything is the
world we want and need. So God is justified, in a way that
might perhaps have surprised him.

3 GOD AND NATURE

The Hebrew Psalmist considered Nature to be a demonstration of the glory of God the creator, for which he was to be praised. 'The heavens declare the glory of God; and the firmament sheweth his handiwork', says Psalm 19, while Psalm 104 provides an eloquent picture of the magnificence of God's cosmos not, as in the concluding chapters of the Book of Job, as something remote from and indifferent to man, but as a subject for praise and rejoicing:

> Bless the Lord, O my soul.
> O Lord my God, thou art very great;
> Thou art clothed with honour and majesty.
>
> Who coverest thyself with light as with a garment,
> Who stretchest out the heavens like a curtain;
>
> Who layest the beams of his chambers in the waters,
> Who maketh the clouds his chariot,
> Who walketh upon the wings of the wind . . . .

The psalm concludes with the Psalmist blessing and praising the Lord.

In neither of these psalms—nor, indeed, anywhere in the Book of Psalms—is the Psalmist arguing that the glories of the natural world prove the existence of God. There is no suggestion that evidence of design in the natural world proves the existence of a divine designer. God's existence is taken absolutely for granted, and far from the facts of Nature proving his existence, it is his existence that gives meaning to the facts of Nature. Psalm 94 asks the question, 'He that planted the ear, shall he not hear? He that formed the eye, shall he not see?' As Professor Kemp Smith pointed out in his 1931 British Academy lecture, *Is Divine Existence Credible?*, 'this is by no means an argument to design. The argument here is that the being who *has been* able to plant the ear and to form the eye, who *is able* to instruct the nations and to teach men knowledge—all of which is taken as being beyond question—that such a Being must surely be omniscient, with powers that utterly transcend those of any of his creatures.' Kemp Smith went on:

The position . . . as regards the convictions of religious writers, whether in the Old Testament or elsewhere, is this. In and through their religious experience of fellowship with God, they have belief in God, and coming to Nature and history with this belief in their minds, they interpret Nature and history freely in accordance therewith. They do not observe order and design, and *therefore* infer a Designer: they argue that order and design must be present even where they are not apparent, because all existences other than God have their source in him. They start, that is to say, from an *immediate* experience of the Divine; and only so are their methods of argument and modes of expression possible at all.

This is worlds away from the eighteenth-century view that the Newtonian order that can be demonstrated to exist in the universe proves the existence of a beneficent divine designer.

> Nature! great Parent! whose directing Hand
> Rolls round the Seasons of the changeful Year,
> How mighty! how majestick are thy Works!
> With what a pleasing Dread they swell the Soul,
> That sees, astonish'd: and, astonish'd, sings!

This is from the first version of James Thomson's 'Winter', which was the first written of the sequence he entitled *The Seasons*. Nature itself seems to be God here (as we find too in the writings of the third Earl of Shaftesbury, who influenced Thomson. 'O Mighty Nature! wise substitute of Providence! impowered creatress! Or thou impowering Deity, supreme creator!' Nature and Nature's God seem here to be virtually identified). Nature is both a manifestation of God and proof of his existence and of his attributes. As Thomson put it in the 'Hymn' which concludes *The Seasons*:

> These, as they change, Almighty Father! these,
> Are but the varied God. The rolling year
> Is full of Thee. Forth in the pleasing Spring
> Thy beauty walks, thy tenderness and love. . . .
>   Mysterious round! what skill, what force divine,
> Deep felt, in these appear! a simple train,
> Yet so delightful mix'd, with such kind art,
> Such beauty and beneficence combin'd . . . .

The beauty of Nature and the evidence it bears of being the work of divine designing intelligence testify to the beneficence of Nature's creator, God. This is a familiar thought in the work of the physico-theologicans of the seventeenth and eighteenth centuries. Belief in a Deity, argued John Ray in the Preface to his book *The Wisdom of God Manifested in the Works of the Creation* (1692), is the foundation of all religion and we must therefore demonstrate 'by Arguments drawn from the Light of Nature, and Works of the Creation' that the required Deity exists. These proofs 'Taken from Effects and Operations, exposed to every Man's view, are not to be denied or questioned by any'. Similar arguments are found in William Derham's *Physico-Theology* (1713) and his *Astro-Theology* (1715), and in George Cheyne's *Philosophical Principles of Religion: Natural and Revealed* (1718). (Ray's and Derham's books, incidentally, were amongst those read by the young Robert Burns.) Cheyne's book, he tells us in his Preface, was 'for the Use of the Younger Students of *Philosophy*, who while they were taught the most probable account of the *Appearance of Nature* from the Modern Discoveries, might thereby have the *Principles of Natural Religion* insensibly instill'd into them at the same time'.

The assumption that we can prove the existence of an almighty and benevolent God through examining his works with our human senses can provide a justification of the ways of God to men very different from that attempted by Milton. Pope, in his *Essay on Man*, made it quite clear that he thought that God's ways could be justified in just that way:

> Say first, of God, above, or Man below,
> What can we reason, but from what we know?
> Of Man what see we, but his station here,
> From which to reason, or to which refer?
> Thro' worlds unnumbered tho' the God be known,
> 'Tis ours to trace him only in our own.
> He, who thro' vast immensity can pierce,
> See worlds on worlds compose our universe,
> Observe how system into system runs,
> What other planets circle other suns,
> What vary'd being peoples ev'ry star,
> May tell why Heav'n has made us as we are.
> But of this frame the bearings, and the ties,
> The strong connections, nice dependencies,
> Gradations just, has thy pervading soul
> Look'd thro'? or can a part contain the whole?

> Is the great chain, that draws all to agree,
> And drawn supports, upheld by God, or thee?

The answer is, of course, that the Great Chain of Being,
the proper ordering of every element in the universe, is upheld
by God. The general laws through which God operates the
universe do not necessarily and always make for individual
happiness.

> Better for Us, perhaps, it might appear,
> Were there all harmony, all virtue here;
> That never air or ocean felt the wind;
> That never passion discompos'd the mind:
> But ALL subsists by elemental strife;
> And Passions are the elements of Life.
> The gen'ral ORDER, since the whole began,
> Is kept in Nature, and is kept in Man.

The general order requires occasional disasters and even evils
both in the natural world and in the moral world of man. That
is the price of order, and the universal laws of order are what
govern the universe. What we have, in fact, is the best of all
possible worlds:

> Cease then, nor Order Imperfection name:
> Our proper bliss depends on what we blame.
> Know thy own point: This kind, this due degree
> Of blindness, weakness, Heav'n bestows on thee.
> Submit—In this, or any other sphere,
> Secure to be as blest as thou canst bear:
> Safe in the hand of one disposing Pow'r,
> Or in the natal, or the mortal hour.
> All Nature is but Art, unknown to thee;
> All Chance, Direction, which thou canst not see;
> All Discord, Harmony, not understood;
> All partial Evil, universal Good:
> And, spite of Pride, in erring Reason's spite,
> One truth is clear, 'Whatever IS, is RIGHT.'

In his note on this passage, Professor John Butt drew reader's
attention to *Paradise Lost*, Book VIII, lines 167-84, as 'the best
commentary' on it, adding that the lines from *Paradise Lost*
'come close to summarizing the argument of this Epistle' (that
is, this section of Pope's *Essay on Man*).[1] I do not think so. In the

---

[1] *The Poems of Alexander Pope*, ed. John Butt, London, 1963, p. 515.

passage from *Paradise Lost* Raphael tells Adam that he should
not enquire too curiously about the details of astronomy:

> Sollicit not thy thoughts with matters hid,
> Leave them to God above, him serve and feare;
> Of other Creatures, as him pleases best,
> Wherever plac't, let him dispose: joy thou
> In what he gives to thee . . .
>   be lowlie wise:
> Think only what concerns thee and thy being;
> Dream not of other Worlds, what Creatures there
> Live, in what state, condition or degree,
> Contented that thus farr hath been reveal'd
> Not of Earth only but of highest Heaven.

There is a superficial resemblance between this and Pope's
argument, but the whole mental framework is different. Behind
Pope's lines lies the thought, expressed strongly and clearly
earlier in the poem, that the conclusion is reached by our rea-
soning 'from what we know' from experience. Adam, on the
other hand, is told to be content with what has been revealed to
him. He could not possibly have known about the revolt in
Heaven and its consequences unless Raphael had told him. And
the conclusion is not that 'whatever is, is right', for the abuse of
free will by Satan and his followers was not right, any more
than the later abuse of free will by Eve and Adam was to be
right. The doctrine of the 'fortunate fall' is not handled by
Milton in such a way as to suggest that all partial evil is universal good. Evil for Milton remained evil, something called forth
by the Fall and subsequently to be constantly fought against.
Milton would have thought Pope's formulation altogether too
slick. His own sterner view of the nature of evil and the root
cause of all human suffering had its own contradictions and
paradoxes, but it certainly did not involve advising man to
accept the world he found himself in, with all its imperfections,
as the inevitable consequence of order in the universe. One can
imagine the cold comfort to be had, say, in a concentration
camp or *en route* to the gas chamber by being told that

> All Nature is but Art, unknown to thee;
> Not Chance, Direction, which thou canst not see;
> All Discord, Harmony, not understood;
> All partial Evil, universal Good.

It would not perhaps be any more comforting to be told by
Milton that it was part of the consequences of the Fall, but at
least Milton would not have denied the reality of the suffering
and of the evil it represented.

Pope was a Roman Catholic, but there is no trace of Catholic
theology in his *Essay on Man*. The deism of so many eighteenth-
century writers ignored totally the specific theological differ-
entia of the Christian religion—the doctrine of Original Sin, of
the Atonement, of the Trinity, for example—to concentrate on
a view of God as the Great Designer of a well-ordered machine.
(Dr Johnson is of course quite different: he believed in the
Christian scheme of things and rejected any kind of optimistic
deism). Pope at least conceded that there was 'partial evil', that
the system of order in the universe operated through general
laws which required occasional incidents of dislocation and suffering. Thomson took the more conventional deistic view, at
least in some of his moods, in seeing everything as perfect and
delightful. Here are some lines from his 'Summer':

> With what a perfect, World-revolving Power
> Were first the unwieldy Planets launch'd along
> Th'illimitable Void! thus to remain,
> Amid the Flux of many thousand Years,
> That oft has swayed the busy Race of Men
> And all their labour'd Monuments away,
> Unresting, changeless, matchless in their Course;
> To Day, and Night, and the delightful Round
> Of Seasons, faithful; not excentric once:
> So pois'd, and perfect, is the vast Machine . . . .

But *is* the machine so poised and perfect? Can we infer from
the universe as we know it that it was created by an all-powerful and benevolent Deity? It was to this question that David
Hume addressed himself in his *Dialogues on Natural Religion*,
where Philo voices objections to the argument both *to* and *from*
design, maintaining that there is no true analogy between the
universe and humanly designed machines within it, if only
because the former is unique, and also pointing out, more
damagingly so far Thomson's argument is concerned, that, if
we accepted the analogy, we would have to find the universe a
pretty botched-up job. 'The misery and ill of the universe'

would have to arise from 'the inaccurate workmanship of all the springs and principles of the great machine of nature'.

One would imagine, that this grand production had not received the last hand of the maker; so little finished is every part, and so coarse are the strokes, with which it is executed. Thus, the winds are requisite to convey the vapours along the surface of the globe, and to assist men in navigation: But how oft, rising up to tempests and hurricanes, do they become pernicious? Rains are necessary to nourish all the plants and animals of the earth: But how often are they defective? how often excessive? Heat is requisite to all life and vegetation; but is not always found in the due proportion. On the mixture and secretion of the humours and juices of the body depend the health and prosperity of the animal: But the parts perform not regularly their proper function. What more useful than all the passions of the mind, ambition, vanity, love, anger? But how oft do they break their bounds, and cause the greatest convulsions in society? There is nothing so advantageous in the universe, but what frequently becomes pernicious, by its excess or defect; nor has nature guarded, with the requisite accuracy, against all disorder or confusion. The irregularity is never, perhaps, so great as to destroy any species; but is often sufficient to involve the individuals in ruin and misery.[2]

Philo concedes that 'if the goodness of the Deity . . . could be established on any tolerable reasons *a priori*, these phenomena, however untoward, would not be sufficient to subvert that principle; but might easily, in some unknown manner, be reconcilable to it'. In fact he takes very much the view that Kemp Smith takes in the lecture from which I have quoted, that while the existence of an omnipotent and benevolent God cannot be inferred from an examination of nature and human life as they are, a pre-knowledge of such a divine existence (obtained, Kemp Smith argues, not by inference but by direct intuitive experience) could be reconciled with the situation as we experience it. Divine existence, one might say, is credible but not demonstrable.

It is, however, the Psalmist's belief that 'The Heavens declare the glory of God' that has most appealed to the poets, even those who came after Hume. Wordsworth, in direct opposition to the voice of God at the end of the Book of Job, declared that

---

[2] *Hume's Dialogues on Natural Religion*, ed. Norman Kemp Smith, Oxford, 1935, p. 258 (Part XI).

there was a profound correlation between the workings of
Nature and the mind of man and, further, that pleasure was a
principle that ran through Nature:

> Through primrose tufts, in that green bower,
> The periwinkle trailed its wreaths;
> And 'tis my faith that every flower
> Enjoys the air it breaths.
>
> The birds around me hopped and played,
> Their thoughts I cannot measure:—
> But the least motion which they made,
> It seemed a thrill of pleasure.
>
> The budding twigs spread out their fan,
> To catch the breezy air;
> And I must think, do all I can,
> That there was pleasure there.

And there is Wordsworth's classic expression of the relation
between Nature and man in those well-known lines from *Tintern
Abbey*:

> For I have learned
> To look on nature, not as in the hour
> Of thoughtless youth; but hearing oftentimes
> The still, sad music of humanity,
> Nor harsh, nor grating, though of ample power
> To chasten and subdue. And I have felt
> A presence that disturbs me with the joy
> Of elevated thoughts; a sense sublime
> Of something far more deeply interfused,
> Whose dwelling is the light of setting suns,
> And the round ocean and the living air,
> And the blue sky, and in the mind of man . . . .

Aldous Huxley, in his essay 'Wordsworth in the Tropics',
pointed out that such a view is possible only if one lives in a
very tamed and moderate nature:

In the neighbourhood of latitude fifty north, and for the last hundred years or thereabouts, it has been an axiom that Nature is divine
and morally uplifting. For good Wordsworthians . . . a walk in the
country is the equivalent of going to church, a tour through West-
morland is as good as a pilgrimage to Jerusalem. To commune with
the fields and waters, the woodlands and the hills, is to commune,

according to our modern and northern ideas, with the visible manifestations of the 'Wisdom and Spirit of the Universe.'

The Wordsworthian who exports this pantheistic worship of
Nature to the tropics is liable to have his religious convictions
somewhat rudely disturbed. Nature, under a vertical sun, and
nourished by the equatorial rains, is not at all like that chaste, mild
deity who presides over the *Gemüthlichkeit,* the prettiness, the cosy
sublimities of the Lake District. The worst that Wordsworth's goddess ever did to him was to make him hear

> Low breathings coming after me, and sounds
> Of undistinguishable motion, steps
> Almost as silent as the turf they trod;

was to make him realize, in the shape of 'a huge peak, black and huge,'
the existence of 'unknown modes of being.' He seems to have imagined
that this was the worst Nature *could* do. A few weeks in Malaya or
Borneo would have undeceived him. Wandering in the hothouse
darkness of the jungle, he would not have felt so serenely certain of
those 'Presences of Nature,' those 'Souls of Lonely Places', which he
was in the habit of worshipping on the shores of Windermere and
Rydal. The sparse inhabitants of the equatorial forest are all believers
in devils. When one has visited, in even the most superficial manner,
the places where they live, it is difficult not to share their faith. The
jungle is marvellous, fantastic, beautiful; but it is also terrifying, it is
also profoundly sinister. There is something in what, for lack of a
better word, we must call the character of great forests—even in those
of temperate lands—which is foreign, appalling, fundamentally and
utterly inimical to intruding man.[3]

This is not so very far from the view proclaimed in the
Theophany in *Job*: the universe was not made for man's con-
venience and contains dark mysteries that are far beyond him.
But Huxley is also suggesting that Wordsworth, and indeed
most of us, project subjective feelings on to Nature and then
imagine that they emanate from Nature. I am not sure that
Wordsworth would have wholly disagreed with this, or that he
would have considered Huxley's argument as damaging to his
position as Huxley himself felt it to be. It was after all Coleridge, who was Wordsworth's disciple so far as his view of
Nature went, who wrote

> we receive but what we give,
> And in our life alone does Nature live,

[3] *Do What You Will,* by Aldous Huxley, London, 1931, pp. 113-14.

thus conceding the subjective nature of man's feeling for
Nature. Without what he called in the same poem the 'shaping
spirit of Imagination', Nature remained dead. Wordsworth
never proclaimed that contemplation of Nature led to a belief
in a benevolent designing Deity. But he did believe that a
properly developed imagination could see and feel some profound correspondence between the goings on of nature ('goings
on' was a favourite phrase of his) and the mind of man. Faced
with the tropics he could have said that indeed horrors in the
tropics had their echoes in horrors in the human mind; the correspondence between Nature and the human mind did not
mean that all was always sweetness and light. At the same
time, he did believe in a universal pleasure principle at work in
Nature, and that would be as difficult to reconcile with the
Huxleyan view of tropical Nature as with the Tennysonian
view of Nature red in tooth and claw.

Let us return for a moment to Pope and his optimistic faith
that all partial evil is universal good. This would seem to be an
odd point of view to be held by one of the greatest satirists of
our language. One cannot help feeling that Pope was speaking
more from the centre of his being in the bitingly satiric eloquence of the *The Dunciad* than in the neatly turned aphorisms
of the *Essay on Man*. The picture of the end of civilization that
concludes the *Dunciad* is presented with nightmare conviction:

> She comes! she comes! the sable Throne behold
> Of *Night* Primaeval, and of *Chaos* old!
> Before her, *Fancy's* gilded clouds decay
> And all its varying Rain-bows die away.
> *Wit* shoots in vain its momentary fires,
> The meteor drops, and in a flash expires.
> As one by one, at dread Medea's strain,
> The sick'ning stars fade off th' ethereal plain;
> As Argus' eyes by Hermes's wand opprest,
> Clos'd one by one to everlasting rest;
> Thus at her felt approach, and secret might,
> *Art* after *Art* goes out, and all is Night.
> See skulking *Truth* to her old Cavern fled,
> Mountains of Casuistry heap'd o'er her head!
> *Philosophy*, that lean'd on Heav'n before,
> Shrinks to her second cause, and is no more.
> *Physic* or *Metaphysic* begs defence,

> And *Metaphysic* calls for aid on *Sense!*
> See *Mystery* to *Mathematics* fly!
> In vain! they gaze, turn giddy, rave, and die.
> *Religion* blushing veils her sacred fires,
> And unawares *Mortality* expires.
> Nor *public* Flame, nor *private*, dares to shine;
> Nor *human* Spark is left, nor Glimpse *divine*!
> Lo! thy dread Empire, CHAOS! is restor'd
> Light dies before thy uncreating word:
> Thy hand, great Anarch! lets the curtain fall;
> And Universal Darkness buries All.

This is a picture of uncreation, of the reversal of God's original bringing of order out of chaos to create the universe and a return to the primal chaos. And this destruction of order—order which he had so praised in the *Essay on Man*—comes about as a consequence of the victory of dullness, of bad poetry, the forces of anti-culture. It does not say much for the grand scheme of order in the universe that it can be overthrown by a handful of bad poets. And even if we do not take this literally, there can be no doubt that this nightmare vision of Pope's represents a real fear, a real sense of the precariousness of culture and civilization, not merely a getting his own back at a few personal literary enemies.

The truth is that the forces of optimism and rationality that critics and literary historians used to see as so characteristic of the eighteenth century (a century that George Saintsbury characterized as 'a place of rest and refreshment') were very precariously balanced indeed. The age of reason could equally well be called the age of madness. Dr Johnson, that eminently reasonable critic, was afflicted by a recurring melancholia that he himself considered to be verging on the brink of madness. Christopher Smart was considered mad by his contemporaries. William Cowper suffered from intervals of madness. William Collins, after long suffering from mental depression, died insane. The great Jonathan Swift himself, the supreme apostle of man as a creature *rationis capax*, if he did not, in Dr Johnson's words, 'expire a driveller and a show' was certainly deemed in his last few years to be 'of unsound mind and memory'. On the one hand belief in man as a rational animal could lead to such frustration in the face of the daunting facts of experience that a man might be driven almost out of his mind; on the other, dependence on inner religious conviction might lead to desperately unsettling doubts of one's own salvation.

The century that followed Newton, for all its belief that, as Pope put it,

> Nature and Nature's Laws lay hid in Night.
> God said, *Let Newton be*! and All was Light,

was thus not altogether committed to the belief that, divine order in the universe having been satisfactorily proved and explained, there was no cause for alarm and despondency. Quite apart from the seething social inequities and the positively frightening disparity between the lives of genteel Newtonian deists and the lives of those at the bottom of the social and economic scale, there were many evidences in both England and Scotland throughout the eighteenth century of a desperate sense of living in a state of unstable equilibrium from which one could easily fall into madness. For, although the argument from design was widely accepted in discussions about proofs of the existence of God, it did not really take David Hume to prove that if we argued from design we might well come to have grave doubts about the intentions or abilities of the designer. In his *Vanity of Human Wishes* Dr Johnson gives a devastating account of the ills that await mortals, however gifted or good. Even the virtuous, temperate, benevolent conscience-free man will be attacked by fate:

> Yet ev'n on this her load Misfortune flings,
> To press the weary minutes flagging wings:
> New sorrow rises as the day returns,
> A sister sickens, or a daughter mourns.
> Now kindred Merit fills the sable bier,
> Now lacerated Friendship claims a tear.
> Year chases year, decay pursues decay,
> Still drops some joy from with'ring life away;
> New forms arise, and diff'rent views engage,
> Superfluous lags the veteran on the stage,
> Till pitying Nature signs the last release,
> And bids afflicted worth retire to peace.

This may remind some readers of Michael's grim picture of the afflictions of men that he presents to Adam in Book XI of *Paradise Lost*:

                                                Immediately a place
           Before his eyes appeard, sad, noysom, dark,
           A Lazar-house it seemd, wherein were laid
           Numbers of all diseas'd, all maladies,
           Of gastly Spasms or racking torture, qualmes
           Of heart-sick Agonie, all feavorous kinds,
           Convulsions, Epilepsies, fierce Catarrhs,
           Intestin Stone and Ulcer, Colic pangs,
           Daemoniac Phrenzie, moaping Melancholie,
           And Moon-struck madness, pining Atrophie,
           Parasmus and wide-wasting Pestilence,
           Dropsies, and Asthma's, and Joint-racking Rheums.
           Dire was the tossing, deep the groans, despair
           Tended the sick busiest from Couch to Couch;
           And over them triumphant Death his Dart
           Shook, but delaid to strike, though oft invok't . . . .

And even if a man observed all the rules of virtue and tem-
perance, Michael goes on, and lives long as a result, until he
drops into the lap of earth 'like ripe fruit',

                                     then thou must outlive
           Thy youth, thy strength, thy beauty, which will change
           To witherd weak and gray; thy Senses then
           Obtuse, all taste of pleasure must forgoe,
           To what thou hast, and for the Aire of youth
           Hopeful and cheerful, in thy blood will reigne
           A melancholy damp of cold and dry
           To weigh thy Spirits down, and last consume
           The Balme of Life.

   To Milton, these horrors were part of the consequences of
the Fall, and could be mitigated by man's looking to the
'paradise within'. Similarly Johnson, at the conclusion of *The
Vanity of Human Wishes*, advises that man should pray for
obedience and resignation and

              For love, which scarce collective man can fill;
              For patience sov'reign o'er transmuted ill;
              For faith, that panting for a happier seat,
              Counts death kind Nature's signal of retreat:
              These goods for man the laws of heav'n ordain,
              These goods he grants, who grants the pow'r to gain;
              With these celestial wisdom calms the mind,
              And makes the happiness she does not find.

Man cannot find happiness in the world, however well designed it was. He must *make* it for himself.

Milton lived in the pre-Newtonian world (though his life overlapped with that of Newton) and in spite of his great interest in contemporary science had no concept of a Newtonian natural religion. Johnson knew very well about a Newtonian natural religion, but he rejected it. He really agreed with Hume's Philo (though of course he detested Hume) that argument from the nature of the universe to the nature of a divine designer could yield very disturbing results. He made this clear in his review of Soame Jenyns's *Free Enquiry into the Nature and Origin of Evil*. Jenyns had argued that the world as it is is a happy and perfectly conducted place, with no undeserved suffering and with the apparent misfortunes of the virtuous neatly compensated, so that, for example, the poor man has more hopes, fewer fears, and greater health than the rich. The whole structure of facile optimism raised by Jenyns was fiercely attacked by Johnson, who believed the argument could more plausibly be turned round the opposite way. When Jenyns raised the possibility that just as men hunt animals for their pleasure, so there may be beings who deceive or destroy men for their own pleasure and utility (and this suggestion was put forward as a 'justification' of the divine order!), Johnson's comment was grim:

I cannot resist the temptation of contemplating this analogy, which, I think, he might have carried further, very much to the advantage of the argument. He might have shown, that these 'hunters, whose game is man' have many sports analagous to our own. As we drown whelps and kittens, they amuse themselves, now and then, with sinking a ship, and stand round the fields of Blenheim, or the walls of Prague, as we encircle a cockpit. As we shoot a bird flying, they take a man in the midst of his business or pleasure, and knock him down with an apoplexy. Some of them, perhaps, are virtuosi, and delight in the operations of an asthma, as a human philosopher in the effects of an air-pump. To swell a man with a tympany is as good sport as to blow a frog. Many a merry bout have these frolick beings at the vicissitudes of an ague, and good sport it is to see a man tumble with an epilepsy, and revive and tumble again, and all this he knows not why. As they are wiser and more powerful than we, they have more exquisite diversions; for we have no way of procuring any sport so brisk and so lasting, as the paroxysms of the gout and

stone, which, undoubtedly, must make high mirth, especially if the
play be a little diversified with the blunders and puzzles of the blind
and deaf. We know not how far their sphere of observation may
extend. Perhaps, now and then, a merry being may place himself in
such a situation, as to enjoy, at once, all the varieties of an epidemical
disease, or amuse his leisure with the tossings and contortions of
every possible pain, exhibited together.

So much for the argument from design: its message is a
hopeless one. Johnson, a devout Christian, did not believe any
more than Milton that life on this earth for post-lapsarian man
was anything but miserable. He clung to his belief in revealed
Christianity as the only possible comfort: neither the structure
of the universe nor the behaviour and fate of man on earth
proved anything in the least bit encouraging. In spite of his
eminent rationality in ordinary affairs of life and indeed in his
literary criticism, Johnson in the last resort believed that the
only hope was in revealed religion, and even that hope could
not be absolutely certain. When Boswell once asked him if any
man had the same conviction of the truth of religion that he had
in the common affairs of life, Johnson answered, 'No, Sir!' He
was afraid of dying and of being sent to Hell. Talking with Dr
William Adams in Oxford some six months before his death, he
expressed his fears. This is Boswell's account of the conversation, in which he took part:

JOHNSON: 'That [God] is infinitely good, as far as the perfection of
his nature will allow, I certainly believe; but it is necessary for good
upon the whole, that individuals should be punished. As to an *individual*, therefore, he is not infinitely good; and as I cannot be *sure* that
I have fulfilled the conditions on which salvation is granted, I am
afraid I shall be one of those who shall be damned.' (looking dis-
mally.) DR ADAMS: 'What do you mean by damned?'
JOHNSON: (passionately and loudly) 'Sent to Hell, Sir, and punished
everlastingly.'

Johnson believed that only a belief in rewards and punishment after death could induce men to lead even approximately
moral lives on earth. Boswell worried constantly about what he
termed a 'future state', and we know the familiar story of his
haunting the death-bed of David Hume to watch in horrified
incredulity how a man who did not believe in a future state

could face death in total calm. Though the argument from design could bring the conclusion that the designer was imperfect or even malicious, the alternative way to God, through revealed religion, brought to many in eighteenth-century Britain despair and madness. It was William Cowper's conviction of his own damnation that drove him mad. The Wesleyan religious revival, that reacted so strongly against Enlightenment thought, brought its own crop of sufferers, of doubters in their salvation whose doubt drove them to despair and madness. In Scotland, twenty-four-year-old Robert Fergusson, having been reminded by the Revd. John Brown of Haddington of the exceeding 'madness of those who, heedless of the awful account which is before them, waste the precious moments of life in idle and profitless gaiety and licence', fell into a fit of religious melancholia which turned into something worse after being awakened one night by the cries of his pet starling being consumed by a cat. As an early biographer wrote: 'The words of John seemed to be written before him in characters of fire, "I will come on thee as a thief, and thou shalt not know what hour I will come upon thee."' Shortly afterwards Fergusson died in the public bedlam of Edinburgh.

But of course the pattern was more complex than all this might suggest. Optimistic believers in a divinely designed Newtonian universe, those who believed that the argument from design if accepted as sole proof of the existence and nature of God could lead to most disturbing conclusions about his motives or abilities or both, those who sought the comforts of revealed religion, and those who, seeking the comforts of revealed religion, found it also threatening their sanity by inducing worries about eternal damnation—these far from exhaust the reactions to science and religion in the Enlightenment. Christopher Smart was locked up as mad by his contemporaries because he took his religion seriously and would insist on praying in public, going down on his knees in parks, streets, and assembly rooms. But his poetry shows no trace whatever of the religious melancholia that afflicted such a poet as Cowper. They are poems of joyful praise to God and his creatures partly in the spirit of the Hebrew Psalms of praise and partly in that of his own happy pleasure in the created world. The famous praise of his cat Jeoffry from *Jubilate Agno* illustrates this very well:

> For I will consider my Cat Jeoffry.
> For he is the servant of the Living God and duly and
>   daily serving him.
> For at the first glance of the glory of God in the
>   East he worships in his way.
> For is this done by wreathing his body seven times
>   round with elegant quickness.
> For then he leaps up to catch the musk, which is
>   the blessing of God upon his prayer.
> For he rolls upon prank to work it in.
> For having done duty and received blessing he begins
>   to consider himself.
> For this he performs in ten degrees.
> For first he looks upon his fore-paws to see if they
>   are clean.
> For secondly he kicks up behind to clear away there;
> For thirdly he works it upon stretch with his fore-paws
>   extended.
> For fourthly he sharpens his paws by wood.
> For fifthly he washes himself.
> For sixthly he rolls upon wash.
> For Seventhly he fleas himself, that he may not be
>   interrupted upon the beat.
> For Eighthly he rubs himself against a post.
> For Ninthly he looks up for his instructions.
> For Tenthly he goes in quest of food.
> For having consider'd God and himself he will consider
>   his neighbour.
> For if he meets another cat he will kiss her in
>   kindness.
> For when he takes his prey he plays with it to give
>   it a chance.
> For one mouse in seven escapes by his dallying.
> For when his days work is done his business more
>   properly begins.
> For he keeps the Lord's watch in the night against
>   the adversary.
> For he counteracts the powers of darkness by his
>   electrical skin and glaring eyes.
> For he counteracts the Devil, who is death, by
>   brisking about the life.

The celebration of the cat concludes:

> For I perceived God's light about him both wax
>   and fire.
> For the electrical fire is the spiritual substance,
>   which God sends from heaven to sustain the bodies
>   both of man and beast.
> For God has blessed him in the variety of his movements.
> For, though he cannot fly, he is an excellent clamberer.
> For his motions upon the face of the earth are more
>   than any other quadrupede.
> For he can tread all the measures upon the music.
> For he can swim for life.
> For he can creep.

These lines are, in their way, as religious as Smart's long
and passionate *Song to David* where he shows the Psalmist's joy
in God's creation and God's power through listing the themes
of David's psalmody in verse of great power and rhythmic
force:

> He sung of God—the mighty source
> Of all things—the stupendous force
>   On which all strength depends;
> From whose right arm, beneath whose eyes,
> All period, power, and enterprise
> Commences, reigns, and ends.

This is not Newtonian deistic poetry nor is it poetry of natural
theology. It belongs to a different area—and era—of sensibility, while at the same time reflecting Smart's own strong
individuality. Smart's praise of God, 'the stupendous force', is
really very different from Thomson's seeing divine planning in
the seasons or Addison's seeing in 'the spacious firmament on
high' signs of a divine designer:

> What though, in solemn Silence, all
> Move round the dark terrestial Ball?
> What tho' nor real Voice nor Sound
> Amid their radiant Orbs be found?
> In Reason's Ear they all rejoice,
> And utter forth a glorious Voice,
> For ever singing as they shine,
> 'The Hand that made us is Divine.'

Of course even the poets who succumbed to religious melancholia had their moments of what might be called devotional peace, as Cowper's *Olney Hymns* show very clearly. Simple devotion—and this is true of other eighteenth-century hymn-writers also—often cuts across moods of doubt and despair to produce verse of religious serenity:

> How blest thy creature is, O God,
>   When with a single eye,
> He views the lustre of thy word,
>   The day-spring from on high!

This Olney Hymn, entitled 'The Happy Change', is one of Cowper's most serene poems. It is hard to believe that it came from the same poet who in his last poem, 'The Castaway', compares himself to a sailor fallen overboard in mid-ocean for whom the ship, sailing fast before the wind, is unable to stop:

> No voice divine the storm allay'd,
>   No light propitious shone;
> When, snatched from all effectual aid,
>   We perish'd, each alone:
> But I beneath a rougher sea,
> And whelm'd in deeper gulphs than he.

Immediate experience might, as Kemp Smith pointed out and as Hume's Philo would have agreed, produce a conviction of the existence of God that could not be satisfactorily produced by the arguments of the natural theologians. But, while immediate experience had its own great compensations, it also had its own dangers, and those poets who trusted to it in the eighteenth century sometimes found themselves in the madhouse. Perhaps it was the climate of the Enlightenment that produced this effect on religious natures. For there is little sign of such an effect in, say, the metaphysical poets of the seventeenth century or in religious poets of still earlier periods.

4 POETIC ATTITUDES TO GOD FROM THE PSALMS TO DANTE

I ended my last lecture by observing that while in the eighteenth century religious natures were sometimes driven to madness by a fear of their own ultimate damnation there is little trace of this in earlier periods, at least not in the poetry. Of course self-doubt and melancholia arising from worry about one's personal salvation is always a possibility among believers in a religion that makes personal salvation in eternity man's supreme goal. The Hebrew Psalmist did not hold this view: the bitter complaints that we find among the Psalms are addressed to God for allowing the wicked to prosper or the Psalmist's enemies to prevail or for abandoning him to misery and misfortune. 'Why standest thou afar off, O Lord', is the cry with which Psalm 10 opens, while Psalm 22 opens with the great cry, 'My God, my God, why hast thou forsaken me?' This does not mean that the hope of eternal salvation has been withdrawn from him, but that he is overcome by enemies who are destroying him.

There are several ways in which the poet can place himself in relation to God. He can *address* him, in prayer or praise or complaint. Again, the Psalms are prime examples here as well as much subsequent devotional poetry. 'Batter my heart, three person'd God', exlaims Donne. And again

> Thou hast made me, And shall thy works decay?
> Repair me now, for now mine end doth haste . . . .

Or there is Herbert:

> Throw away thy rod,
> Throw away thy wrath:
>   O my God,
> Take the gentle path.

There is, in a later age, Gerard Manley Hopkins echoing the Psalmist:

> Thou art indeed just, Lord, if I contend
> With thee; but sir, so what I plead is just.
> Why do sinners' ways prosper? and why must
> Disappointment all I endeavour end?

There are innumerable writers of hymns that address God: 'O God our help in ages past' can stand for a whole class. Hymns, however are to be distinguished from devotional poetry by their more communal nature. They do not, as a rule, represent the voice of the individual seeking an encounter with God, but rather formulate sentiments suitable for a congregation to sing together, so that they tend to lack the personal passion (sometimes the personal anguish) of the writer of devotional poems. The Psalms include poems that could be called hymns—the songs of praise to God, for example—as well as passionate personal poetry.

The poet can do something quite different from addressing God: he can tell his readers *about* God, as Milton does in *Paradise Lost* (although this includes putting words into God's mouth). Milton's epic *presents* God, displays him as a character who acts and speaks. This is not at all the same thing as the 'thus saith the Lord' of the Hebrew prophets, who do not so much tell their auditors about God as act out what they are convinced is God's message. It is different, too, from the theophany in Job where a mysterious God speaks in a quite different way from Milton's coldly logical God.

A third way in which the poet may stand in relation to God is the way of visionary experience. The poet may relate such an experience, in which he encounters either God or some symbolic representation of him. There is nothing visionary in Milton's description of Heaven in *Paradise Lost*, but Dante's picture in his *Paradiso* is visionary. Dante's *Divina Commedia* alternates in a most remarkable way between the visionary and the almost pedantically explanatory. It is a very special kind of visionary poetry, more complex and challenging than a visionary lyric such as Henry Vaughan's 'The World' with its striking first line: 'I saw Eternity the other night.'

Then, as we have seen, the poet may find God indirectly through proof of his working in Nature or evidence of design in the structure of the universe. And finally, as well as addressing God, telling about God, communicating a visionary experience of God, and finding God through his works, the poet can agonize about God's existence. This last is a much more modern approach, and first appears significantly in the nineteenth century. Tennyson's *In Memoriam* is a central example of this while Matthew Arnold's 'Dover Beach' illustrates another aspect of a similar phenomenon. As well as these five ways of positioning himself in relation to God, as it were, it is possible for the poet simply to deny his existence, as James Thomson did in his *City of Dreadful Night* and as Thomas Hardy did in his poem 'Hap'. It is also possible to write deliberately agnostic poetry, as Wallace Stevens did memorably in 'Sunday Morning'.

To return to the Psalms, we find in this extraordinary collection of religious poems the fullest examples of the first mode, the poet *addressing* God, examples that have inspired innumerable poets, both Jewish and Christian, to attempt similar work. There are appeals to God: 'Hear me when I call, O God of my righteousness' (Psalm 40); 'O Lord, rebuke me not in thine anger, neither chasten me in thy hot displeasure' (Psalm 6); 'Help, Lord; for the godly man ceaseth' (Psalm 12); 'Hear the right, O Lord, attend unto my cry' (Psalm 17); 'Unto thee will I cry, O Lord my rock' (Psalm 28); 'Be merciful unto me, O God, be merciful unto me' (Psalm 56). These are statements of confidence in God: 'The Lord is my shepherd; I shall not want' (Psalm 23); 'God is our refuge and strength, a very present help in trouble' (Psalm 46). Then there is the large category of Psalms which simply praise God: 'Great is the Lord, and greatly to be praised' (Psalm 48); 'Make a joyful noise unto God, all ye lands: sing forth the honour of his name: make his praise glorious' (Psalm 66); and the series of 'Hallelujah' psalms that conclude the collection. 'Hallelujah' is simply the imperative plural of the Hebrew word *hilel*, 'to praise' coupled with 'jah', the short form of the name of God; 'praise ye the Lord'. (I might remark incidentally that it is quite different from *hosanna*, which is often used in Christian tradition as though it meant the same thing: *hosanna* is not an exclamation of praise, but of supplication. It is the Hebrew *hoshah-na*, where *hosha* (or *hoshia*) is the imperative singular of the verb 'to save' and '*na*' is a particle of supplication or entreaty, so that the expression means 'Save, pray!' and is addressed to God, whereas 'hallelujah' is addressed to the people.) It might be said that these Psalms of praise are not strictly poems in which the poet *addresses* God, for he is addressing the people, telling them to praise God. But this is in a sense

a quibble, for the whole tone of the 'Hallelujah' Psalms is that
of an address to God.

Praise of God was regarded from very early in the development of the Hebrew religious tradition as a prime duty of man.
God deserved praise and enjoyed it. His function was very
largely to be praised—and this is how Milton saw it too in
Paradise Lost. In Christian tradition the angels spend their time
in praising God, and so do the blessed in Paradise. In both
Jewish and Christian religious tradition praise is seen as a form
of prayer, and prayer and praise are closely associated. George
Herbert considered praise of God to be man's chief function:

> Of all the creatures both in sea and land
> Onely to Man thou hast made known thy wayes,
> And put the penne alone into his hand,
> And made him Secretarie of thy praise.
>
> Beasts fain would sing; birds dittie to their notes;
> Trees would be tuning on their native lute
> To thy renown: but all their hands and throats
> Are brought to Man, while they are lame and mute.
>
> Man is the worlds high Priest: he doth present
> The sacrifice for all; while they below
> Unto the service mutter an assent,
> Such as springs use that fall, and windes that blow.
>
> He that to praise and laud thee doth refrain,
> Doth not refrain unto himself alone,
> But robs a thousand who would praise thee fain,
> And doth commit a world of sin in one.

These lines are from Herbert's poem 'Providence'. In his
poem entitled 'Miserie' he laments the difficulty of imperfect
man's praising perfect God, yet the attempt must be made:

> My God, Man cannot praise thy name:
> Thou art all brightnesse, perfect puritie;
> The sunne holds down his head for shame,
> Dead with eclipses, when we speak of thee:
> How shall infection
> Presume in thy perfection?
>
> As dirtie hands foul all they touch,
> And these things most, which are most pure and fine:
> So our clay hearts, ev'n when we crouch

To sing thy praises, make them lesse divine.
                Yet either this,
            Or none, thy portion is.

The long religious tradition, both Jewish and Christian, of
praising and thanking God has probably produced more religious poetry than any other theme. In that section of the
Talmud entitled *Berachot* ('Benedictions'), which deals with the
various occasions and the various ways in which God should be
blessed and praised, there is a charming little four-line poem
which expresses with attractive simplicity what one might call
a mood of innocent devotion. It is intended as a benediction to
be recited by one 'who goes outside during the month of Nisan
[March-April] and sees trees budding'. I quote it first in the
original Hebrew:

בָּרִיךְ שֶׁלֹּא חָסַר בְּעוֹלָמוֹ כְּלוּם

וּבָרָא בּוֹ בְּרִיּוֹת טוֹבוֹת

וְאִילָנוֹת טוֹבוֹת

לְהִתְנָאוֹת בָּהֶם בְּנֵי אָדָם.

Blessed is he who has left nothing at all out of his world,
Who has created in it beautiful creatures
And beautiful trees
That men may look on them with delight.

The ninth-tenth-century medieval Jewish philosopher
Sa'adiah Gaon, in a poem entitled גָּדַלְתָּ מְאֹד, 'You are
Great Indeed', praised God for His creative and designing
power. Here are the first two stanzas in the translation by
T. Carmi:[1]

> You are far greater than all architects:
> for they fix the lower, then erect the
> upper part above it; but You first fixed
> the heavens, then stretched the earth
> beneath them as a haven. *O Lord my
> God, You are great indeed!*

> You are far greater than all those who
> have hearing: for they cannot grasp the
> words of two people who address them

[1] *The Penguin Book of Hebrew Verse*, ed. and trans. T. Carmi, Harmondsworth, 1981, p. 253.

at the same time; but You hear what is
said by all the ends of the earth, as well
as the islands of the sea; nothing
escapes You. *O Lord my God, You are*
great indeed!

The poem concludes by praising God as the greatest of all
artists: גָּדַלְתָּ מִכָּל הַצַּיָּרִים :

You are far greater than all artists: for
they can only make forms by the light
of day or fire; but You form all life
within the entrails, in the hidden
recesses and innermost chambers.
O Lord my God, You are great indeed!

Poetry of what I have called innocent devotion is not of
course concerned with demonstrating or justifying anything.
What the author of Job saw as a deep and incomprehensible
mystery, with which man must be content, the great Hebrew
poet of twelfth-century Spain, Jehudah Halevi, saw as simple
cause for praise: in his short poem beginning כָּל כּוֹכְבֵי בֹקֶר
לְךָ יָשִׁירוּ , 'All the stars of the morning sing to thee', he takes
the phrase from Chapter 38 of Job about the morning stars singing together and associates himself with their glorifying of God.
At the same time Halevi could see the paradox of God's being
both hidden and revealed. In his poem 'Thy Glory fills the
World' he expresses this paradox directly:

יָהּ אָנָה אֶמְצָאֲךָ מְקוֹמְךָ נַעֲלָה וְנֶעְלָם
וְאָנָה לֹא אֶמְצָאֲךָ כְּבוֹדְךָ מָלֵא עוֹלָם

Lord, where shall I find thee?
Thy place is high and hidden.
And where shall I not find thee?
Thy glory fills the world.[2]

God is both a *deus absconditus* and revealed in Nature. This is
not the Newtonian argument from design that we find, for ex-

---

[2] T. Carmi, op. cit. 338. The translation here is not Carmi's but my own.

ample, in James Thomson, for it is not an argument at all, nor an inference, but a statement of what is seen as fact.

God's Work is interpreted in the light of God's Word. George Herbert saw the latter as more legible than the former:

> Starres are poore bookes, and oftentimes do misse:
> This book of starres lights to eternall blisse.
>
> ('The Holy Scripture', II)

For Herbert Nature was a divine hieroglyph that could be properly interpreted only through the light of God's word:

> Indeed mans whole estate
> Amounts (and richly) to serve thee:
> He did not heav'n and earth create,
> Yet studies them, not him by whom they be.
>
> Teach me thy love to know;
> That this new light, which now I see,
> May both the work and workman show:
> Then by a sunne-beam I will climbe to thee.

Like Sa'adiah Gaon, Herbert saw God the great architect and artist everywhere, but in Herbert's view God is not only the architect of Nature, he is also, as such a poem as 'The Church-floore' shows, the architect of man's salvation who builds in human hearts:

> Blest be the *Architect*, whose art
> Could build so strong in a weak heart.

God's art is a challenge to human art, whose sole justification is to be put at God's service:

> Wherefore with my utmost art
> I will sing thee.
>
> ('Praise (II)')

The clearest statement of the devotional position that holds that God's work can be seen as reflecting his glory only if the viewer already loves God in the proper way is revealed in Jehudah Halevi's poem, מִי כָמוֹךָ , 'Who is Like Thee?':

> The Creator who brings forth all from nothing
> Is revealed to the heart, but not to the eye . . . .

Francis Bacon distinguished between God's Word, as revealed by Him and studied by His ministers, and God's Work, the natural world, the province of scientific enquiry, and he was content to assign the former to divines so that he and those like him could study the natural world unhindered by any other considerations. Herbert, who admired Bacon—he called him 'The Prince of Theories, the High Priest of Truth' in a poem written in his praise—nevertheless interpreted Bacon's distinction between the two sources of truth quite differently from Bacon himself, as we have seen. The parallels between the great apostle of inductive science and the devotional poet who believed in submitting himself to God's grace in order to be able to see God at work in Nature and even then regarding God's revealed word as the more assured source of truth, are in some ways surprisingly close, as Joseph Summers pointed out in the appendix on 'Bacon and Herbert' in his study *George Herbert: His Religion and Art*. There are passages in Book Three of *The Advancement of Learning*, such as the praise of 'that divine state of mind' where charity 'comprehendeth and fasteneth all virtues together', with which Herbert would have been in wholehearted agreement. Bacon's insistence, in *The Great Instauration*, that 'it was not that pure and uncorrupted natural knowledge whereby Adam gave names to the creatures' that is suspect, but 'the ambitious and proud desire of moral knowledge to judge of good and evil, to the end that man may revolt from God and give laws to himself', and his defence of charity (of which 'there can be no excess') in the same passage, again would have been acceptable to Herbert. There was as yet no conflict seen—certainly not by Herbert—between science and religion. Nor was there yet an attempt to resolve the problem through natural theology. Thomas Burnet, in his *Sacred Theory of the Earth*, reconciled the study of God's Work and God's Word by the perhaps surprising argument that God's handwriting was equally difficult to read in both.

The *difficulty* of writing religious poetry was seen and expressed in different ways by Dante, Milton, and Herbert. Herbert felt the paradox that while the true Christian poet owed God the best artistic language he could form, yet in the end he must be willing to surrender his subtle craftsmanship to the simplicities of faith:

Farewell sweet phrases, lovely metaphors.
But will ye leave me thus? when ye before
Of stews and brothels onely knew the doores,
There did I wash you with my tears, and more,
    Brought you to Church well drest and clad:
My God must have my best, ev'n all I had.

Lovely enchanting language, sugar-cane,
Hony of roses, whither wilt thou flie?
Hath some fond lover tic'd thee to thy bane?
And wilt thou leave the Church, and love a stie?
    Fie, thou wilt soil thy broider'd coat,
And hurt thy self, and him that sings the note.

Let foolish lovers, if they will love dung,
With canvas, not with arras, clothe their shame:
Let follie speak in her own native tongue.
True beautie dwells on high: ours is a flame
    But borrow'd thence to light us thither.
Beautie and beauteous words should go together.

Yet if you go, I passe not; take your way:
For, *Thou art still my God*, is all that ye
Perhaps with more embellishment can say.
Go birds of spring: let winter have his fee;
    Let a bleak palenesse chalk the doore,
So all within be livelier then before.
                  ('The Forerunners')

Milton, aware of the daring nature of his unprecedented
attempt to justify the ways of God to men in an epic poem,
appealed for illumination and support to the divine creative
Spirit that formed the universe:

                    What in me is dark
Illumin, what is low raise and support;
That to the highth of this great Argument
I may assert Eternal Providence
And justifie the wayes of God to men.

Dante, at the very beginning of the *Inferno*, expressed his
sense of the difficulty of conveying his experience to the reader:

Ah quanto a dir qual era è cosa dura . . . .

His sense of the difficulty of expression is naturally even
greater in the *Paradiso*. There is the passage in Canto XXXIII
where language seemed to fail him:

> Da quinci innanzi il mio veder fu maggio
>   che 'l parlar nostro, ch'a tal vista cede,
> E cede la memoria a tanto oltraggio.

From then my vision was greater than our speech, which fails at such a
sight, and memory fails too at such excess.

And later in the same Canto Dante exclaims:

> O quanto è corto il dire e come fiòco
>   al mio concetto!

O how limited is speech and how feeble to my conception!

There is too the great cry in Canto XXX, reminiscent of
Milton's appeal for divine aid:

> O isplendor di Dio, per cu' io vidi
>   l'alto triunfo del regno verace,
>   dammi virtù a dir com' io il vidi!

O splendour of God by which I saw the high triumph of the true
kingdom, give me power to say what I saw there!

Dante shares with Sa'adiah Gaon and George Herbert a sense
of God as the wondrous architect, and with the Psalmist the
view that the heavens declare the glory of God. But, unlike
the others, Dante felt it necessary to be quite specific about
the astronomical details that show how good God's workmanship is.

> Leva dunque, lettore, all'alte ruote
>   meco la vista, dritto a quella parte
>   dove l'un moto e l'altro si percuote;
> e lì commincia a vagheggiar nell'arte
>   di quei maestro che dentro a sè l'ama.
>   tanto che mai da lei occhio non parte.
> Vedi come da indi so dirama
>   l'oblico cerchio che i pianeti porta,
>   per sodisfare al mondo che li chiama.
> E se la strada lor non fosse torta,
>   molta virtù nel ciel sarebbe in vano,
>   e quasi ogni potenza qua giù morta;

> e se dal dritto più o men lontano
> fosse 'l partire, assai sarebbe manco
> e giù e su dell'ordine mondano.

Lift up thine eyes with me then, reader, to the lofty wheels, directing them on that part where the one motion strikes the other, and from that point take thy pleasure in the art of the Master, who so loves it in His heart that His eye never leaves it. See how from there the circle branches obliquely that bears the planets to satisfy the world which calls for them. And if their track were not aslant much virtue in the heavens would be vain and almost every potency down here dead, and if it parted farther or less far from the straight course much would be lacking both above and below in the order of the world.

(Paradiso, X, trans. J. D. Sinclair[3])

Dante explains the workings of the heavens in the conviction that this is evident testimony to God's divine genius and that he himself knows the astronomical facts, in which he clearly delights. Again, this is not the argument from design; God as the creator is not deduced but is a prior assumption.

While Dante delights in explaining with schoolmasterly precision the astronomical facts as he understands them, he is also aware that there are aspects of astronomical reality that are beyond language, such as the nature of the sun:

> Perch' io lo 'ngegno e l'arte e l'uso chiami
> sì nol direi, che mai s' imaginasse;
> ma creder puossi e di veder si brami.
> E se le fantasie nostre son basse
> e tanta altezza, non e maraviglia;
> chè sopra 'l sol non fu occhio ch'andasse.

Were I to summon genius and skill and practice I should never tell of it so that it might be imagined, but we can believe it, and let us long for the sight; and if our imagination is too low for such a height it is no wonder, for never did eye see light greater than the Sun.

(*Paradiso*, X, trans. J.D. Sinclair)

The grand workings of the universe are both to be explained to men and not to be explained to men. Dante's vision, which in the *Paradiso* rises to its supreme heights, is meant to be both instructive and exalting to his readers; but there remain

---

[3] Those passages from Dante translated by J.D. Sinclair are from his three-volume edition and translation of the *Divine Comedy*, London, 1948. Unattributed translations are my own.

mysteries in the working of God's design that are inexpressible
and indeed can be disturbing to the human enquirer. As Dante
says in Canto III of the *Purgatorio*

> Matto è chi spera nostra ragione
> possa trascorrer la infinita via
> che tiene una sustanza in tre persone.
> State contenti, umana gente, al *quia* . . .

Foolish is he who hopes that our reason can trace the infinite way that
one substance in three persons takes. Be content, humankind, with
the *quia*.

Moral questions can be more disturbing than problems of
astronomical design. Why did God allow men to be born with
different talents and different inclinations? Are there not signs
of defective workmanship sometimes?

> Se fosse a punto la cera dedutta
> e fosse il cielo in sua virtù suprema,
> la luce del suggel parebbe tutta;
> ma la natura la dà sempre scema,
> similemente operando all'artista
> c' ha l'abito dell'arte e man che trema.

If the wax were moulded perfectly and the heavens were at the height
of their power, all the brightness of the seal would be seen; but nature
always gives it defectively, working like the artist who has the skill of
his art and a hand that trembles.

(Paradiso, XIII, trans. Sinclair)

True, Dante goes on to say here that *il caldo amor*, the burning
love, that is the primal force in the universe, can turn all to perfection. But the problem remains. The *prima materia* does not
always answer to the demands of that primal force. Is God's
power then limited? We are reminded of Fitzgerald's Omar
Khayyám:

> What! did the Hand then of the Potter shake?

This is exactly Dante's 'man che trema'.

While there is no trace in the *Divina Commedia* of the cumulative counter-poem that is built up by the imagery and by other
means in Milton's *Paradise Lost*, there are tensions in Dante's
poem between what might be called his human affections and

his sense of the divine order that give it a special kind of reson-
ance. The very fact that it is Virgil who leads Dante through
Hell and Purgatory, Virgil who is Dante's hero, the supreme
poet, *dolcissimo patre*, sweetest father, *delli altri poeti onore e lume*,
glory and light of the other poets, vibrates with paradox. Virgil,
the supreme poet of Rome, whose empire was in Dante's view
divinely ordained to provide for the coming of Christianity, the
poet who prophesied not only the greatness of the Roman
Empire, but, in his fourth Eclogue, the coming of Christ, was
none the less a pagan and could never enter Paradise. When,
in the thirtieth canto of the *Purgatorio*, Beatrice appears to him,
Dante is so overcome that he turns to Virgil

> col rispitto
> col quale il fantolin corre alla mamma
> quando ha paura o quando elli è afflitto

with the trust of a little child running to his mother when he is afraid
or he is in trouble.

But Virgil has left him; he cannot proceed further and share the
beatific vision with Dante; and Dante weeps, to be comforted
by Beatrice herself:

> Dante, perchè Virgilio se ne vada,
> non pianger anco, non piangere ancora . . . .

But the comfort is also a stern reproof. He will have something
else to weep about, she tells him, addressing him by his name
which here appears for the only time in the whole *Divina Commedia*, and goes on to reproach him for following *via non vera*
after her death so that the only way his salvation could be at-
tained would be by taking him through Hell and Purgatory to
see *le perdute genti* and to learn penitence.

There is a paradox here, too, for although Dante is here to
learn and to become a regenerate man as a result of what he
learns, throughout the poem he puts into the mouths of a variety
of characters whom he meets, in Hell and Purgatory and Paradise equally, the most confident pronouncements about his
views of the corruption of the Church, the degeneracy of the
Papacy, the role of the Roman Empire in establishing Christianity, the future role of the Holy Roman Empire in relation to
the Church, as well as explicit condemnations of his enemies

and praise of those he admired. Yet he does not simply put his
enemies in Hell and those he admires in Paradise. Far from it.
As I have observed, Virgil, who has Dante's supreme admiration, can never enter Paradise. And there is the whole question
of the virtuous heathen and indeed the vast majority of people
who were born before Christ and who, therefore, unless privi-
leged with some special pre-vision of the Christian scheme of
redemption (and this was a tiny minority), were forever excluded
from salvation. The virtuous heathen are in the first circle of
that Hell over whose gate is written PER ME SI VA NELL' ETTERNO
DOLORE, 'through me one goes to eternal pain'. Here he meets
the great poets of ancient Greece and Rome, Homer and Horace
and Ovid and Lucan, whom he describes in the most admiring
terms and who honour him as a poet by making him one of
their number. He also sees other great characters from Greek
and Roman history, including Socrates and Plato and Aristotle.
These are all characters whom Dante admires immensely, yet
they are part of the lost people, *la perduta gente*, living in eternal
pain in a region entry to which is marked by the abandonment
of all hope for ever. Divine Power, supreme Wisdom, and
primal Love created it this way, we are told.

Dante has his own justification of the ways of God to men,
much more succinct than Milton's. Why, he asks in Canto
XIX of the *Paradiso*, should someone born on the banks of the
Indus, with none to speak or read or write of Christ, even
though all his desires are towards good and he lives without sin
so far as he can, be eternally condemned simply because, as a
result of a geographical accident, he dies unbaptized, without
faith?

> ov'è la questa giustizia che 'l condanna?
> ov'è la colpa sua, se ei non crede?

Where is this justice that condemns him? Where is his fault if he does
not believe?

The answer is that human minds are too gross to comprehend
the divine truth that

> La prima volontà, ch'e da sè bona,
> da sè, ch'è sommo ben, mai non si mosse.
> Cotanto è giusto quanto a lei consona:

> nullo creto bene a sè la tira,
> ma essa, radiando, lui cagiona.

The Primal Will, which is good in itself and of itself, which is the Supreme Good, never was moved. Everything is just to the degree that it accords with it. No created good draws it to itself but, shining out in rays, it creates that good.

Divine goodness is the sole source of justice and the only measure of justice; one cannot apply any external standard of justice to it. Dante leaves it at that; it is a mystery, and human minds must be content with that. (The theophany in Job makes a similar point in a wholly different way. There is no suggestion in Job that there is a profound philosophical truth at the heart of the matter; the point in Job is that God's ways in Nature are wondrous and marvellous, incomprehensible to man and not devised for him. Dante would never have distinguished the God of Nature from the God of human justice.)

More moving than the passages from the *Paradise* that I have quoted, and more indicative of the tensions in Dante between his personal moral feeling and the Christian truths imparted to him in his visionary journey, are such passages as the account of his meeting with Francesca of Rimini in Canto V of the *Inferno* and her speech to him, his conversation with the deeply admired teacher Brunetto Latini in Canto XV, the great speech of Ulysses in Canto XXVI describing his final journey, and Ugolino's account of the sufferings and death of his children in Canto XXXIII.

All these characters are damned for eternity in Hell, yet they move Dante to pity and sometimes admiration rather than to moral indignation (as some others of the damned characters do). After Francesca has told him the story of how she and Paolo fell in love Dante 'swooned in pity as though he had died'. To Brunetto Latini Dante pays passionately admiring tribute:

> chè 'n la mente m' è fitta, e or m'accora,
> la cara e buona imagine paterna
> di voi quando nel mondo ad ora ad ora
> m'insegnavate come l'uom s'etterna:
> e quant' io l'abbia in grado, ment' io vivo
> convien che nella mia lingua si scerna.

the dear and kind parternal image of you when many a time in the
world you taught me how man makes himself immortal; and how
much I am grateful for it my tongue, while I live, must needs
declare . . . .

(Trans. Sinclair)

And when at the end of the canto Brunetto Latini turns to leave
him, Dante sees him as the victor in a race, a localised race in
Verona, which gives a special feeling of intimacy and reality to
the image:

> Poi si rivolse, a parve di coloro
>   che corrono a Verona il drappo verde
>   per la campagna; a parve di costoro
> quelli che vince, non colui che perde.

Then he turned round, and seemed like those who run the race for the
green flag in Verona, and he appeared the winner among them, not
the loser.

The reference to the annual race for the green flag in Verona is
one of those many local references—to rivers, towns, hills, and
other places in Italy—that emerge periodically throughout the
Divina Commedia to provide a kind of refreshment in this extraordinary visionary story of travel through Hell, Purgatory, and
Paradise. It helps to establish Dante the narrator as a real person, of a real time and place, with real memories, desires, and
emotions. Theoretically, theologically, this world is nothing
compared to the realities of experience after death (and in this
respect Dante is far removed from the Psalmist), but in the
actual conduct of his story Dante often uses it as a touchstone of
reality.

Ulysses is far down in the eighth circle of Hell, with the false
counsellors, for Dante like so many of his age saw the Trojans
as heroes and those who contrived to assist in the fall of Troy as
villains, and he also saw Ulysses' final voyage (which he seems
to have invented) as an example of inhumanity and arrogance.
But the grandeur of his account of the fatal voyage—on which
Dante makes no comment—tells its own story. Sinclair quotes
Croce: 'No one of his age was more deeply moved than Dante
by the passion to know all that is knowable, and nowhere else
has he given such noble expression to that noble passion as in
the great figure of Ulysses.' Sinclair himself sees here 'conspic-

uously a tension between the poet and the mediaeval theologian, more properly between two ideals and motives; on the one hand, of sheer human craving and daring to know all that men at every mortal cost, can attain to know, and on the other, of the submission of the spirit to the deeper and still costlier disciplines of obedience to providence and grace. Here, if anywhere, Dante's imagination beats at the bars of his day and creed.'

I think perhaps the situation is more complex than this, and it is only the modern mind that sees a simple contrast between what we admire and what we morally disapprove of. Milton after all was to face a similar dilemma in *his* attitude to knowledge, and it is one deeply built into the whole tradition about admissible and forbidden knowledge symbolized in the myth of the eating of the forbidden fruit of the Tree of Knowledge in the Garden of Eden. As Milton saw, knowledge is both dangerous and desirable, and for him the dangers are worth risking. Dante never hinted at this in the way Milton did as I discussed in an earlier lecture. But then Dante's whole technique was very different from Milton's.

In *Paradise Lost* Milton is the omniscient author who is *telling* us. He tells us what goes on in Heaven, Hell, and the Garden of Eden and what the various characters, including God and Satan, say. Dante is telling the reader too, but in a quite different way: he is sharing a visionary experience in which he himself, as well as the reader, is being continuously informed and educated. True, at intervals he launches into informative lectures on doctrinal or astronomical matters, but the general texture of the work is that of sharing with the reader an enlightening and extraordinary visionary experience. Dante's final vision of God, Infinite Goodness visualized as Eternal Light, is very different from Milton's argumentative Deity chopping logic about free will and foreknowledge. Dante's handling of this problem is couched in terms of scholastic philosophy but is at the same time subdued to the terms of his vision. In Canto XVII of the *Paradiso* Dante's ancestor Cacciaguida addresses him on the subject with amor paterno, 'paternal love':

> La contingenza, che fuor del quaderno
> della vostra matera non si stende,
> tutta e depinta nel cospetto etterno:
> necessità però quindi non prende

> se non come dal viso in che si specchia
> nave che per corrente giù discende.

Contingency, which does not extend beyond the volume of your material world, is all depicted in the Eternal Vision, yet does not thence derive necessity, any more than does a ship that drops downstream from the eyes in which it is mirrored. (Trans. Sinclair)

In the end, in Dante all argument is subsumed in vision, for sight is the primary sense throughout the poem, and light the supreme symbol of God. (Milton's appeal to Holy Light at the beginning of Book III of *Paradise Lost* may seem Dantesque, especially the words

> since God is light,
> And never but in unapproached light
> Dwelt from Eternitie,

but this is a unique statement in the poem and a sense of light and of vision does not permeate it as it does Dante's *Paradiso*.) For Dante the vision, the visual experience, is paramount. At the end of *Paradiso* he is in the presence of the *luce etterna* and strives for words to convey the experience. 'Fantasía', which he described in the *Convito* as 'the power by which the intellect represents what it sees', cannot cope with this vision, and in the end Love comes to the rescue:

> All'alta fantasía qui mancò possa;
> ma già volgeva il mio disio e 'l velle,
> sì come rota ch' igualmente e mossa,
> l'amor che move il sole e l'altre stelle.

Here power failed the high fantasy; but now my desire and will, like a wheel which is moved with equal motion, were revolved by the Love that moves the sun and the other stars.

In the end God takes over his faculties and Dante is subsumed in the universal motion of all things. How different from the ending of *Paradise Lost* where Milton's fallen couple go out together to face the challenge of a now imperfect world. 'The world was all before them.' But for Dante the world—that world that he lovingly re-created through the poem in innumerable little touches of description and recollection—was behind him, even though we know he would have to return to it and indeed the purpose of his visionary experience was to enable him to return to it a better person. The climax of a visionary poem is the ultimate vision, which is too transcendent to be properly described but which can be suggested by the proper placing of simple, elemental words such as 'love', 'sun', 'stars'. For of course the *Divina Commedia* is a work of high poetic art and to discuss its ideas without reference to its artful handling of language is to strip it of an essential dimension. It would be for someone more skilled in Italian poetics than I am to demonstrate Dante's verbal art; but in any case my subject in these lectures necessarily leads to more discussion of content than of technique in the works of the poets taken up. In true poetry, however, form and content are bound inextricably up with each other, and I hope that some sense of this comes through in my discussion.

5 MOOD POETRY: THE DILEMMA OF SOLIPSISM

In an age of religious faith a poet had to pit his own experience of life against the creed handed down to him, in which he implicitly believed. Sometimes this creed encouraged religious states of mind that could be expressed in devotional poetry. But often there is a tension between what religion tells him and what experience tells him. Both messages are true, but they are far from identical. The tension between taught religious truth and personally encountered truth produces the special characteristics of certain kinds of religious poetry, such as *Paradise Lost*, as I have tried to show. Tensions, though of a different kind, exist in Dante, for whom experienced truth did conform to the religious truth he learned from his teachers but for whom at the same time personal feeling and personal religious conviction were not always one. For certain kinds of mystical and visionary poets, taught religious truth and personally encountered truth could be one, but in general it is in the tensions between the two kinds of truth that poetry in ages of faith has found its most memorable expression. Those tensions disappear in an age that has lost its implicit religious faith and, instead of having two poles to work between, the poet has only one, his brooding self. The doubting or agnostic poet tends to be a brooder. His poetry tends to lose itself in sad-sweet melancholy or break out into hysteria.

One of the first to diagnose what happened to English poets when they had to fall back on their personal experience without being able to counterpoint it against a truth that came from elsewhere was the American Walt Whitman. In the first of three anonymous reviews which Whitman wrote of his own *Leaves of Grass* soon after its publication in 1855, he compared the English and the American poet and, in particular, Tennyson and himself. He saw English poetry as incurably aristocratic, and he meant by this term not simply a social attitude but a tendency to use culture and leisure in order to cultivate emotional self-indulgence in isolation. Tennyson, he says, 'is the bard of ennui and of the aristocracy, and their combination into love'. He

goes on to say that this kind of love-poetry 'seeks nature for
sickly uses. It goes screaming and weeping after the facts of the
universe, in their calm beauty and equanimity, to note the
occurrence of itself, and to sound the news, in connection with
the charms of the neck, hair, or complexion of a particular
female.' Whitman was probably thinking of *Maud*, which had
just been published. But he was thinking also of nineteenth-
century English poetry in general and of its tendency to use
nature as a background for introspective brooding, to 'seek
nature for sickly uses'. He continues:

Poetry, to Tennyson and his British and American *élèves*, is a gentleman
of the first degree, boating, fishing, and shooting genteelly through
nature, admiring the ladies, and talking to them, in company, with
that elaborate half-choked deference that is to be made up by the
terrible license of men among themselves. The spirit of the burnished
society of upper-class England fills this writer and his effusions from
top to toe. Like that, he does not ignore courage and the superior
qualities of men, but all is to show forth through dandified forms. He
meets the nobility and gentry half-way. The models are the same both
to the poet and the parlors. Both have the same supercilious elegance,
both love the reminiscences which extol caste, both agree on the
topics proper for mention and discussion, both hold the same under-
tone of church and state, both have the same languishing melancholy
and irony, both indulge largely in persiflage, both are marked by the
contour of high blood and a constitutional aversion to anything
cowardly and mean, both accept the love depicted in romances as the
great business of a life or a poem, both seem unconscious of the
mighty truths of eternity and immortality, both are silent on the
presumptions of liberty and equality, and both devour themselves in
solitary lassitude.[1]

This is a brilliant if malicious portrait, coloured, it is true, by
Whitman's self-conscious Americanism and his desire to follow
Emerson's advice in freeing himself from the courtly muses of
Europe, but at the same time specifying with cunning accuracy
some important elements in what might be called the Tennysonian tradition. Precisely what Whitman means by 'dandified'
I shall discuss later. First I should like to follow Whitman's
diagnosis of 'languishing melancholy' and 'solitary lassitude'
and try to show that this represents a clear insight into an

[1] *The Poetry and Prose of Walt Whitman*, p. 543.

important characteristic of much Victorian poetry. Whitman is here describing what I call, for lack of a better phrase, the Victorian elegiac mode. Victorian poetry ran to elegy and Victorian poets tended to believe that what was most elegiac was most poetical; their movement towards elegy, that is to say, was bound up with their deepest feelings about the nature of poetry. Again and again we find in Victorian poetry the poet removing himself from the workaday world in a mood of controlled self-pity to lose himself in sad-sweet meditation:

> And the stately ships go on
>   To their haven under the hill;
> But O for the touch of a vanish'd hand,
>   And the sound of a voice that is still!
>   ('Break, break, break')

The prospect of the world at work or at play sends the poet, not outward to imagine the reality of those other lives around him (as Whitman imagined them), but inward to intensify his isolation. 'The noise of life' is the signal for the poet's renewed cultivation of elegy:

> He is not here; but far away
>   The noise of life begins again,
>   And the ghastly through the drizzling rain
> On the bald street breaks the blank day.

The resolution of problems or of woes through the cultivation of a mood in which they can dissolve and become part of a generalized sense of loss or loneliness is related to the romantic tendency to throw the poet back on to his own personality as the only reality, for in a post-religious age he sees no other source of truth. There is a line in nineteenth-century poetry that moves steadily towards solipsism. We see it clearly first in Keats, the source of so much in the Tennysonian tradition:

> When I have fears that I may cease to be
>   Before my pen has glean'd my teeming brain,
> Before high-piled books, in charactery,
>   Hold like rich garners the full ripen'd grain;
> When I behold, upon the night's starr'd face,
>   Huge cloudy symbols of a high romance,
> And I think that I may never live to trace

> Their shadows, with the magic hand of chance;
> And when I feel, fair creature of an hour,
>   That I shall never look upon thee more,
> Never have relish in the faery power
>   Of unreflecting love;—then on the shore
> Of the wide world I stand alone, and think
> Till love and fame to nothingness do sink.

The contrast between this sonnet and Milton's sonnet on his blindness is striking. While Keats can find comfort only in a mood of dissolving introspection, Milton appeals outside his own mood to another truth, and trusts in God:

> When I consider how my light is spent
>   E're half my days, in this dark world and wide,
>   And that one Talent which is death to hide,
>   Lodg'd with me useless, though my Soul more bent
> To serve therewith my Maker, and present
>   My true account, least he returning chide,
>   Doth God exact day-labour, light deny'd,
>   I fondly ask; But patience to prevent
> The murmur, soon replies, God doth not need
>   Either man's work or his own gifts, who best
>   Bear his mild yoak, they serve him best, his State
> Is Kingly. Thousands at his bidding speed
>   And post ore Land and Ocean without rest:
>   They also serve who only stand and waite.

The tone of Keats's sonnet is common in Tennyson; for Tennyson too a characteristic pose is to stand on the shore alone and muse grief into sadness. We see it often in Matthew Arnold:

> Listen! you hear the grating roar
> Of pebbles which the waves draw back, and fling,
> At their return, up the high strand,
> Begin, and cease, and then again begin,
> With tremulous cadence slow, and bring
> The eternal note of sadness in.

It is true that Arnold in 'Dover Beach' is not altogether alone; but his companion is merely an extension of his own lonely self, and the emphasis is on their dual isolation from the meaningless confusion of the world:

> Ah, love, let us be true
> To one another! for the world, which seems

To lie before us like a land of dreams,
So various, so beautiful, so new,
Hath really neither joy, nor love, nor light,
Nor certitude, nor peace, nor help for pain;
And we are here as on a darkling plain
Swept with confused alarms of struggle and flight,
Where ignorant armies clash by night.

The function of natural scenery in this kind of poetry tends to be the setting of a mood; natural objects are used so that we may move at once from them to the sensibility that responds to them—very different from the use of natural objects in Gerard Manley Hopkins, who never employs the Victorian elegiac mode. In his early poetry Tennyson may do this excessively:

Upon the middle of the night,
    Waking she heard the night-fowl crow:
The cock sung out an hour ere light:
    From the dark fen the oxen's low
Came to her: without hope of change,
In sleep she seem'd to wake forlorn,
    Till cold winds woke the gray-eyed morn
About the lonely moated grange.

                                        (*Mariana*)

Even in love poetry, as Whitman perceived, there is a rejection of the external world as of any interest in itself; it exists to reflect more interest on to the lovers, who remain in dual isolation. Consider the imagery in 'Now sleeps the crimson petal' (*The Princess*, vii). There is no interest in the flowers as flowers, no attempt to render their 'quiddity', their own individual reality. The natural images set the mood, they suggest the poet's state of mind and emotion. 'Now droops the milkwhite peacock like a ghost, / And like a ghost she glimmers on to me.' 'Glimmer' is a favourite Tennysonian verb; it has a merging and dissolving function. Everything, even the poet's beloved, is finally merged in the poet himself: 'So fold thyself, my dearest, thou, and slip / Into my bosom and be lost in me.' The crimson and white petals, the gold fin, the porphyry font, the silent meteor, and all the other visualized objects point only to the self and to isolation: they exist in order to invite sympathy with the mood of the observer. The Victorian poet's use of *objects*

very often has this function, as in the opening stanza of
Mariana:

> With the blackest moss the flower-plots
>   Were thickly crusted, one and all:
> The rusted nails fell from the knots
>   That held the pear to the gable-wall . . . .

The Pre-Raphaelites developed the use of objects with a
more self-conscious feeling for the symbolic values of simple
things, and this line is a steady one in Victorian poetry. To
name things precisely in order to set up a vague feeling of what
they mean or suggest—it is exactly what we find in Edward
Lear:

> They sailed to the Western Sea, they did—
> To a land all covered with trees;
> And they bought an owl, and a useful cart,
> And a pound of rice, and a cranberry-tart,
>   And a hive of silvery bees;
> And they bought a pig, and some green jackdaws,
> And a lovely monkey with lollipop paws,
>   And forty bottles of ring-bo-ree,
>   And no end of Stilton cheese.

The piling-up of objects here is of course deliberately aimless
and exaggerated, and the result is parody, yet even here we
cannot help feeling that there is an appropriate *mood* to which
these objects point, and the mixture of the exotic and the familiar achieves a teasing mixture of nostalgia and adventure that
is not unimpressive. There are exceptions, of course—Browning
in one direction and Hopkins in the other—but on the whole it
might be said that the Victorian poet is not interested in objects
or places or other people except in so far as by naming them he
may help to build up a mood which emanates from and returns
to his own emotional state. Swinburne is the last stage in this
development—his naming of objects never leads us to the objects
at all, but stops at the names and exploits their suggestiveness
by hinting, through rhythmic and other devices, at possible
contexts in which these names might carry an overpowering
emotional charge. This is essentially the poetry of agnosticism:
nothing is known except individual mood.

The Victorian poet tended to see the external world in the

mirror of his own introspection, and if he turned away to
look at it directly the curse came upon him as it came upon
the Lady of Shalott: he became garrulous and pretentious.
(There are exceptions to this rash generalization, of course, but
it nevertheless represents a real truth.) The paradox is that the
world in the mirror could be described in the most accurate and
meticulous detail; some of Tennyson's natural descriptions, for
example, are remarkably precise and show most careful observation; yet his purpose in such descriptions is to lead back to
himself or to the character with whom he identifies himself. For
my point is not that the Victorian poet always talks about himself; the Victorian elegiac mode can operate equally well in the
dramatic monologue—as in Tennyson's *Œnone* and *Ulysses* or
in pseudo-epic narrative poetry, as in *Morte d'Arthur*. But there
is always a focus for the mood, some stand-in for the poet, as it
were, round whom the proper emotional atmosphere gathers.
Nothing is more characteristic of this phase of Victorian poetry
than the modulation of the heroic into the elegiac which we find
in Tennyson and Arnold—in 'The Lotos-Eaters' and *Morte
d'Arthur*, for example, and in Arnold's *Sohrab and Rustum* and
Tristram and Iseult.

The opening of 'The Lotos-Eaters' provides an excellent
illustration of this sort of modulation. It opens on a heroic note—

'Courage!' he said, and pointed toward the land . . .

but almost immediately the heroic fades into the languid:

> In the afternoon they came unto a land
> In which it seemed always afternoon.
> All round the coast the languid air did swoon,
> Breathing like one that hath a weary dream.
> Full-faced above the valley stood the moon;
> And like a downward smoke, the slender stream
> Along the cliff to fall and pause and fall did seem.

Notice the adjectives—'*languid* air', '*weary* dream', which assist
the suggestions of the natural objects described so carefully.
For another two stanzas Tennyson develops natural images,
organized and presented in order to assist the mood of languor
and pleasing sadness—'slow-dropping veils', 'wavering lights
and shadows', 'slumbrous sheet of foam', 'gleaming river',

'silent pinnacles of aged snow', 'sunset-flushed', 'shadowy
pine', 'charmed sunset', 'winding vale'—until he is ready to
introduce the culminating symbolic figures, 'the mild-eyed
melancholy Lotos-eaters'. In some sense the lotos-eaters stand
for the poet or for the poetic mood. Lotos-eating does not yield
happiness, but pleasing sadness:

> Eating the Lotos day by day,
> To watch the crisping ripples on the beach,
> And tender curving lines of creamy spray;
> To lend our hearts and spirits wholly
> To the influence of mild-minded melancholy;
> To muse and brood . . . .

Even where the theme of the poem is heroic assertion, as in
Ulysses, the imagery evokes elegiac suggestions:

> I will drink
> Life to the lees: all times I have enjoy'd
> Greatly, have suffer'd greatly, both with those
> That loved me, and alone; on shore, and when
> Thro' scudding drifts the rainy Hyades
> Vext the dim sea . . . .

The adjective 'dim' gives notice of the modulation into elegy
that takes place more completely later in the poem, when,
paradoxically, the final assertion of heroic purpose becomes
plangent and charged with sadness:

> something ere the end,
> Some work of noble note, may yet be done,
> Not unbecoming men that strove with Gods.
> The lights begin to twinkle from the rocks:
> The long day wanes: the slow moon climbs: the deep
> Moans round with many voices.

Tennyson's most strenuous artifice is generally put at the
service of the elegiac mood; here, the long vowel sounds ('the
slow moon climbs: the deep moans round'), the careful patterning and balancing of the vowels ('the long day wanes'), the
use of alliteration, and other devices, transpose the mood of
Ulysses almost to that of 'Break, break, break'. We see the same
thing if we compare Malory's Arthurian stories with Tennyson's
versions: everywhere the heroic turns to the elegiac. It is true

that there is something of this in Malory's own account, particularly in his account of the final collapse of the fellowship of
the Round Table with its sense of nostalgia for a lost age of
chivalry; but Tennyson emphasizes it and draws out the melancholy cadence wherever he can:

> So saying, from the pavement he half rose,
> Slowly, with pain, reclining on his arm,
> And looking wistfully with wide blue eyes
> As in a picture.
>
> *(Morte D'Arthur)*

This is almost pre-Raphaelite, the situation presented pictorially
in order to evoke the proper subdued response. Elsewhere, the
emphasis on loneliness and isolation draws everything into
a single context of withdrawal and loss:

> and from them rose
> A cry that shiver'd to the tingling stars,
> And, as it were one voice, an agony
> O lamentation, like a wind that shrills
> All night in a waste land, where no one comes,
> Or hath come, since the making of the world.
>
> (Ibid.)

The withdrawal is from time as well as space: the individual on
this lonely shore is all of human history and geography.

The view that lies behind this kind of poetic practice seems to
be that the most effective poetic image is one which concen-
trates and isolates. The final meaning of the tragedy of Sohrab
and Rustum emerges at the end of Arnold's poem in terms of
a lonely landscape very like that 'waste land, where no one
comes' at the end of *Morte d'Arthur.*

> But the majestic river floated on,
> Out of the mist and hum of that low land,
> Into the frosty starlight, and there moved,
> Rejoicing, through the hush'd Chorasmian waste,
> Under the solitary moon . . . .

The word 'rejoicing' here is somewhat surprising, both in its
unexpected use of the 'pathetic fallacy' and in the note of joy
which it introduces; but it is clear in the light of the total context of these lines that the river is rejoicing to have escaped

from populated areas to solitariness and silence. It is the same
joy in melancholy that is associated with lotos-eating in Tennyson. In the very last lines of the poem, when it looks as though
Arnold is going to give us a picture of the thundering ocean as
the river's final goal, we find instead that even the dash of
waves is subdued to the tranquil starlight and the poem ends in
an enchanted starlit silence, characteristic of many a nineteenth-
century poetic setting.

> till at last
> The long'd-for dash of waves is heard, and wide
> His luminous home of waters opens, bright
> And tranquil, from whose floors the new-bathed stars
> Emerge, and shine upon the Aral Sea.

The scene is impersonal, removed from the characters of the
poem and from the poet himself; yet can we not call it the
'objective correlative' of a mood, the same mood projected
autobiographically in 'Dover Beach' and in the opening of
'A Summer Night'?

> In the deserted, moon-blanch'd street,
> How lonely rings the echo of my feet!
> Those windows, which I gaze at, frown,
> Silent and white, unopening down,
> Repellent as the world . . . .

Both natural objects and the world at work tend to increase
the Victorian poet's sense of loneliness and point back to his
musing self; the invitation to eat the lotos is always in the background, if it is not in the foreground. How utterly different, in
its use of language and in its placing of the poet's self, is the
poetry of Walt Whitman! I began by quoting Whitman's
remarks—both admiring and disapproving—on Tennyson,
because I believe that Whitman's insight into some important
aspects of Tennyson's art is bound up with his own clear intention of avoiding precisely what he describes so well. Whitman
is a poet of the self in a very different way from Tennyson. Both
poets fall back upon themselves, their moods, their responses to
their environment, without any appeal to a third force—that is,
in addition to the poet and his environment—of the kind that is
found in overtly religious poets. Each illustrates in a different
way the dilemma, or at least the practice, of a poet when an

objectively existing God is no longer a factor in the poet's consciousness. Whitman uses what might be called the imagery of association rather than the imagery of introspection, and though he talks about himself even more than the Victorian poets he uses that self in a unique way. Consider, for example, the well-known opening of *Song of Myself*:

> I celebrate myself, and sing myself,
> And what I assume you shall assume,
> For every atom belonging to me as good belongs to you.
>
> I loafe and invite my soul,
> I lean and loafe at my ease observing a spear of summer grass.

The tone here is direct, familiar, even slangy. And the poem is *addressed* to a reader, addressed with studied negligence. The initial statements are presumptuous, bordering indeed on the absurd. 'And what I assume you shall assume.' But the poet is aware of this; the claim is made half-humorously, with a deliberate air of careless exaggeration. What he means by these extraordinary remarks becomes clear as the poem proceeds; the opening arrests and invites. Further, for all its apparent egocentricity the poem is not focused on the poet's own self and his own mood, as so much English nineteenth-century poetry is; it takes real cognizance of other people and other things. 'I lean and loafe at my ease observing a spear of summer grass.' The spear of grass is of course a basic Whitmanesque symbol; nevertheless, the important thing here is not so much what it is as that the poet is looking at it for what it is. He is 'loafing'. Whitman's loafing is wholly different from the mood of elegiac introspection in Tennyson and Arnold; it represents a deliberate angling of his sensibility towards the external world, towards other people and other things; it represents an induced mood of receptivity. Whitman is as aware as any European romantic poet or any English Victorian poet of the demands of the self and is as determined as they are to keep himself in the centre of his poems; but by radiating out from the centre the self can achieve community, even in a sense identity, with other selves. The otherness of other people remains a mystery to Whitman as it remained to D.H. Lawrence (who castigated Whitman for believing in 'merging' with other people instead of seeing that real love was the awareness of the mystical core of otherness in the other person), but for him the mystery is a continual challenge. How can one pose the self so that it can enter into the otherness of other people?

> Trippers and askers surround me,
> People I meet, the effect upon me of my early life or the ward
>   and city I live in, or the nation,
> The latest dates, discoveries, inventions, societies, authors old
>   and new,
> My dinner, dress, associates, looks, compliments, dues,
> The real or fancied indifference of some man or women I love.
>
> The sickness of one of my folks or of myself, or ill-doing or loss
>   or lack of money, or depressions or exaltations,
> Battles, the horrors of fratricidal war, the fever of doubtful
>   news, the fitful events;
> But they are not the Me myself.
>
> Apart from the pulling and hauling stands what I am,
> Stands amused, complacent, compassionating, idle, unitary,
> Looks down, is erect, or bends an arm on an impalpable
>   certain rest,
> Looking with side-curved head curious what will come next,
> Both in and out of the game and watching and wondering at it.

The language here is completely free of the brooding introspective cadence, that sense of reducing all light to twilight or starlight or moonlight, the transcendental hush of lonely genius communing with itself, that is so common in Victorian poetry. Whitman's poetic self is both separate and isolate *and* participating, part of a community, 'both in and out of the game and watching and wondering at it'. The self observes, half humorously, a little wryly, the self observing. The first requirement of the poetic self is full realization of its position, of its uniqueness and its share in humanity, its capacity for withdrawal and its capacity for community, and only after this realization can the poet proceed to test his imaginative capacity for entering into the life of others. Such entering into the life of others is, for Whitman, essential for any man who claims to be a poet; if a poet knows how to clarify his own identity he can turn it on others and in imagination absorb theirs. To Tennyson standing on the shore in his lonely grief, the sound of others at work or at play only emphasized his own isolation and sadness: 'And the stately ships go on / To their haven under the hill.' But

Whitman, when he sees a ship go by, is moved to wonder what
it must be like to be a member of its crew or to be its captain; he
is moved by the staggering fact of other people's lives existing,
really existing as other selves, and it is his very awareness of his
own unique self that makes it possible for him to project his
imagination into other unique selves:

> I understand the large hearts of heroes,
> The courage of present times and all times,
> How the skipper saw the crowded and rudderless wreck of the
>   steam-ship, and Death chasing it up and down the storm,
> How he knuckled tight and gave not back an inch, and was
>   faithful of days and faithful of nights,
> And chalk'd in large letters on a board, *Be of good cheer, we will*
>   *not desert you*;
> How he follow'd with them and tack'd with them three days
>   and would not give it up,
> How he saved the drifting company at last,
> How the lank loose-gown'd women look'd when boated from
>   the side of their prepared graves,
> How the silent old-faced infants and the lifted sick, and the
>   sharp-lipp'd unshaved men;
> All this I swallow, it tastes good, I like it well, it becomes mine,
> I am the man, I suffer'd, I was there.
>
>   (ll. 822-32)

The progression here is from understanding to identity,
beginning with 'I understand the large hearts of heroes' and
ending with 'I am the man, I suffer'd, I was there.' From this
point the poem becomes for a time an exhibition of the poet's
capacity for identifying himself with all who suffer: 'I am the
hounded slave, I wince at the bite of the dogs', or 'I am the
mash'd fireman with breastbone broken.'

In his Preface to *Leaves of Grass* Whitman describes the im-
pulse behind it as 'a feeling or ambition to articulate and faith-
fully express in literary or poetic form, and uncompromisingly,
my own physical, emotional, moral, intellectual, and aesthetic
Personality, in the midst of, and tallying, the momentous spirit
and facts of its immediate days, and of current America—and
to exploit that Personality, identified with place and date, in a
far more candid and comprehensive sense than any hitherto
book or poem'. And later in the same Preface he insists that his

poetry represents 'an attempt, from first to last, to put a *Person*, a human being (myself, in the latter half of the Nineteenth Century, in America), freely, fully and truly on record'. This Preface ought to be compared with Wordsworth's famous Preface to the second edition of *Lyrical Ballads* for they represent different ways of putting truth before artistic tradition just as *Leaves of Grass* ought to be set beside *The Prelude* as prime examples of different ways in which egotism can work cognitively. 'No one', proclaims Whitman, 'will get at my verses who insists upon viewing them as a literary performance, or as aiming mainly toward art or aestheticism', and though Wordsworth would not have expressed himself in this way, he would have understood and endorsed the principle.

A 'dandy' for Whitman is someone who sinks his individuality in fashions derived merely from tradition or merely from society or some other external source. In the extension to his Preface which appeared as an appendix to the second edition of *Leaves of Grass* Whitman described the young men of America as 'a parcel of helpless dandies, who can neither fight, work, shoot, ride, run, command—some of them devout, some quite insane, some castrated—all second-hand, or third, fourth, or fifth hand—waited upon by waiters, putting not this land first, but always other lands first, talking of art, doing the most ridiculous things for fear of being called ridiculous, smirking and skipping along, continually taking off their hats—no one behaving, dressing, writing, talking, loving, out of any natural and manly tastes of his own, but each looking cautiously to see how the rest behave, dress, write, talk, love . . .'. The poet is for Whitman a first-hand personality, who realizes himself by looking inward and then looks clearly outward. The process of 'loafing' is the process of self-preparation for that self-knowledge which alone can achieve truly inward knowledge of others. The polarity of the self and others is always present in Whitman, present as a challenge and a paradox. The most affluent man', he wrote, 'is he that confronts all the shows he sees by equivalents out of the stronger wealth of himself.' In the end, the true poet is a microcosm of all life, and that is what makes sympathy possible: we cannot sympathize with what we cannot truly imagine, and we cannot truly imagine what we do not inwardly know. 'One's-self I sing, a simple separate person, / Yet utter the word Democratic, the word En-Masse.' This is a rather clumsy way of putting it (Whitman's use of phrases like 'en masse' is often embarrassing), but the essence of Whitman's poetic aim is there. The self moves from *myself* to *one's* self through first the integrity of its self-awareness and then the extension of that self-awareness through following the implications of its own microcosmic nature; 'one' is the intermediate term between the self and other selves, between 'me' and 'you'. If the poet's self is so intrigued by traditions of artistic expression that he employs them whether or not they are adequate to contain his own essential vision, then his work is 'dandified'. In calling Tennyson dandified Whitman was calling attention to the degree to which, as it seemed to him, Tennyson tailored his vision to achieve an expression which conformed to the public idea of poetry in his time.

It seems, then, that in idiom and imagery Whitman deliberately repudiated the Victorian elegiac mode and refused to see poetry as concerned essentially with isolation and introspection. Yet in spite of himself the note of elegy creeeps in. (I am not here concerned with his ostensible elegies such as *When lilacs last*, but still with *Song of Myself*.) *Song of Myself* ends on the familiar Victorian note of loneliness and longing, though it is true that it is loneliness and longing with a difference. The identifying imagination, after its leap into the lives of others, sinks back exhausted, and the poet is left making gestures towards others without any real assurance that they are received and accepted. Perhaps only in death can the individual self fully enter into the selves of others—the very reverse of A.E. Housman's belief that 'When we two are spilt on air / Long we shall be strangers there'. Yet even this hope, expressed in the end wistfully rather than confidently, is asserted with a robust and effective vulgarity of speech ('If you want me again to look for me under your boot-soles') that is far removed from anything in the Victorian tradition. It is a remarkable ending to a remarkable poem:

> The last scud of day holds back for me,
> It flings my likeness after the rest and true as any on the
>   shadow'd wilds,
> It coaxes me to the vapor and the dusk.

I depart as air, I shake my white locks at the runaway sun,
I effuse my flesh in eddies, and drift it in lacy jags.

I bequeath myself to the dirt to grow from the grass I love,
If you want me again look for me under your boot-soles.

You will hardly know who I am or what I mean,
But I shall be good health to you nevertheless,
And filter and fibre your blood.

Failing to fetch me at first keep encouraged,
Missing me one place search another,
I stop somewhere waiting for you.

(11. 1334-46)

Whitman had begun the poem by saying that 'every atom belonging to me as good belongs to you', confident of the reality of communion between selves. He ends on a note of patience and muted hope: 'I stop somewhere waiting for you.' In the end the sense of identity resists assimilation and the paradox of the fully known self being most able to enter into other selves remains only a wish. The twilight mood of Victorian poetic loneliness almost enters the poem here, but the idiom of its expression is wholly different from anything in Tennyson or Arnold and, further, its function is not to emphasize the poet's lonely brooding self but rather to use the fading light to dissolve the poet's personality so that he can participate in the lives and personalities of others:

> The last scud of day holds back for me,
> It flings my likeness after the rest and true as any on the
> shadow'd wilds,
> It coaxes me to the vapor and the dusk.

How sternly Whitman resists the cadence of meditation, and how different in tone and idiom this setting of the poet in a twilight scene not only from anything in Tennyson and Arnold but also from the great prototype of all twilight meditation in English poetry, Gray's 'Elegy'! The three lines just quoted are not dissimilar in content, but worlds away in form and feeling, from:

> The curfew tolls the knell of parting day,
>   The lowing herd wind slowly o'er the lea,
> The ploughman homeward plods his weary way,
>   And leaves the world to darkness and to me.

Whitman as a rule achieves his effects by accumulation, by pointing, naming, listing persons, places, and things in all their teeming individuality; he exposes his poetic self to the world of other people and objects, and the result is the exciting movement between identity and assimilation that I have tried to describe. Different though his poetic mode is from that characteristic of nineteenth-century poets, Whitman does share their refusal to use the apparatus of any pre-formulated set of ideas, religious or philosophical, in order to focus the implication of his insights. For Tennyson and Arnold the meaning of the poetic experience (and for them poetry was the record of an experience) lay in the poet's sensibility and in that only; for Whitman, too, the poet's response created everything; there is not in either case any counterpointing of traditional belief and individual insight of the kind we find in Dante or Milton or Herbert. The Victorian poet tends towards solipsism inevitably, one might say, because his own moods are the only demonstrable reality, and Whitman avoids solipsism by his presentation of the poetic self as a self specially prepared, specially poised and angled, to achieve projection into the selves of others. There is no third party. That is what makes the poetry of Gerard Manley Hopkins so radically different from either the other English Victorian poets or from Whitman. For Hopkins there *is* a third party, and the problem of the relation between the poetic self and other selves and objects can only be solved by an appeal to it.

Oddly enough, there are impressive similarities as well as differences between Hopkins and Whitman. Hopkins himself once wrote to Robert Bridges: 'I always knew in my heart Walt Whitman's mind to be more like my own than any other man's living.' He added. 'As he is a very great scoundrel this is not a pleasant confession.' The similarity lies in the sense of 'thisness', of what Duns Scotus and Hopkins following him called *hacceitas*, the sense of distinctive individuality which made an individual thing or creature what it was. In his Preface to *Leaves of Grass* Whitman also wrote about the individuality of things: 'Each precise object or condition or combination or process exhibits a beauty . . . the multiplication table its—old age its—the carpenter's trade its—grand-opera its . . . .' This can be set beside Hopkins's discussion of 'inscape' and selfhood

and distinctiveness; Hopkins, like Whitman, sought to avoid
dandified poetry and to achieve, in his own phrase, what was
'beautiful to individuation'. But Hopkins's sense of self and
distinctiveness was not left to work its way out to a poetic
insight by simply operating, as it were; he was a religious poet,
and a confidence in religious truths emerges in all his poems as
either ultimate implication or as original assumption. In
imagery he is closer to Whitman than to Tennyson or Arnold,
though his oddities are not Whitman's oddities.

Here is a poem by Hopkins that is very Whitmanesque in
subject and in some respects in style, yet very unlike Whitman
in the way the total meaning is generated as well as in some
other aspects of style. It is 'The Lantern out of Doors':

> Sometimes a lantern moves along the night,
>   That interests our eyes. And who goes there?
> I think; where from and bound, I wonder, where,
> With, all down darkness wide, his wading light?
>
> Men go by me whom either beauty bright
>   In mould or mind or what not else makes rare:
>   They rain against our much-thick and marsh air
> Rich beams, till death or distance buys them quite.
>
> Death or distance soon consumes them: wind
>   What most I may eye after, be in at the end
> I cannot, and out of sight is out of mind.
>
> Christ minds: Christ's interest, what to avow or amend
>   There, éyes them, wánts, care haúnts, foot fóllows kínd
> There ránsom, théir rescue, ánd first, fást, last friénd.

The poem begins with the self observing. But the poet's
sense of other people passing him in the darkness does not lead
back to the isolated meditating self as it so often does in Tennyson and Arnold. Like Whitman, Hopkins tries to project
himself into the life of the casually met other person. But the
attempt is perfunctory, or at least it is not sustained, for it leads
almost at once to a reflection on the way we lose contact with
those who pass us by in life, and that in turn leads to the appeal
to the third party, the introduction of Christ as the protector
and friend who never loses contact. The surface thought of the
poem is simple enough. We meet people in daily life who
interest us momentarily, but our paths cross only briefly and

they disappear and we forget about them, because 'out of sight is out of mind'. But Christ never forgets people; he is always interested in them; he is their ransom, rescue, and their eternal friend.

The paraphrasable content of Hopkins's poem seems a mere commonplace of religious thought; almost, one might say, a piece of arrant sentimentality: 'Christ is man's best friend.' The power and distinction of the poem derives from its idiom, a mingling of the ordinariness and the unexpected which is both like and unlike the idiom of Whitman. We notice, in the first place, the deliberate way in which Hopkins imposes a collo-quial tone on a highly formal structure (Whitman, using a much freer verse, never has the problem or the achievement of counterpointing the colloquial and the formal in this way).

> Sometimes a lantern moves along the night,
>   That interests our eyes. And who goes there?
>   I think . . .

—the word 'interests' is not a normal poetic word; it arrests us by its very unpoetic ordinariness. In the light of the way the poem is developed, this word 'interests' comes to suggest not only its obvious, primary meaning, but its financial meaning, to lend at interest. People whose character makes them valuable pass by but soon disappear when they are *bought* by death or distance. Death or distance buys and consumes them, and they are lost to sight.

> Men go by me whom either beauty bright
>   In mould or mind or what not else makes rare:
>   They rain against our much-thick and marsh air
> Rich beams, till death or distance buys them quite.
>
> Death or distance soon consumes them: wind
>   What most I may eye after, be in at the end
> I cannot, and out of sight is out of mind.
>
> Christ minds: Christ's interest, what to avow or amend
>   There, éyes them, heart wánts, care haúnts, foot fóllows kínd,
> Their ransom, théir rescue, ánd first, fást, last friénd.

Notice Hopkins's introduction of the colloquial English pro-verb, 'Out of sight is out of mind', into the midst of this very formally constructed sonnet. People, however valuable, who are bought by death or distance go out of our minds. But Christ

continues to 'mind' them—in the sense of remember them
and also in the sense of look after them, as a man minds his
property. Christ's *interest* is their *ransom*; the implication is that
Christ gives the interest on his property to ransom man—but of
course the word 'interest' is also used in its more obvious and
usual meaning.

But let me return to the earlier part of the poem. I have
already mentioned the crossing of the formal with the colloquial in

> And who goes there?
> I think; where from and bound, I wonder, where,
> With, all down darkness wide, his wading light?

The language here is both colloquial and odd. 'With, all down
darkness wide, his wading light' is a most unusual word-order
in English, and 'wading', which normally means 'paddling' (as
in the sea), is here used in a special sense. Hopkins himself
explains his use of the word 'wading' in a note, connecting it
with Old English *wadan* to walk and quoting Spenser's line,
'Vertue gives her selfe light, through darknesse for to wade'.
The light, carried by a passer-by as he walks at night down the
street away from the poet, wades through the darkness. The
particular order in which Hopkins places the words conveys the
sense first of the wide darkness enveloping the road and secondly of the lantern wading through it and diminishing in the
distance. 'With, all down darkness wide, his wading light.'

The second group of four lines begins:

> Men go by me whom either beauty bright
> In mould or mind or what not else makes rare:

these passers-by are made valuable by their 'mould'—that is,
their shape, their physical beauty—or their 'mind', their
qualities of intellect and intelligence. But 'mould' does not
mean only shape; it also means soil and, specifically, the earth
of the grave. Men beautiful in mould, in shape, disappear into
the mould, the grave: their very beauty suggests their mortality. And men distinguished in mind pass out of mind; no one
minds (looks after) them, no one minds (remembers) them. But
Christ does. His relationship to men is not that of the casual
passer-by mentioned in the first stanza: he looks after them, he

interests himself in them, helping them to acknowledge their
true selves or to improve themselves ('what to avow or amend
there'); Christ's heart wants men, his care haunts them, his
'foot follows kind'—that is, Christ follows men in kindness,
and he follows them because he too is man, of the same 'kind',
of humankind; and he ransoms and rescues them:

> Christ minds: Christ's interest, what to avow or amend
> There, éyes them, heart wánts, care háunts, foot fóllows kínd,
> Their ránsom, théir rescue, ánd first, fást, last friénd.

In this poem Hopkins also achieves through his use of language a remarkable sense of *dailiness*, or ordinary quotidian
experience, and in doing so suggests that religion is not something special, something only for sabbaths and holy days, but is
bound up with the routine concerns of every day. The formality
of the poet's *form* and the deliberate eccentricity of some elements in the diction, suggest what is special and important
about religion, while the colloquial elements in the diction and
the use of language that brings in echoes of day-to-day human
affairs suggest what is ordinary and omnipresent about it. And
so the third party, the a priori resolution, Christ as solver of the
problem, is seen at the end not to be an outsider at all, but part
of the world we are already familiar with. God—and this is true
in all of Hopkins's poems—is never a *deus ex machina*, because
Hopkins through his idiom and imagery makes clear that God
only emerges because he has been there all the time.

Writing religious poetry in an age when the most sophisticated sensibilities tended to be agnostic (in spite of the manifold
manifestation of Victorian religion) Hopkins could not fall
back easily on a traditional devotional poetry or indeed on any
kind of poetry that assumed a consensus about the existence
and nature of God on the part of his public. True, he wrote his
poems as much for himself as for any audience, but his letters
make clear that he did want an audience in spite of that and he
was at pains to explain to his friends just how his poetry should
be read in order to be appreciated. He had to shock his readers
into attention to the presence of divinity in Nature. Nothing
could be more removed from the nature poetry of natural theology that we find in the eighteenth century than such a poem as
'The Windhover' or even, to take a simpler example, 'Pied

Beauty': God's presence in Nature is not deduced or inferred
in these poems, nor is it taken for granted; it is, one might
almost say, *generated* by the way imagery and insight reinforce
each other.

'The Windhover' (kestrel) is dedicated 'To Christ our
Lord', which provides some clue as to how to read it. It opens
with a sudden and passionate description of the poet's seeing
the bird soaring and swooping in the sky: the bird is 'morning's
minion' (darling), 'kingdom of daylight's dauphin', the phrase
suggesting overtones of chivalry and splendour; there follows a
series of images comparing the bird in its movement to a horse
circling round its trainer at the end of a long rein and then to a
skater's heel:

>   how he rung upon the rein of a wimpling wing
> In his ecstasy! then off, off forth on swing,
>   As a skate's heel smooth on a bow-bend: the hurl and gliding
>   Rebuffed the big wind. My heart in hiding
> Stirred for a bird,—the achieve of, the mastery of the thing!

His heart is in hiding: he is a priest dedicated to God, not to the
recording of moments of pleasure in watching God's creatures,
but the glory of the bird's flight stirs him in spite of himself.
The union of animal beauty and pride of movement (suggestive
again of chivalric pomp) astonishes the poet, and in this union
he sees both beauty and danger:

>   Brute beauty and valour and act, oh, air, pride, plume here
>   Buckle! AND the fire that breaks from thee then, a billion
>   Times told lovelier, more dangerous, O my chevalier!

The windhover is the poet's marvellous knight of chivalry: the
conjunction of 'air, pride, plume' suggests the famous description of Prince Henry in the first Part of Henry IV, Act IV, 'I
saw young Harry with his beaver on' and this makes contact
with 'chevalier' two lines further down. The danger lies in the
temptation to admire mere courage and splendour, and to forget the importance of suffering and sacrifice. The last three
lines of the sonnet illuminate thie point in a very Hopkinsesque
manner:

>   No wonder of it: sheer plod makes plough down sillion
> Shine, and blue-bleak embers, ah my dear,
>   Fall, gall themselves, and gash gold-vermilion.

'No wonder': Christ's humility and suffering are bound up with his glory and pride: many things include their opposites; 'sheer plod' can make the ploughshare shine as it cuts its furrow, and a black coal in a burning fire can fall over and break and reveal its red-hot interior, its 'gold-vermilion' gashes suggesting on the one hand beauty and on the other Christ's wounds and suffering.

This is religious poetry of a deeply personal kind, yet not personal in the Tennysonian brooding manner, nor indeed in the manner of the metaphysical religious poets of the seventeenth century, though Hopkins has more in common with the latter than with the former. Nature speaks of God in a complex and paradoxical manner, suggesting the complexities and paradoxes of God's working with man and man's relation to God. Nor is this the poetry of simple devotion. Hopkins's poems prove his faith by the way he works through a cluster of contradictory yet mutually illuminating images.

A poem such as 'Pied Beauty' is on the surface much simpler, with its straightforward opening line

> Glory be to God for dappled things.

But in his exploration of the significance of dappling and stippling in Nature, Hopkins opens out the poem to celebrate all the difficulties, contradictions, puzzles, contraries in Nature and in man. All is produced by God, who is 'past change':

> All things counter, original, spare, strange;
>   Whatever is fickle, freckled (who knows how?)
>   With swift, slow; sweet, sour; adazzle, dim;
> He fathers-forth whose beauty is past change:
>   Praise him.

The simple conclusion, the short line 'Praise him' that swells out like a final organ chord, belies the complexity of the poem, yet it emerges naturally from the poem's meaning. God, who is above and beyond change, created all these contraries and changes for he delights in the complexities of individuation. This is the theme of many of Hopkins's poems. Sometimes he takes a traditional religious statement, like his adaptation of the opening of Psalm 19 in 'God's Grandeur'

> The world is charged with the grandeur of God

('The heavens declare the glory of God', says the Psalmist) before proceeding to explore and illustrate and complicate the statement in a poem which projects in its imagery man's warping and concealing of Nature with his daily activities over the generations before suggesting, in a remarkable turn in the sestet of the sonnet, that in spite of this each dawn brings a reminder of the freshness and love of the first creation. This is a kind of religious poetry that is, as it were, fought for and not easily won. As the reader familiarizes himself with the rhythms and the imagery he is drawn into a complex and difficult experience. Projecting the relation between man and God is not easy.

Hopkins never falls into the elegiac mode of much Victorian poetry, a mode of which Tennyson and Arnold were masters. He has his own difficulties, including the difficulty of reconciling a love of Nature and of poetry with his priestly vocation—we sense a continual tension in Hopkins's poetry that appears to be bound up with this. The moments of near-despair (but never despair itself), of the dark night of the soul, are memorably recorded in such a poem as 'Carrion Comfort'. The poem opens with a great anguished cry against God the 'terrible', but the second stanza produces a remarkable turn and concludes with a startling picture of his emerging from the darkness to find himself, wrestling, astonishingly, with his God.

> That night, that year
> Of now done darkness I wretch lay wrestling with (my God!)
> my God.

There are of course echoes of Jacob's experience here, but this is essentially Job's problem presented not through a dramatic poem, as in the Book of Job, but in a highly wrought personal lyric. Like Job, Hopkins gets his encounter with God, but it is of a very different kind.

In my last lecture I referred to Tennyson's mood poetry and described it as in some ways the poetry of agnosticism, where the poet falls back into himself because he has nothing outside of himself to turn to. Yet Tennyson was not a happy agnostic, and he fought hard to achieve a faith in beneficent divinity. One of the great differences between eighteenth-century scepticism and Victorian scepticism is that the former was regarded as a liberation, and produced (notably in the case of David Hume) cheerfulness, whereas the latter was always a source of *worry*. Many of the Victorian sceptics were reluctant and troubled sceptics who spent much energy endeavouring to find a way out of their unbelief based on a redefinition of faith or of God or on some kind of reconciliation between scientific and religious truth. Such an eighteenth-century Nature poet as James Thomson had been able quite readily to put science at the service of a belief in a beneficent designing Deity, as I discussed in my third lecture. But it was more difficult for the Victorian poet, not because he accepted Hume's destruction of the 'argument from design' in his *Dialogues on Natural Religion*— in fact, Hume's argument had very little impact in the nineteenth century, as is made clear by the important part played in Victorian higher education by William Paley's *Evidences of Christianity* (1794), which uses the 'argument from design' without any awareness of Hume's attack on it—but because geology presented threats to religious belief that Newtonian science had not presented.

There was, however, another factor at work which made it increasingly difficult to see the great scientific and philosophical prophets of the late seventeenth century, Newton and Locke, in the way they were often seen in the early and mid-eighteenth century, as thinkers who could be prayed in aid of a benevolent deism. That factor emerges with striking force in the work of William Blake, who fiercely attacked the whole tradition of Western thought since the seventeenth century:

Thus the terrible race of Los & Enitharmon gave
Laws and Religions to the sons of Har, binding them more
And more to Earth, closing and restraining,
Till a Philosophy of Five Senses was complete.
Urizen wept & gave it into the hands of Newton & Locke.
                              ('The Song of Los')

And again, more succinctly:

                        May God us keep
          From single vision & Newton's sleep![1]

Newton and Locke are the villians of the piece for Blake, as
they were to be more than a century later for W.B. Yeats:

          Locke sank into a swoon;
          The Garden died;
          God took the spinning-jenny
          Out of his side.

A 'Philosophy of the Five Senses', an industrial, materialist
society, and middle-class Philistinism were, on this view,
equated or closely related. And though one current in the
Romantic movement was in fact pro-scientific as we see clearly
in Shelley (whose poem 'The Cloud' is meteorologically exact,
and who combined a high neo-Platonic idealism with the traditional Platonic interest in the mathematical sciences) and, in a
different way, later in Tennyson—the anti-scientific current
that manifests itself so vividly in Blake was strong enough to
reach into the next century. The lines on Newton that Wordsworth added after 1830 to Book III of the Prelude (lines 61-3)
show Newton as a hero:

          Newton with his prism and silent face,
          The marble index of a mind for ever
          Voyaging through strange seas of Thought, alone.

Wordsworth had not immediately joined in drinking a famous
toast proposed by Keats many years earlier. 'And don't you
remember', Haydon wrote later to Wordsworth, 'Keats pro-
posing "Confusion to the memory of Newton," and upon your
insisting on an explanation before you drank it, his saying:

---

[1] In a letter to Thomas Butts, 22 Nov. 1802. In *The Poetry and Prose of William Blake*,
ed. G. Keynes, London, 1932, p. 1068.

"Because he destroyed the poetry of the rainbow by reducing it to a prism."'[2]

Wordsworth was in fact notable among the Romantic poets in agreeing with the late-seventeenth- and early-eighteenth-century writers who believed that poetry could be enriched by science; he went further, and argued that poetry could and should *absorb* science.

> Poetry is the breath and finer spirit of all Science . . . . If the labours of Men of science should ever create any material revolution, direct or indirect, in our condition, and in the impressions which we habitually receive, the Poet will sleep then no more than at present: he will be ready to follow the steps of the Man of science, not only in those general indirect effects, but he will be at his side, carrying sensation into the midst of the objects of the science itself.

And Wordsworth specifically names 'the remotest discoveries of the Chemist, the Botanist, or Mineralogist' as proper objects of the poet's art 'if the time should ever come when these things shall be familiar to us as enjoying and suffering beings'. The poet, to Wordsworth, brings out the human relevance of scientific knowledge. So we understand why he was reluctant to joint Keats in denouncing Newton. Nor would he have agreed with Keats's famous lines in 'Lamia':

> Do not all charms fly
> At the mere touch of cold philosophy?
> There was an awful rainbow once in heaven:
> We know her woof, her texture; she is given
> In the dull catalogue of common things.
> Philosophy will clip an Angel's wings,
> Conquer all mysteries by rule and line,
> Empty the haunted air, and gnomed mine—
> Unweave a rainbow, as it erewhile made
> The tender-person'd Lamia melt into a shade.

Neither Wordsworth nor Shelley, for different reasons, would have accepted Keats's position here. Wordsworth himself accepted quite specifically that 'the beauty in form of a plant or an animal is made not less but more apparent as a whole by more accurate insight into its constituent properties and

---

[2] *Correspondence and Table-Talk of Benjamin Haydon*, with a Memoir by Frederick Wordsworth Haydon, London, 1876, II. 54-5.

powers'. Shelley, who classed Francis Bacon with Dante, Shakespeare, and Milton as ideally a 'poet' who firmly believed that poetry and science should go hand in hand, only criticized adversely the effects of a science unaccompanied by 'the poetical faculty'. In 'Defence of Poetry' he conceded that the Baconian aim of dominating nature could have bad results:

The cultivation of these sciences which have enlarged the limits of the empire of men over the external world, has, for want of the poetical faculty, proportionately circumscribed those of the internal world: and man, having enslaved the elements, remains himself a slave. To what but a cultivation of the mechanical arts in a degree disproportioned to the presence of the creative faculty, which is the basis of all knowledge, is to be attributed the abuse of all inventions for abridging and combining labour, to the exasperation of the inequality of mankind.

This side of Shelley's thought brings him close to the Victorian 'prophets' Carlyle and Ruskin, with their suspicion of mechanism, where they were at one with Blake and with Coleridge. But theirs was not, as Blake's was, a fundamental suspicion of the whole basis of modern science. Coleridge objected to what M.H. Abrams has conveniently called 'the mistaken and unbounded metaphysical pretensions of atomism and mechanism—in Coleridge's view, a useful working hypothesis for physical research which had been illicitly converted first into fact, and then into a total world-view'.[3] The suspicion of science and the suspicion of a mechanistic philosophy, though they sometimes went together, were far from being the same thing.

In his notes on Joshua Reynolds's *Discourses* (*c*.1808), Blake had written: 'To Generalize is to be an Idiot. To Particularize is the Alone Distinction of Merit, General Knowledges are those Knowledges that Idiots possess.' This is a virulent version of a long tradition, which goes back at least to Joseph Warton's *Essay on the Writings and Genius of Pope* (1756): Warton saw the selection and description of minute particulars as characteristic of poetry as distinct from history, and thus flatly contradicted both Aristotle (who saw poetry as more universal than history) and Dr Johnson (who objected to the poet's

[3] *The Mirror and the Lamp*, by M.H. Abrams, New York, 1953, p. 310.

numbering 'the streaks of the tulip' because his business was 'to remark general properties and large appearances'). That poetry is concrete and science general became more and more accepted as the nineteenth century progressed. 'Generalization is necessary to the advancement of knowledge, but particularity is indispensable to the creatures of imagination', wrote Macaulay in his essay on Milton (1825). This tradition was given a new lease of life in the twentieth century by the Imagist movement, and has entered into modern critical theory as a fairly central and orthodox view. For John Crowe Ransom in 1934, 'pure poetry ' was 'a kind of Physical Poetry' that is 'the basic constituent of any poetry', and 'its visible context is a thing-context.' What he called 'Platonic poetry'[4] only pretended to deal in things; it really dealt in general ideas and was therefore bad.

Another distinction that came to be made more and more as the nineteenth century advanced concerned the role of poetry and of imaginative literature in general in the education of the feelings. It is what things are to human sensibility, not to the analysing instruments and classifying mind of the scientist, that matters in man's emotional life, and the emotional life is the true inner life. 'The difference between the mere botanist's knowledge of plants, and the great poet's or painter's knowledge of them', wrote Ruskin in the Preface to *Modern Painters* (1843), is that 'the one notes their distinctions for the sake of swelling his herbarium, the other, that he may render them vehicles of expression and emotion.'

The distinction between science (which addressed itself to the individual's belief) and poetry (which addresses itself to his feelings) is closely related to the distinction between scientific and poetic truth, about which critics have argued since Aristotle. Coleridge's famous remark about the 'willing suspension of disbelief' that poetry produces in us is only one shot in a long battle. The general lines on which the idea of poetic truth was developed are indicated partly by J.S. Mill's view that the poet's duty is to feel and communicate feeling, whereas the scientist's is to know and communicate truth (in a letter to G.H. Lewes he defined poetry as 'feeling expressing itself in the

---

[4] Poetry: A Note in Ontology', in *Critiques and Essays in Criticism 1920-1948*, ed. R.W. Stallman, New York, 1949, pp. 30 ff.

forms of thought'), and partly by Matthew Arnold's argument in trying to rescue religion from its dependence on the literal historicity of the Bible:

Our religion has materialised itself in the fact, in the supposed fact; it has attached its emotion to the fact, and now the fact is failing it. But for poetry the idea is everything; the rest is a world of illusion, of divine illusion. Poetry attaches its emotion to the idea; the idea *is* the fact. The strongest part of our religion today as its unconscious poetry.[5]

In spite of his somewhat misleading emphasis on 'the idea', Arnold is not here pleading for poetry as primarily a philosophical or intellectual activity; he is trying to differentiate the kind of meaning that language bears in poetry from that which it bears in history of science. I.A. Richards quoted with approval this passage of Arnold's, forty-six years later, when, in his book *Science and Poetry* (1926), he distinguished between the scientific and the poetic uses of language. Richards had already—with C.K. Ogden, in *The Meaning of Meaning* (1923)—differentiated between 'emotive meaning' (which 'tells us, or should tell us, nothing') and 'scientific' of 'referential' meaning. In *Science and Poetry* he developed his point further. 'In its use of words poetry is just the reverse of science. Very definite thoughts do occur, but not because the words are so chosen as logically to bar all possibilities but one. No. But because the manner, the tone of voice, the cadence and the rhythm play upon our interests and make *them* pick out from an indefinite number of possibilities the precise particular thought which they need.' Ultimately, this line of thought goes right back to Sir Philip Sidney, who in his *Apologie for Poetrie* (first published anonymously in 1595) had argued that the poet 'nothing affirmes, and therefore never lyeth'. But the concern of both Arnold and Richards was not to defend poets against the ancient charge of being liars: it was, for Arnold, to defend and define the central value to civilization of a kind of discourse that was not necessarily (or even preferably) true in any historical or scientific way; and, for Richards, to define as scientifically as possible the non-scientific use of language in

[5] Introduction to T.H. Ward's *English Poets*, London, 1880; Arnold quoted it again in his *Essays in Criticism*, 2nd Series, 1888.

poetry, and to show the psychological value of reading and responding to works written in that non-scientific kind of language. Arnold was also concerned to save religion from biblical fundamentalism, because the higher criticism of the Bible was daily making a literal-historical reading of some parts of the Bible more difficult. If there is a truth of the imagination, a truth of feeling, a religious truth—and these terms were increasingly being associated—then the Bible can be saved as poetry, to rank with the *Iliad* as a work in which 'perfect plainness of speech is allied with perfect nobleness' (*On Translating Homer*, 1861), and religion can be redefined as 'morality touched by emotion' (*Literature and Dogma*, 1873).

The higher criticism of the Bible, no less than new ideas in geology and biology, represented a threat from science to fundamental religion; and in subsuming religion in poetry, Arnold was extending to it the kind of protection that critics had for some time been developing for imaginative literature. As we have seen, the 'argument from design' had enabled eighteenth-century thinkers to reconcile science and religion, although at the cost of transforming the latter from a dogmatic Christianity into a generalized deism. But the evangelical movements of the late eighteenth and early nineteenth century and the increasing commitment, when challenged, not only of Nonconformism but also of a considerable section of the Church of England as well as of the Church of Scotland to a biblical fundamentalism, together with the new interest in dogma, ritual, and theology illustrated by the Oxford Movement, now made the simple equation of religion with belief in the existence of a Great Designer impossible for many religious people. It was not, in Bacon's terms, God's Work but God's Word that was the subject of debate. If what the scientist told us about the age and development of the natural world (including man) contradicted what was told in holy writ, then arguments about a Great Designer were beside the point. The question was whether the ways of discovering truth open to the natural scientist were the only ways; and if they were not, what kind of insights, discovered in what way, communicated in what kind of language, were represented by the 'truths' of religion—and poetry. There is an interesting corollary here. If religion is saved as poetry, and is still seen as representing something central in civilization, then poetry must take on the prestige of religion and be valued as something central in civilization, and the task of defining what Arnold called 'the best' poetry becomes the high function of the priest-critic. This line of thought eventually leads us to F.R. Leavis's concept of the 'great tradition' in a national literature, to be interpreted and transmitted by the dedicated apostle of literary culture. Just as the biblical canon was distinguished from the Apocrypha, so there was to be a literary canon from which everything not in the 'great tradi-tion' was to be excluded.

It was not on these lines, however, that Tennyson tried to reconcile what he had learned from modern science with a belief in a caring God of love. Like many others of his time, he had felt the impact of the work of geologist and biologists— notably of Sir Charles Lyell's *Principles of Geology* (1830-4) and *The Geological Evidences of the Antiquity of Man* (1863), and of Robert Chambers's pre-Darwinian *Vestiges of the Natural History of Creation* (1844); the influence on him of Darwin's *On the Origin of Species*, which was not published until 1859, came later, after Tennyson had completed and published *In Memoriam*. The conflict between science and religious orthodoxy produced by these books is vividly illustrated in Edmund Gosse's *Father and Son* (1907), which gives an account of his father P.H. Gosse, a distinguished biologist, who was at the same time a member of the Plymouth Brethren and an uncompromising biblical fundamentalist. This conflict between the scientist and the man of religion within the same person is a classic case. P.H. Gosse's book *Omphalos* (1857) is an ingenious but basically preposterous attempt to reconcile geological evidence with the biblical account of the Creation. Even where there was no direct con-flict there were varieties of doubt and even anguish that are reflected in literature. It was Lyell's *Principles of Geology*, which Tennyson read in 1837, that first provoked Tennyson's worry about the way Nature works, expressed in Canto LV:

> Are God and Nature then at strife,
>   That Nature lends such evil dreams?
>   So careful of the type she seems,
> So careless of the single life;
>
> That I, considering everywhere
>   Her secret meaning in her deeds,

> And finding that of fifty seeds
> She often brings but one to bear.

> I falter where I firmly trod,
>   And falling with my weight of cares
>   Upon the great world's altar-stairs
> That slope through darkness up to God,

> I stretch lame hands of faith, and grope,
>   And gather dust and chaff, and call
>   To what I feel is Lord of all,
> And faintly trust the larger hope.

In Memoriam moves towards a willed optimism, a determination to believe in a beneficent God of love in spite of conflicting evidence, but at this stage in the poem the belief is little more than an undefined feeling and a faint trust. The next canto virtually withdraws that trust. (We must remember that the cantos on evolution in *In Memoriam* were written before the publication either of Robert Chambers's *Vestiges of Creation* or of Darwin's *Origin of Species*.)

> Man, her last work, who seemed so fair,
>   Such splendid purpose in his eyes,
>   Who rolled the psalm to wintry skies,
> Who built him fanes of fruitless prayer,

> Who trusted God was love indeed
>   And love Creation's final law—
>   Though Nature, red in tooth and claw
> With ravine, shrieked against his creed—

> Who loved, who suffered countless ills,
>   Who battled for the True, and Just,
>   Be blown about the desert dust,
> Or sealed within the iron hills?

> No more? A monster then, a dream,
>   A discord. Dragons of the prime,
>   That tare each other in their slime,
> Were mellow music matched with him.

> O life as futile, then, as frail!
>   O for thy voice to soothe and bless!
>   What hope of answer, or redress?
> Behind the veil, behind the veil.

Earlier in the poem, in Canto LIV, Tennyson had given classic expression to the combination of scepticism with a will to believe that is so characteristic of one aspect of Victorian thought:

> Oh yet we trust that somehow good
>   Will be the final goal of ill,
>   To pangs of nature, sins of will,
> Defects of doubt, and taints of blood;
>
> That nothing walks with aimless feet;
>   That not one life shall be destroyed,
>   Or cast as rubbish to the void,
> When God hath made the pile complete;
>
> Behold, we know not anything;
>   I can but trust that good shall fall
>   At last—far off—at last, to all,
> And every winter change to spring.
>
> So runs my dream: but what am I?
>   An infant crying in the night:
>   An infant crying for the light:
>   And with no language but a cry.

Throughout *In Memoriam* the poet trusts, then wavers in his trust, then trusts again, trying to will himself to faith. Perhaps the dead really are 'breathers of an ampler day', perhaps evolution is moving man steadily upward to work out the beast and let the ape and tiger die. Perhaps.

> Contemplate all this work of Time,
>   The giant labouring in his youth;
>   Nor dream of human love and truth,
> As dying Nature's earth and lime;
>
> But trust that those we call the dead
>   Are breathers of an ampler day
>   For ever nobler ends. They say,
> The solid earth whereon we tread
>
> In tracts of fluent heat began,
>   And grew to seeming-random forms,
>   The seeming prey of cyclic storms,
> Till at the last arose the man;
>
> Who throve and branched from clime to clime,
>   The herald of a higher race,
>   And of himself in higher place,
> If so he type this work of time

Within himself, from more to more;
   Or, crowned with attributes of woe
   Like glories, move his course, and show
That life is not as idle ore,

But iron dug from central gloom,
   And heated hot with burning fears,
   And dipt in baths of hissing tears,
And battered with the shocks of doom

To shape and use. Arise and fly
   The reeling Faun, the sensual feast;
   Move upward, working out the beast,
And let the ape and tiger die.

Is his dead friend, for whom the poem was written, really living eternally 'in conclusive bliss' or, as he goes on to suggest in the same stanza as that in which this hope is expressed, is this just grief playing with symbols? Is this doubt itself a higher form of faith?

You say, but with no touch of scorn,
   Sweet-hearted, you, whose light-blue eyes
   Are tender over drowning flies,
You tell me, doubt is Devil-born.

I know not: one indeed I knew
   In many a subtle question versed,
   Who touched a jarring lyre at first,
But ever strove to make it true:

Perplext in faith, but pure in deeds,
   At last he beat his music out.
There lives more faith in honest doubt,
   Believe me, than in half the creeds.

The willed optimism of the concluding cantos is reflected in the Prologue, which is really an Epilogue:

Strong Son of God, immortal Love,
   Whom we, that have not seen thy face,
   By faith, and faith alone, embrace,
Believing where we cannot prove;

Thine are these orbs of light and shade;
   Thou madest Life in man and brute;
   Thou madest Death; and lo, thy foot
Is on the skull which thou has made.

> Thou wilt not leave us in the dust:
> Thou madest man, he knows not why,
> He thinks he was not made to die;
> And thou hast made him: thou are just . . . .

Tennyson is reported as having said of *In Memoriam* that 'it was meant to be a kind of *Divina Commedia*, ending with happiness' and when reading the poem to James Knowles he said: 'It is rather the cry of the whole human race than mine.' It is also the cry of Victorian worry about God, of Victorian dissatisfaction with a scepticism that keeps challenging faith. It is significant that he also said to Knowles when reading the poem to him: 'It's too hopeful, this poem, more than I am myself.'[6] Tennyson never ceased worrying about the problem of faith in the face of the realities of man's history. He returned to the subject at the age of seventy-seven in *Locksley Hall, Sixty Years After*. Is Evolution part of a beneficent divine plan to bring man to perfection, or does it produce an endless see-sawing between cosmos and chaos?

> Chaos, Cosmos! Cosmos, Chaos! once again the sickening game;
> Freedom, free to slay herself, and dying while they shout her name.

And, later in the poem:

> Forward, backward, backward, forward, in the immeasurable sea,
> Sway'd by vaster ebbs and flows than can be known to you or me.
>
> All the suns—are these but symbols of innumerable man,
> Man or Mind that sees a shadow of the planner or the plan?
>
> Is there evil but on earth? or pain in every peopled sphere?
> Well, be grateful for the sounding watchword 'Evolution' here,
>
> Evolution ever climbing after some ideal good,
> And Reversion ever dragging Evolution in the mud.

But the will to optimistic belief persisted. In his eightieth year Tennyson wrote a poem entitled 'By an Evolutionist' which concludes with Old Age answering an Old Man's doubts and pessimism. The willed optimism is back:

> If my body come from brutes, though somewhat finer than their own,
> I am heir, and this my kingdom. Shall the royal voice be mute?

---

[6] *The Poems of Tennyson*, ed. Christopher Ricks, London, 1969, p. 859.

No, but if the rebel subject seek to drag me from the throne,
Hold the sceptre, Human Soul, and rule thy Province of the brute.
I have climbed to the snows of Age, and I gaze at a field in the Past,
Where I sank with the body at times in the sloughs of a low desire,
But I hear no yelp of the beast, and the Man is quiet at last
As he stands on the heights of his life and with a glimpse of
a height that is higher.

In spite of this determination to believe and to hope on the part of Tennyson and many others, the shaking of traditional beliefs by the joint forces of biblical criticism, geology, and biology lay behind the sense of loss that we find echoed in so many ways in Victorian poetry. 'There is not a creed which is not shaken, not an accredited dogma which is not shown to be questionable, not a received tradition which does not threaten to dissolve', wrote Arnold at the beginning of his essay on 'The Study of Poetry'. I quoted Arnold's 'Dover Beach' in my last lecture as an example of the Victorian elegiac mode, the poetry of introspective isolation, but the poem is also a classic expression of the mid-century sense of loss of faith:

The Sea of Faith
Was once, too, at the full, and round earth's shore
Lay like the folds of a bright girdle furled.
But now I only hear
Its melancholy, long, withdrawing roar,
Retreating, to the breath
Of the night-wind, down the vast edges drear
And naked shingles of the world.

This is the Victorian version of Donne's line, 'The new Philosophy calls all in doubt', though Donne never suggested that it called the Christian faith in doubt. In 'Stanzas from the Grande Chartreuse' Arnold spoke of himself as

Wandering between two worlds, one dead,
The other powerless to be born . . . .

His friend A.H. Clough faced the question more directly:

Matthew and Mark and Luke and holy John
Evanished all and gone!

And sometimes with genuine anguish (in 'Easter Day, Naples, 1849'):

Where they have laid Him there is none to say!
No sound, nor in, nor out; no word
Of where to seek the dead or meet the living Lord;
There is no glistering of an angel's wings,
There is no voice of heavenly clear behest:
Let us go hence, and think upon these things
In silence, which is best.
        Is He not risen? No—
      But lies and moulders low—
        Christ is not risen.

It is true that Clough answers this with a counter-poem, also called 'Easter Day', in which he asserts

    In the great Gospel, and true Creed,
    He is yet risen indeed;
       Christ is yet risen.

Clough interspersed his sceptical or anguished or ironical poems with such cries of willed optimistic belief, as in the famous 'Say not the struggle nought availeth' (which may have been written as a reply to Arnold's 'Dover Beach'), but it is the former note that is sounded more memorably. Sometimes he is the most explicit of all Victorian poets on the science-religion theme, as in 'When Israel Came Out Of Egypt':

    And as of old from Sinai's top
      God said that God is one,
    By Science strict so speaks He now
      To tell us, There is None!
    Earth goes by chemic forces; Heaven's
      A Mécanique Céleste!
    And heart and mind of human kind
      A watch-work as the rest!

The eighteenth-century Deists saw God the Divine Watch-maker as a guarantee of order and purpose in the universe. Clough sees the same God as no God, but a guarantee of emptiness both in the universe and in the human mind. Yet even for Clough the assertion of some kind of optimism about life was a kind of Victorian duty. His unfinished verse play, 'The Mystery of the Fall', ends with Adam addressing Cain after Cain's murder of Abel:

> In spite of doubt, despondency, and death,
> Though lacking knowledge alway, lacking faith
> Sometimes, and hope; with no sure trust in ought
> Except a kind of impetus within,
> Whose sole credentials were that trust itself;
> Yet, in despite of much, in lack of more,
> Life has been beautiful to me, my son,
> And if they call me, I will come again.

It is not the Divine Watchmaker, however, who inspires this desperate hope; it is 'a kind of impetus within': salvation is achieved not by God's intervention or even by a reverent noting of God's Work, but by willed introspection. Again, the eighteenth-century James Thomson drew quite different conclusions from observation of the workings of Nature, but his namesake, the nineteenth-century James Thomson ('B.V.') took a similar view to Clough's on this point:

> The world rolls round forever like a mill;
> It grinds out death and life and good and ill;
> It has no purpose, heart or mind or will.

These lines from Thomson's *City of Dreadful Night* express the view that to see the universe as a machine, which is how the poet sees it in one of its aspects, is to take up a position that precludes all hope. Thomson's poem is avowedly atheistic, one of the few explicitly atheistic long poems in European literature: it does not seek a way out, as Tennyson's *In Memoriam* does, but is concerned to communicate with what might be called masochistic force a dark vision of a hopeless world ruled by a mindless Necessity. The variety of devices employed by Thomson to achieve this end is striking: he showed himself in this poem to be a rhetorical poet of great skill and originality. *The City of Dreadful Night* is an *Inferno* without a *Purgatorio* or a *Paradiso*, an *Inferno*, moreover, which is not for those after death (for there is nothing after death) but for those living now in a modern city. Thomson's Hell is London at night (with some suggestions of Glasgow: he was born in Port Glasgow) experienced as a Waste Land more terrible than Eliot's (for there is no possibility of regenerating rain ever coming), a symbol of the horror and the meaningless of existence, peopled with images and objects whose only function is to suggest that horror and that meaningless.

Thomson's function is not to convert the reader, but to evoke recognition of the reader's own experience. He writes for his fellow-despairers:

> If any cares for the weak words here written,
> It must be someone desolate, Fate-smitten,
>   Whose faith and hope are dead, and who would die.
>
> Yes, here and there some weary wanderer
>   In that same city of tremendous night,
> Will understand the speech, and feel a stir
>   Of fellowship in all-disastrous fight;
> 'I suffer mute and lonely, yet another
> Uplifts his voice to let me know a brother
>   Travels the same wild paths though out of sight.'
>
> O sad Fraternity, do I unfold
>   Your dolorous mysteries shrouded from of yore?
> Nay, be assured; no secret can be told
>   To any who divined it not before:
> None uninitiate by many a presage
> Will comprehend the language of the message,
>   Although proclaimed aloud for evermore.

Thomson's city is full of gloom and immense 'soundless solitudes', but it is not uninhabited:

> The street-lamps burn amidst the baleful glooms,
>   Amidst the soundless solitudes immense
> Of rangèd mansions dark and still as tombs.
>   The silence which benumbs or strains the sense
> Fulfils with awe the soul's despair unweeping:
> Myriads of habitants are ever sleeping
>   Or dead, or fled from nameless pestilence!
>
> Yet as in some necropolis you find
>   Perchance one mourner to a thousand dead,
> So there; worn faces that look deaf and blind
>   Like tragic masks of stone. With weary tread,
> Each wrapt in his own doom, they wander, wander,
> Or sit foredone and desolately ponder
>   Through sleepless hours with heavy drooping head . . .
>
> The City is of Night, but not of Sleep;
>   There sweet sleep is not for the weary brain;
> The pitiless hours like years and ages creep,
>   A night seems termless hell. This dreadful strain
> Of thought and consciousness which never ceases,

> Or which some moments' stupor but increases,
>   This, worse than woe, makes wretches there insane.
> They leave all hope behind who enter there . . . .

This is not argument, as Tennyson's *In Memoriam* is often argument, but impressionist evocation by means of images that do not necessarily cohere into a consistent symbolic pattern. Thomson keeps changing his symbols, changing the point of vantage from which to penetrate to the reader's recognition of his own state. Sometimes he speaks in his own person, sometimes he evokes other figures to speak for him. The famous incantatory stanzas in Part IV are spoken in the poet's own person:

> As I came through the desert thus it was,
> As I came through the desert: All was black,
> In heaven no single star, on earth no track;
> A brooding hush without a stir or note,
> The air so thick it clotted in my throat;
> And thus for hours; then some enormous things
> Swooped past with savage cries and clanking wings:
>   But I strode on austere;
>   No hope could have no fear.
>
> As I came through the desert thus it was,
> As I came through the desert: Eyes of fire
> Glared at me throbbing with a starved desire;
> The hoarse and heavy and carnivorous breath
> Was hot upon me from deep jaws of death;
> Sharp claws, swift talons, fleshless fingers cold
> Plucked at me from the bushes, tried to hold:
>   But I strode on austere;
>   No hope could have no fear.

The images in this section are not specific symbols to be explained as signifying a particular aspect of experience; they are atmospheric in function, as is the appalling image of the eclipsed sun later in the same section:

> As I came through the desert thus it was,
> As I came through the desert: On the left
> The sun arose and crowned a broad crag-cleft;
> There stopped and burned out black, except a rim
> A bleeding eyeless socket, red and dim;

Whereupon the moon fell suddenly south-west,
And stood above the right-hand cliffs at rest:
    Still I strode on austere;
    No hope could have no fear.

Ian Campbell has remarked of this passage: 'Whether the reader's mind responds by calling up pictures of Gloucester's blinding, of Biblical crucifixion, of Wells's later nightmare vision from *The Time Machine* of the end of life on Earth, or simply of the unnatural atmosphere of total eclipse, nothing can prevent the physical flinching at the use of the eye-socket comparison to the sun.'[7] Yet it does not *mean* anything beyond that effect of flinching it is designed to create. When Dante uses astronomical imagery it is part of a fully articulated view of a benignly structured universe, and we know exactly why it is introduced at any given point and what part it plays in the whole. Thomson's Inferno has no meaning other than that it is meaninglessly hellish.

The preacher in the dark cathedral of section XIV uses a parodic biblical language to proclaim an atheistical creed:

And now at last authentic word I bring,
Witnessed by every dead and living thing;
    Good tidings of great joy for you, for all:
There is no God; no Fiend with names divine
Made us and tortures us; if we must pine,
    It is to satiate no Being's gall.

This whole passage is powerful and striking, the preacher going on to comfort men by assuring them that death is the end and they can end life when they will 'without the fear of waking after death'. But it is not really comfort; at least, it cannot counteract the prevailing mood of the poem, which is one of the bleakest despair. Thomson does not regard his atheism as a liberation. Though he did not fight his scepticism, as Tennyson did and as even Clough occasionally did, he did not enjoy it either. I have mentioned the masochistic force of the poem: time and again in reading it one is struck by the masochistic relish with which Thomson finds images and incidents with which to assault the reader and bring him to recognize in himself the mood that Thomson is evoking.

[7] *Victorian Poetry*, XVI, 1 and 2, Spring—Summer 1978, p. 131.

The universe is both malevolent and neutral. The neutrality is expressed in another part of section XIV:

> I find no hint throughout the Universe
> Of good or ill, of blessing or of curse;
> 　I find alone Necessity supreme.

But in the end Necessity turns into Melencolia, whose reign is strikingly evoked in section XXI. Thomson is thinking of Albrecht Dürer's 1514 engraving 'Melencolia', to which these stanzas refer and from which their symbolism is taken. But the goddess is given a quite new function here. Melencolia is driven by some compulsion in her own will to carry on the meaningless work of Necessity:

> Baffled and beaten back she works on still,
> 　Weary and sick of soul she works the more,
> Sustained by her indomitable will:
> 　The hand shall fashion and the brain shall pore,
> And all her sorrow shall be turned to labour,
> Till Death the friend-foe piercing with his sabre
> 　That mighty heart of hearts ends bitter war.

> But as if blacker night could dawn on night,
> 　With tenfold gloom on moonless night unstarred,
> A sense more tragic than defeat and blight,
> 　More desperate than strife with hope debarred,
> More fatal than the adamantine Never
> Encompassing her passionate endeavour
> 　Dawns glooming in her tenebrous regard:

> The sense that every struggle brings defeat
> 　Because Fate holds no prize to crown success;
> That all the oracles are dumb or cheat
> 　Because they have no secret to express;
> That none can pierce the vast black veil uncertain
> Because there is no light beyond the curtain;
> 　That all is vanity and nothingness . . .

> The moving moon and stars from east to west
> 　Circle before her in the sea of air;
> Shadows and gleams glide round her solemn rest.
> 　Her subjects often gaze up to her there:
> The strong to drink new strength of iron endurance,
> The weak new terrors; all, renewed assurance
> 　And confirmation of the old despair.

There is a hint of stoical endurance in Thomson's picture of Melencolia. Yet it is not a triumphant stoicism, and, as far as man is concerned, there is no suggestion that there is a triumph in bracing oneself before meaningless darkness. There is nothing here of W.E. Henley's histrionic stoical cry:

> Out of the night that covers me,
>   Black as the Pit from pole to pole,
> I thank whatever gods may be
>   For my unconquerable soul.
>
> In the fell clutch of circumstance
>   I have not winced or cried aloud.
> Under the bludgeonings of chance
>   My head is bloody, but unbowed.
>
> Beyond the place of wrath and tears
>   Looms but the Horror of the shade,
> And yet the menace of the years
>   Finds and shall find me unafraid.
>
> It matters not how strait the gate,
>   How charged with punishments the scroll,
> I am the master of my fate:
>   I am the captain of my soul.

This kind of shouting in the dark is very far from Thomson's utterance, which is one of the bleakest in the poetry of the English language. Yet in a sense Thomson's is more authentic than Henley's, less pure gesture, more determined to take the reader with him. A.E. Housman's stoical gestures are less histrionic:

> The troubles of our proud and angry dust
>   Are from eternity and shall not fail.
> Bear them we can, and if we can we must.
>   Shoulder the sky, my lad, and drink your ale.

But stoicism, which finds expression often in English poetry, in the Renaissance as well as in the Victorian period and later, really represents a very different field of enquiry. There is a Christian stoicism as well as a sceptical stoicism. Even such a committed Christian poet as Christiana Rossetti can strike a stoical note:

> Does the road wind uphill all the way?
>   Yes, to the very end.

But Christina Rossetti is talking of a journey that is very different from James Thomson's walk through the desert without hope or fear.

7 CALVINISM AND THE POETIC IMAGINATION: FROM BURNS TO HOGG PROBLEMS OF ANTINOMIANISM

O thou that in the heavens does dwell!
Wha, as it pleases best thysel,
Sends ane to heaven and ten to hell,
    A' for thy glory!
And no for ony gude or ill
    They've done before thee.

I bless and praise thy matchless might,
When thousands thou has left in night,
That I am here before thy sight,
    For gifts and grace,
A burning and a shining light
    To a' this place.

What was I, or my generation,
That I should get such exaltation?
I, wha deserv'd most just damnation,
    For broken laws
Sax thousand years ere my creation,
    Thro' Adam's cause!

When from my mother's womb I fell
Thou might hae plunged me deep in hell,
To gnash my gooms, and weep, and wail,
    In burning lakes,
Where damned devils roar and yell
    Chain'd to their stakes.

Yet I am here, a chosen sample,
To show thy grace is great and ample:
I'm here, a pillar o' thy temple
    Strong as a rock,
A guide, a ruler and example
    To a' thy flock.

This, of course, in Burns's Holy Willie. I should like to take a look at his background.

In the words of the Confession of Faith reaffirmed by an Act of the Scottish Parliament of 25 April 1690 as the doctrine of the Church of Scotland, 'God according to his eternal and immutable Purpose, and the secret Counsel and Good Pleasure of his Will' has elected and predestined some for eternal life 'without any Foresight of Faith, or good Works, or Perseverance in either of them . . . Neither are any other redeemed by Christ, effectually Called, Justifed, Adopted, Sanctified and Saved, but the Elect only. The rest of mankind God was pleased . . . to pass by.' This spells out the doctrine of predestination defined by Calvin in his *Institutes* as 'the eternal decrees of God by which He has determined with Himself what He would have to become to every man. For . . . eternal life is foreordained for some and eternal damnation for others.'

Scottish preachers in the seventeeth and eighteenth centuries elaborated on this doctrine with ingenuity and passion and were prone to emphasize the implication that no 'good works' on the part of any man or woman had the slightest relevance to his or her eternal fate, for, because of Adam's sin, all were totally depraved from birth. As Henry Gray Graham summed it up in his chapter entitled 'Theological Opinions and Teaching' in his *Social Life of Scotland in the Eighteenth Century*[1] (and though this book is now seen to be inadequate in some respects, this chapter, based on a wide reading of primary sources, has never been challenged): 'The Fall, Original Sin, the total depravity of human nature, redemption of the elect, the woes of hell and joys of heaven' were the main topics of religious preaching. Thomas Boston's *Fourfold State of Man*, that influential work of Scottish divinity first published in 1720, proclaimed that good works of religion performed by an unregenerate man were 'mere sham and dead forms of holiness' and that repentance on the part of a man who was not one of the predestined elect was 'nothing but sin; for man, aye, even the new-born babe, is a lump of wrath, a child of hell'. It is clearly stated in the Westminster Confession: 'Works done by unregenerate man, although, for the matter of them, they may be things which God commands . . . are sinful and cannot please God.'

When Robert Burns was eighteen years old there appeared in Glasgow a book by Hugh Clark entitled *Meditations on the Love of Christ in Redeeming Elect Sinners* which pointed out that all

---

[1] 2 vols., London, 1899. The quotations below from Thomas Boston, Hugh Clark, and Thomas Blackwell will be found in Graham, ch. VIII.

descendants of Adam deserved everlasting and infinite torture since they were 'guilty lumps of hell' as a result of Adam's original sin. The wrath of God was one of Boston's favourite themes in his sermons in his Ettrick kirk, and these when published remained the gospel of the peasantry for generations. 'Everything in God is perfect of its kind, and therefore no wrath can be so perfectly fierce as His.' God's wrath is justly directed at all men, as inheriting Adam's guilt, and those who achieve salvation in spite of this do so 'no for ony gude or ill they've done before thee' but because it was God's arbitrary pleasure, before the beginning of time, to predestine this tiny minority to salvation.

The antinomian implications of this creed were not slow to emerge, and caused some bitter controversy in the eighteenth century. If human actions, however moral, are the products of total human depravity, and salvation depends not on good works but on God's mysterious decree of predestination, then if one was predestined to damnation what could it matter how one behaved? And if on the other hand one was elected to salvation, ones behaviour should be equally irrelevant. What was the individual to do about it? One could seek for evidence of one's election by the way one was moved to a life of godliness, but this could in itself be no proof. Ministers could exhort their congregations 'to get a grip of Christ', 'to close with his offer', 'to be espoused to Him', to accept Christ as their 'surety', but the logic of their doctrine would have to force them to admit that all this might be but shadow-boxing. That logic indeed was made clear in 1717 when the presbytery of Auchterarder insisted on a divinity student's subscribing a number of special articles before he could receive a licence to preach. One of these articles read: 'I believe that it is not sound and orthodox to teach that we must forsake sin in order to our coming to Christ, and installing us in covenant with God.' On declining to subscribe this article the student was denied his licence and appealed to the General Assembly, which condemned what came to be known as the 'Auchterarder Creed' on the grounds of dangerous ambiguity. Ambiguous it may have been, but it was drawing out an implication of a theological position clearly stated in the Westminster Confession which was embodied in the Act of 1690 (which has never been repealed).

Of course there were many in the Church of Scotland in the eighteeth century who did not accept this interpretation of Christian doctrine. The so-called Moderates, among whom were many of the literati, men of the Scottish Enlightenment, people like William Robertson and Hugh Blair, one a Principal and the other a Professor of Edinburgh university and both ministers of the Church of Scotland, took an altogether kindlier view of God's intentions towards man and did not dismiss the significance of moral behaviour as irrelevant to man's eternal fate. Hugh Blair, in the very first of the sermons published in two volumes in 1777, the same year that saw the appearance of Hugh Clark's fearful *Meditations*, discoursed on 'Piety and Morality', arguing that both are necessary, that 'morality without devotion is both defective and unstable' while devotion without morality is vain and impious. Worship and prayers, Blair argues, are 'for the sake of man, not of God; nor that God may be rendered more glorious, but that man may be made better'. This view is in sharp contrast with that expressed earlier in the century by Professor Thomas Blackwell of Aberdeen, who argued that although God from all eternity enjoyed perfect blessedness in the 'contemplation of His own perfection', he decided to create man so that he could get 'an additional revenue of glory by creating rational creatures who would sing eternal hallelujahs'. The whole tone of Blair's theology, like that of so many of the 'Moderates', is in striking opposition to that of some of the passages I have quoted from orthodox Calvinists. 'For what purpose did God place thee in this world', asks Blair, 'in the midst of human society, but that as a man among men thou mightest cultivate humanity; that each in his place might contribute to the general welfare; that as a spouse, a brother, a son, or a friend, though mightest act thy part with an upright and a tender heart; and thus aspire to resemble Him who ever considers the good of his creatures, and whose *tender mercies are over all his works*?' Contrast this with Boston's picture of the fate of the damned. 'God shall not pity them, but laugh at their calamity. The righteous company in heaven shall rejoice in the execution of God's judgment, and shall sing while the smoke riseth up for ever. Natural affection shall be extinguished; parents will not love their children, nor children their parents; the mother will not pity the daughter in the flames, nor the daughter the mother.' Or again 'The godly husband shall say Amen to the damnation of her who lay in his bosom.'

The argument between those who believed that human good works were irrelevant to salvation (even if they could be a sign of salvation's having been predestined for the individual who performed them) and those who believed, in Burns's words, in practice and in morals, had been going on since the previous century. Edward Burt, an English visitor to Scotland in the 1730s, noted the paradox of the Calvinist position. 'To tell the People they may go to Hell with all their Morality at their Back: This surely may insinuate to weak Minds, that it is to be avoided as a kind of sin; at best that it will be of no use to them; And then no wonder they neglect it, and set their enthusiastic Notions of *Grace* in the Place of Righteousness.'[2]

This brings us straight back to Holy Willie. The language of 'Holy Willie's Prayer' is that known as the 'language of the saints', defined by James Kinsley as 'that improbable amalgam of biblical English and colloquial Scots which was characteristic of the Covenanter and the Presbyterian evangelical'.[3] By using the dramatic monologue, Burns enables the speaker to damn the creed he is professing without any awareness that he is doing so. The mixture of self-righteousness, complacency, hypocrisy, and malevolence is presented with a continuous irony which is clear to the reader but of which the speaker is quite unconscious. Holy Willie's confession of 'fleshly lust' is perhaps too blatant in its hypocrisy; the excuse that he was drunk when he had his three encounters with 'Leezie's lass' is more low comedy than controlled satire; but the complacent reflection that follows the confession sets the poem back on the rails of theological satire:

> Maybe thou lets this fleshly thorn
> Buffet thy servant e'en and morn,
> Lest he o'er proud and high should turn,
>   That he's sae gifted;
> If sae, thy hand maun e'en be borne
>   Until thou lift it.

The cursing of his liberal-minded enemy Gavin Hamilton has the pseudo-biblical tone of righteous indignation, while the

[2] *Letters from a Gentleman in the North of Scotland to his Friend in London*, 1754, p. 206.
[3] *The Poems and Songs of Robert Burns*, ed. James Kinsley, Oxford, 1968, p. 1047.

conclusion, with its appeal for an abundance of both 'grace and gear', shows that association of godliness with wordly prosperity that the famous if now not wholly accepted Weber-Tawney thesis about the connection between Protestantism and capitalism was to attempt to explain.

> Lord, in thy day o' vengeance try him!
> Lord, visit them that did employ him!
> And pass not in thy mercy by them,
>   Nor hear their prayer;
> But for thy people's sake destroy them,
>   And dinna spare!
>
> But Lord, remember me and mine
> Wi' mercies temporal and divine!
> That I for grace and gear may shine,
>   Excell'd by nane!
> And a' the glory shall be thine!
>   Amen! Amen!

In spite of the prevalence of the harsher forms of Calvinism in the preaching of many of the ministers of Burns's time and region, Burns himself was brought up in a less rigid Christian code. In the *Manual of Religious Belief, in a Dialogue between Father and Son*, which has come down to us as by William Burnes, Burns's father, it is clearly stated that 'the Moral Law, as a rule of life, must be of indispensable obligation, but it is the glory of the Christian religion, that if we be upright in our endeavours to follow it, and sincere in our repentance, upon our failing and shortcoming we shall be accepted according to what we have, co-operating with our honest endeavours'. Burns was baptized by the Revd Dr William Dalrymple, whom in adult life he admired and whose works he read with appreciation. In his poem 'The Kirk of Scotland's Garland—a new Song', satirizing a theological crisis in Burns's native presbytery of Ayr, when Dr William McGill, one of the Ayr ministers, was charged with heresy, Burns defended McGill (Doctor Mac) and linked him with Dalrymple as humane and sensible men whom the orthodox persecuted. Throughout the poem Burns speaks ironically on behalf of the orthodox:

> Orthodox, Orthodox, who believe in John Knox,
>   Let me sound an alarm to your conscience;
> A heretic blast has been blawn i' the West—

That what is not sense must be Nonsense, Orthodox
That what is not Sense must be Nonsense.

Doctor Mac, Doctor Mac, ye should streek on a rack,
   To strike Evildooers with terror;
To join FAITH and SENSE upon any pretence
   Was heretic, damnable, error, &c . . .

D'rymple mild, D'rymple mild, tho' your heart's like
   a child,
   And your life like the new-driven snaw;
Yet that winna save ye, auld Satan maun have ye,
   For preaching that three's ane and twa, &c.

The great Chambers-Wallace edition of Burns describes Dalrymple's writings as 'expository rather than controversial', adding:

Mildness and gentleness of character are exhibited in everything he wrote, and the reader is ever and again tempted to discover in statements such as that natural passions are not criminal, save when ill directed or ill employed, that no penitent sinners whatever are excluded from pardon, the origins of the poet's working theory of life, as well as of the theological dogmas which he held so loosely.

Dr McGill, whom Burns called in a letter to Mrs Dunlop 'my learned and truly worthy friend', was a more systematic theologian, who incurred the wrath of the orthodox by more than a suspicion of Socinianism in his *Practical Essay on the Death of Jesus Christ* (1786). (Socinianism is a term that embraces quite a range of views, but in general it might be said that it emphasizes Christ's teaching and example rather than his divinity, holds that the soul is pure by nature though contaminated at an early age by evil example and teaching, and stresses the importance of human reason as well as of Scripture.) Burns had great sympathy with McGill's position and despised his persecutors. On 2 August 1788 he wrote to Miss Rachel Dunlop:

I am in perpetual warfare with that doctrine of our Reverend Priesthood that 'we are born into this world bond slaves of iniquity & heirs of perdition, wholly inclined' to that which is evil and wholly disinclined to that which is good until by a kind of Spiritual Filtration or rectifying process Called effectual Calling &c.—The whole business is reversed, and our connections above & below completely

change place.—I believe in my conscience that the case is just quite
contrary—We come into this world with a heart & disposition to do
good for it, untill by dashing a large mixture of base Alloy called
Prudence alias Selfishness, the too precious Metal of the Soul is
brought down to the blackguard Sterling of ordinary currency . . . .

John Goudie, to whom Burns addressed an admiring verse
epistle, wrote *Essays on Various Important Subjects Moral and Divine*
(popularly known as 'Goudie's Bible') and *The Gospel Recovered*
which attacked the literal interpretation of the Scriptures and
totally opposed the doctrine of Original Sin. 'The great cause
of all the moral evil that abounds in the world ariseth, not from
the effect of what they call original sin, proceeding from
ordinary generation, but only from that constitution (being
subject to vanity) to which Adam was created for a proba-
tionary trial, though not proof against but liable to fall.'
Goudie denied that the human race was depraved through
Adam's sin and that if Adam had not sinned man would not
have died, and in general made a frontal attack on central
Calvinist doctrines as interpreted in eighteenth-century Scotland. Burns encouraged him in his polemics and sneered at his
opponents.

> O Gowdie, terror o' the whigs,
> Dread o' black coats and reverend wigs!
> Sour Bigotry on his last legs
>   Girns and looks back,
> Wishing the ten Egyptian plagues
>   May seize you quick!

The clearest statement in Burns's poetry of his disapproval
of the preachers of wrath and his preference for those who
preached the efficacy of good works is found in his 'Holy Fair'.

> Now o'er the congregation o'er,
>   Is silent expectation;
> For Sawnie speels the holy door,
>   Wi' tidings o' damnation:
> Should *Hornie*, as in ancient days,
>   'Mang sons o' God present him,
> The vera sight o' Sawnie's face,
>   To's ain *het hame* had sent him
>   Wi' fright that day.

Hear how he clears the points o' Faith
    Wi' rattlin an' thumpin!
Now meekly calm, now wild in wrath,
    He's stampan, an' he's jumpan!
His lengthen'd chin, his turn'd up snout,
    His eldrich squeel an' gestures,
O how they fire the heart devout,
    Like cantharidian plaisters
                        On sic a day!

But hark! the *tent* has chang'd its voice;
    There's peace an' rest nae langer;
For a' the *real judges* rise,
    They canna sit for anger.
Smith opens out his cauld harangues,
    On *practice* and on *morals*;
An' aff the godly pour in thrangs,
    To gie the jars an' barrels
                        A lift that day.

What signifies his barren shine,
    Of *moral pow'rs* an' *reason*;
His English style, an' gesture fine,
    Are a' clean out o' season.
Like Socrates or Antonine,
    Or some auld pagan heathen,
The *moral man* he does define,
    But ne'er a word o' *faith* in
                        That's right that day.

In guid time comes an antidote
    Against sic poosion'd nostrum;
For Peebles, frae the water-fit,
    Ascends the *holy rostrum*:
See, up he's got the Word o' God,
    An' meek an' mim has view'd it,
While Common-Sense has taen the road,
    An' aff, an' up the Cowgate
                        Fast, fast that day.

'Sawnie' was Alexander Moodie, the noted 'Auld Licht' minister of Riccarton, whom Burns had already satirized in 'The Holy Tulzie'. 'Smith' was George Smith, minister of Galston, 'New Licht' moderate. He was a great grandfather of Robert Louis Stevenson. The description of his sermons as 'cauld harangues on practice and on morals' is of course a defence in the form of an ironic attack, as is the reference to Smith's 'barren shine' and emphasis on the 'moral man'. Burns is ironically assuming the position of Smith's orthodox enemies. He himself was on the side of good works and benevolence. But Burns's irony has been misread by some otherwise perceptive scholars: J.C. Furnas, in his admirable biography of Stevenson, says that Burns here administered 'a stinging flick' at Smith, whereas, of course the attack was aimed at Smith's orthodox opponents, Moodie and Peebles. William Peebles was minister of Newton-upon-Ayr.

In his dedicatory poem to Gavin Hamilton, who was so pursued by the orthodox for his allegedly lax behaviour, Burns pours his irony over the Calvinist suspicion of good works and the whole theological edifice of which it is a part. He is describing the ideal patron:

> I readily and freely grant,
> He downa see a poor man want;
> What's no his ain, he winna tak it;
> What ance he says, he winna break it;
> Ought he can lend he'll no refus 't,
> Till aft his goodness is abus'd;
> And rascals whyles that do him wrang,
> Ev'n *that* he does na mind it lang:
> As Master, Landlord, Husband, Father,
> He does na fail his part in either.

> But then, nae thanks to him for a' that;
> Nae *godly symptom* ye can ca' that;
> It's naething but a milder feature,
> Of our poor, sinfu', corrupt Nature:
> Ye'll get the best o' moral works
> 'Mang black *Gentoos*, and Pagan *Turks*,
> Or Hunters wild on *Ponotaxi*,
> Wha never heard of Orthodoxy.
> That he's the poor man's friend in need,
> The Gentleman in word and deed,
> It's no through terror of Damnation;
> It's just a carnal inclination.

> Morality, thou deadly bane,
> Thy tens o' thousands thou hast slain!
> Vain is his hope, whase stay an' trust is,
> In *moral* Mercy, Truth and Justice!

No—stretch a point to catch a plack;
Abuse a Brother to his back;
Steal thro' the *winnock* frae a whore,
But point the Rake that taks the *door*;
Be to the Poor like onie whunstane,
And haud their noses to the grunstane;
Ply ev'ry art o' *legal* thieving;
No matter—stick to *sound believing.*

Learn three-mile pray'rs, an' half-mile graces,
Wi' weel spread looves, an' lang, wry faces;
Grunt up a solemn, lengthen'd groan,
And damn a' Parties, but your own;
I'll warrant then, ye're nae Deceiver,
A steady, sturdy, staunch *Believer.*

O ye wha leave the springs o' Calvin,
For *gumlie dubs* of your ain delvin!
Ye sons of Heresy and Error,
Ye'll *some day* squeel in quaking terror!
When vengeance draws the sword in wrath,
And in the fire throws the *sheath*;
When Ruin, with his sweeping *besom*,
Just fret s till Heav'n commission gies him;
When o'er the *Harp* pale Misery moans,
And strikes the ever-deep'ning tones,
Still louder shrieks, and heavier groans!

Your pardon, Sir, for this degression,
I maist forgat my *Dedication*;
But when Divinity comes cross me,
My readers still are sure to lose me.

It is difficult to pinpoint Burns's religious beliefs, if only because he was such a superb role taker. He can get carried away into different moods. The picture of family worship in 'A Cotter's Saturday Night' vibrates with real sympathy, even though other parts of the poem seem to be posed for a genteel audience. He is certainly speaking with conviction when he says in his 'Epistle to a Young Friend':

The fear o' Hell's a hangman's whip,
To haud the wretch in order . . .

but when he goes on to say

But where ye feel your *Honor* grip,
Let that ay be your border,

we may wonder how committed Burns is to the concept of
honour as the supreme sanction. The next stanza runs:

> The great Creator to revere,
> > Must sure become the *Creature*;
> But still the preaching cant forbear,
> > And ev'n the rigid feature:
> Yet ne'er with Wits prophane to rage,
> > Be complaisance extended;
> An *atheist-laugh* 's a poor exchange
> > For Deity offended!

There can be no doubt that Burns's antipathy to 'the
preaching cant' and 'the rigid feature', and his belief in a benevolent Creator seems to have been genuine too. The contrast
between 'an atheist laugh' and 'Deity offended' sounds somewhat glib. 'Deity' is a curiously abstract word. But perhaps
it is the right word for Burns, for, in some moods at least, he
seems to have been more a deist than a theist. And like Field-
ing's Tom Jones, he believed in the doctrine of the good
heart and held that kindness, generosity of spirit, and fellow
feeling were the central virtues.

Burns could be mischievously irreverent as well as bitterly
ironical where religion was concerned. He was of course
thoroughly familiar with the language of the Authorized Version of the Bible and of the Presbyterian metrical Psalter, as
well as with the language of the Scottish pulpit of his day, and
he could parody them with wicked effectiveness. When George
III recovered from madness in the spring of 1789 Burns wrote a
psalm of thanksgiving parodying the language and style of the
metrical version of Psalm 144. Burns's poem begins:

> O, sing a new Song to the Lord!
> > Make, all and every one,
> A joyful noise, ev'n for the king
> > His Restoration.

The last three stanzas run:

> And now thou hast restor'd our State,
> > Pity our kirk also,
> For she by tribulations
> > Is now brought very low!

> Consume that High Place, Patronage,
>   From off thine holy hill;
> And in thy fury burn the book
>   Even of that man, McGill.
>
> Now hear our Prayer, accept our Song,
>   And fight thy Chosen's battle:
> We seek but little, Lord, from thee,
>   Thou kens we get as little.

The mood of irreverence in which this mock-psalm was written is sufficiently evidenced by the fact that Burns sent it to the Editor of the London *Star* with a facetious note signed 'Duncan M'Leerie'. 'Duncan Macleerie' is a bawdy song to be found in *The Merry Muses of Caledonia*.

One of the paradoxes of the religious position in Scotland in Burns's day was that the sterner and indeed what may seem to us the crueler forms of religion were preached by the more democratically minded and were popular among the peasantry, while the more humane and liberal doctrines were propounded by the genteel and the well-to-do, who supported the principle of patronage—the appointment of ministers by vested authority rather than election by the congregations concerned. So we find Burns, the great egalitarian and champion of democracy, sneering at those who attacked patronage in favour of democratic election, because he associated the attackers with extreme Calvinist intolerance and the defenders with humane and liberal ideas. Further, it is one of the disappointments of eighteenth-century Scottish culture that the religious doctrine that was set in opposition to Calvinism was more often than not a wishy-washy 'moderatism', a combination of easy-going deism and sentimental morality. Intellectual rigour was with the Calvinists or with the sceptic David Hume (who died when Burns was seventeen). So Burns, passionate critic of social inequality though he was, found himself on the side of the gentry in religious matters. For the gentry tended to be Moderates, while the peasantry tended to be Auld Lichts or, in more general terms, Evangelicals.

The Moderates supported Government and defended patronage, so bitterly opposed by the popular Evangelical party. They became increasingly trapped in reactionary attitudes, their position developing into what Lord Cockburn stigmatized as 'a passive devotion to the gentry'. In justice to them, one might quote Ian Clark's recent analysis:

To the Moderates, acquiescence in patronage was the price which must be paid for their ideal of a Church occupying a central place in the national life. They repudiated the tacitly-held view of their opponents that the Church is a society called out of the world and set over against it. As in their doctrine of salvation they preached the 'Wholeness' of man, appealing to his reason as much as to his emotions, so in their doctrine of the Church the Moderates insisted that Christianity caters not for 'man' in the abstract, but for 'man-in-society'. Man is by nature social, and therefore not only must the Church interpret society, but the Church herself bears an analogy to society.[4]

The Disruption of 1843 showed how the Evangelicals had taken over the role of democrats and patriots, defending the independence of the Kirk against the secular authorities. Lord Cockburn, though he was no Evangelical and perhaps not even in any strict sense a Christian, could not but admire the heroism of the Church free from secular political control. Burns would have been perplexed. For he must have applauded a church that had succeeded in making itself both national and free, while he could not have approved of its theology. But of course the situation was different from what it was in the eighteenth century, if only because it was now the townsfolk at least as much as the peasantry who supported the Evangelical side.

The most sustained attack on the antinomian aspects of some popular Scottish interpretations of Calvinism is in James Hogg's *Private Memoirs and Confessions of a Justified Sinner*, first published anonymously in 1824. Hogg was the 'Ettrick Shepherd', and Thomas Boston, from whose works I have already quoted, had been minister at Ettrick from 1707 to 1732. Hogg must have heard about Boston if he had not also read him, and he must too have picked up many local stories in which the prowess of the Devil stalking the land to see whom he might destroy was luridly portrayed. It seems likely that some such stories, together with an awareness of the nature of Boston's preaching, provided the germ of the *Confessions of a Justified Sinner*. The book is a central work in any discussion of

    [4] *Scotland in the Age of Improvement*, ed. N.T. Philipson and Rosalind Mitchison, Edinburgh, 1970, p. 207.

Calvinism and literature in Scotland. It is the story of a young man brought up in the firm belief in predestination who, from the moment he is convinced of his election to grace, is progressively persuaded that whatever crimes he commits will be to the greater glory of God and could not possibly affect his ultimate salvation which had been predestined since before the beginning of time. The story is told in three parts, first in a straightforward account in the third person, then—the principal and the most powerful part—in the first person as the memoirs of the chief character, and finally in an editorial conclusion that anchors the story in history with contemporary relevance. The *Confessions* can be read either as a psychological probing of the appalling consequences for human character of taking the Calvinist doctrines of predestination and election to extremes; or as a supernatural horror story of how the Devil tempts a convinced Calvinist into horrible crimes through using the implications of the creed he professes; or it can be read as both of these simultaneously, with the reader continually in suspense between a supernatural and a psychological interpretation. The central character, Robert Wringhim, finds himself accompanied by a persuasive and dominating stranger who attaches himself more and more to him and who might be either a figment of Robert's increasingly obsessed imagination or the Devil, as he progressively suspects. The companion calls himself Gilmartin; he continually urges on Robert his duty to rid the world of persons—including his easy-going brother and his equally easy-going father—who are not of the elect and who simply multiply wickedness in the world during their lifetime. Here is a description of one of their conversations:

The two young men came on, in earnest and vehement conversation; but the subject they were on was a terrible one, and hardly fit to be repeated in the face of a Christian community. Wringhim was disputing the boundlessness of the true Christian's freedom, and expressing doubts that, chosen as he knew he was from all eternity, still it might be possible for him to commit acts that would exclude him from the limits of the covenant. The other argued, with mighty fluency, that the thing was utterly impossible, and altogether inconsistent with eternal predestination. The arguments of the latter prevailed, and the laird [Robert Wringhim] was driven to sullen silence . . . .

The autobiographical section of the novel opens thus:

My life has been a life of trouble and turmoil; of change and
vicissitude; of anger and exultation; of sorrow and vengeance. My
sorrows have all been for a slighted gospel, and my vengeance has
been wreaked on its adversaries. Therefore, in the might of Heaven, I
will sit down and write: I will let the wicked of this world know what I
have done in the faith of the promises, and justification by grace, that
they may read and tremble, and bless their gods of silver and gold
that the minister of Heaven was removed from their sphere before
their blood was mingled with their sacrifices.

After Robert has been assured by the Calvinist minister he
calls his reverend father and his fanatically pious mother, the
minister's devoted friend and follower, that he is in fact a
justified person, predestined to salvation with his redemption
'sealed and sure', he has his first encounter with Gilmartin,
who congratulates him on his enviable state and says he has
come to be his humble disciple. Under the influence of Gilmartin's arguments, always absolutely orthodox in terms of logic
but somehow disturbing even to Robert who cannot but accept
them, Robert's character steadily changes.

From the moment, I conceived it decreed, not that I should be a
minister of the gospel, but a champion of it, to cut off the enemies of
the Lord from the face of the earth; and I rejoiced in the commission,
finding it more congenial to my nature to be cutting sinners off with
the sword than to be haranguing them from the pulpit, striving to
produce an effect which God, by his act of absolute predestination,
had for ever rendered impracticable. The more I pondered on these
things the more I saw of the folly and inconsistency of ministers in
spending their lives striving and remonstrating with sinners in order
to induce them to do that which they had not it in their power to do.
Seeing that God had from all eternity decided the fate of every individual that was to be born of woman, how vain was it in man to
endeavour to save those whom their Maker had, by an unchangeable
decree, doomed to destruction. I could not disbelieve the doctrine
which the best of men had taught me, and towards which he made the
whole of the Scripture to bear, and yet it made the economy of the
Christian world appear to me as an absolute contradiction. How
much more wise would it be, thought I, to begin and cut sinners off
with the sword! For till that is effected, the saints can never inherit the
earth in peace. Should I be honoured as an instrument to begin this
great work of purification, I should rejoice in it. But, then, where had

I the means, or under what direction was I to begin? There was one
thing clear, I was now the Lord's and it behoved me to bestir myself
in His service. Oh that I had an host at my command, then would I
be as a devouring fire among the workers of iniquity!

Gilmartin keeps up the pressure by a mixture of flattery and
argument. 'We conversed again till the day was near a close;
and the things that he strove most to inculcate on my mind
were the infallibility of the elect, and the pre-ordination of all
things that come to pass.' When Robert suggests that there
must be 'degrees of sinning which would induce the Almighty
to throw off the elect', Gilmartin replies:

'Why sir . . . by vending such an insinuation, you put discredit on
the great atonement, in which you trust. Is there not enough of merit
in the blood of Jesus to save thousands of worlds, if it was for these
worlds that he died? Now, when you know, as you do (and as every
one of the elect may know of himself) that this Saviour died for you,
namely and particularly, dare you say that there is not enough of
merit in His great atonement to annihilate all your sins, let them be as
heinous and atrocious as they may? And, moreover, do you not
acknowledge that God hath pre-ordained and decreed whatever
comes to pass? Then, how is it that you should deem it in your power
to eschew one action of your life, whether good or evil? Depend on it,
the advice of the great preacher is genuine: "What thine hand findeth
to do, do it with all thy might, for none of us knows what a day may
bring forth." That is, none of us knows what is pre-ordained, but
whatever is pre-ordained we *must* do, and none of these things will be
laid to our charge.'

It is impossible to convey the power and indeed the terror of
The Confessions of a Justified Sinner by a series of brief extracts. It
is a much richer and subtler work than Burns's 'Holy Willie's
Prayer' and it is not, as is Burns's poem, an ironic exposure of
a special kind of hypocrisy and malevolence made possible by a
particular religious creed, but a complex exploration of the
psychological as well as the moral consequences of pursuing the
logic of that creed to what appears to be its irresistible conclusion. It raises fundamental questions about the relation between God's will and power and man's fate. Douglas Gifford
sees as the centre of the novel 'an untruth which lies at the
heart of Christian theology, and allows the whole fabric of
"justified" egotism and social evil to result'. I would demur at

Gifford's use of the term 'Christian theology' here; it is far too blanket a term; but if one substituted 'one strain in Calvinist theology' it would be hard to disagree with him.

Johan Agricola, the sixteenth-century German Protestant theologian, separated himself from Luther in 1536 by taking up an antinomian position similar to that found in some eighteenth-century Scottish preachers. In Agricola's view, good works cannot bring salvation nor do evil works necessarily hinder it: a child of grace, being once assured of salvation, cannot sin; what would be sins in others are not sins in him. Robert Browning was fascinated by the kind of person who could hold this belief. Unlike Burns, whose concern was to pillory Holy Willie, Browning tried to understand Agricola. Here is the latter part of his poem, 'Johannes Agricola in Meditation' —like 'Holy Willie's Prayer' a dramatic monologue, but of a very different kind:

> ay, God said
> This head this hand should rest upon
> Thus, ere He fashioned star or sun.
> And having thus created me,
> Thus rooted me, He bade me grow,
> Guiltless for ever, like a tree
> That buds and blooms, nor seeks to know
> The law by which it prospers so:
> But sure that thought and word and deed
> All go to swell His love for me,
> Me, made because that love had need
> Of something irrevocably
> Pledged solely its content to be.
> Yes, yes, a tree which must ascend,
> No poison-gourd foredoomed to stoop!
> I have God's warrant, could I blend
> All hideous sins, as in a cup,
> To drink the mingled venom up,
> Secure my nature will convert
> The draught to blossoming gladness fast,
> While sweet dews turn to the gourd's hurt,
> And bloat, and while they bloat it, blast,
> As from the first its lot was cast.
> For as I lie, smiled on, full fed
> By unexhausted power to bless,

I gaze below on Hell's fierce bed,
  And those its waves of flame oppress,
Swarming in ghastly wretchedness;
Whose life on earth aspired to be
  One altar-smoke, so pure!—to win
If not love like God's love to me,
  At least to keep His anger in;
And all their striving turn to sin.
  Priest, doctor, hermit, monk grown white
With prayer, and broken-hearted nun,
  The martyr, the wan acolyte,
The incense-swinging child,—undone
Before God fashioned star or sun!
God, whom I praise; how could I praise,
  If such as I might understand,
Make out and reckon on His ways,
  And bargain for His love, and stand,
Paying a price, at His right hand?

By Browning's time this kind of antinomianism had become more a historical curiosity than a living faith to be challenged by those who disagreed with it. Browning could afford to exercise his psychological curiosity and his historical imagination in trying to project Agricola's state of mind. The whole thing is very much distanced—more distanced, we feel, than his evocation of Bishop Blougram's state of mind in his 'Bishop Blougram's Apology'. For that poem was about the relation between doubt and faith, a very Victorian preoccupation, as I tried to show in an earlier lecture. When Bishop Blougram talks of faith he does not specify any particular theology, but simply a faith in the truth embodied somehow by the Church and its rituals. The best-known lines in the poem refer not to adherence to a faith but to the emergence of a mood. It is the mood that challenges and even conquers scepticism:

Just when we are safest, there's a sunset-touch,
A fancy from a flower-bell, some one's death,
A chorus-ending from Euripides,—
And that's enough for fifty hopes and fears
As old and new at once as Nature's self,
To rap and knock and enter in our soul,
Take hands and dance there, a fantastic ring,
Round the ancient idol, on his base again,—

The grand Perhaps! we look on helplessly,—
There the old misgivings, crooked questions are—
This good God,—what He could do, if He would,
Would, if He could—then must have done long since:
If so, when, where, and how? some way must be,—
Once feel about, and soon or late you hit
Some sense, in which it might be, after all.
Why not, 'The Way, the Truth, the Life?'

It might be. Why not? The eighteenth-century Scottish preachers would have looked askance at such a cavalier way with theology.

8 THE AMERICAN EXPERIENCE : FROM PURITANISM THROUGH POST-PURITANISM TO AGNOSTICISM EDWARD TAYLOR EMILY DICKINSON WALLACE STEVENS

No other Calvinist community produced a poem quite like Burns's 'Holy Willie's Prayer'. In New England, which had its own long Puritan tradition and its own versions of Calvinist theology, an enormous amount of intellectual and imaginative energy was spent in defining, propounding, defending, and preaching a variety of interpretations of Calvinism, sometimes as uncompromisingly as in some of the eighteenth-century Scottish preachings I quoted in my last lecture but more often with what appears to be a genuine concern for the spiritual welfare of hearers and readers. The Americans tended to exhort more than they denounced, and though their theological arguments could be as rigidly legal as anything to be found in Scotland—notably in the area of Covenant theology, with its distinction between the Covenant of Works, which Adam broke, and the succeeding Covenant of Grace which God in his mercy then drew up for those whom he would move by his grace to accept it—they never provoked the kind of reaction that the antinomian implications of Calvinism provoked in Scotland. This may have been partly because American theologians came to terms more directly with the problems of combining a confidence of being a justified person with working effectively in one's calling. The lines of this argument were laid down in the seventeenth century, notably by John Cotton. 'A true believing Christian', wrote John Cotton in his *Christian Calling*, 'a justified person, he lives in his vocation by his faith.' He went on to argue that this involved his civil life in this world as well as his spiritual life. For

faith draws the heart of a Christian to live in some warrantable calling. As soon as ever a man begins to look towards God and the ways of His grace, he will not rest till he find out some warrantable calling and employment.

What makes a calling warrantable is that God has given a man gifts for it. He exercises those gifts for the glory of God, and if

as a result he shines 'for grace and gear', as Holy Willie prayed
to be enabled to do, that too is for the glory of God. Indeed, in
John Cotton's 'Spiritual Milk for American Babes, Drawn out
of the Breasts of Both Testaments for their Souls Nourishment',
which formed a conspicuous part of the *New England Primer*,
a work first published as late as about 1790 and enormously
popular well into the next century, while it is emphasized (in
a series of questions and answers) that every child is 'conceived
in Sin & born in Iniquity' and that the child's 'corrupt Nature
is empty of Grace, bent unto Sin, only unto Sin, and that
continually', it is also asserted that the 'Ministry of the Gospel'
can 'raise [the child] up out of this estate' by teaching him 'the
Value & Virtue of the Death of Christ and the Riches of his
Grace to lost Sinners, by revealing the Promise of Grace to
such, and by ministering the Spirit of Grace to apply to Christ
and his Promise of Grace unto [the child] and to keep [him] in
him'. The *Primer* also includes the Westminster Shorter
Catechism, in which it is stated that 'God having out of his
meer good Pleasure, from all eternity, elected some to
everlasting Life, did enter into a Covenant of Grace to deliver
them out of a State of Sin and Misery', yet any antinomian
implications of this are contradicted by later emphasis on the
Moral Law as well as on faith in Jesus Christ, on the importance of Repentance as a saving grace and on the effectiveness
of the Preaching of the Word in 'convincing and converting
Sinners'. The paradox of the coexistence of belief in predestination with belief in the effectiveness of preaching in
converting sinners runs through much Calvinist thought, and
has been much discussed by theologians. The point I wish to
make here is that it was the persuasive power of preaching
rather than the unavoidable fate of the damned or the self-
satisfaction of the elect that was most stressed by New England
divines.

When New England Puritanism declined, it gave way first
to Unitarianism, what Emerson called 'the corpse-cold Unitarianism of Brattle Street and Harvard College', and then
to the more luxuriant appeal of Transcendentalism. Resem-
bling in some ways the Moderates in Scotland, the Unitarians,
revolting against the New England Puritan tradition, liberal-
ized and rationalized Christianity to the point at which it
became a genteel creed which replaced theology by *belles-lettres*

and religious enthusiasm by a cultured urbanity. But just as the polite deism of eighteenth-century England had opened the way to the Wesleyan counter-attack and the polite conservatism of the Scottish Moderates was challenged by the Disruption, so the elegance and liberality (by the 1830s hardened into a deep conservatism) of the Unitarians forced those who thirsted after a more immediate kind of religious experience into new habits of thought. The Calvinists of Princeton, who stuck to the old orthodoxy, could only rub their hands with an 'I-told-you-so' when the Unitarians found Transcendentalism flourishing on their left wing: that was what happened when you abandoned orthodox theology. It was all very paradoxical, because, having rescued religion from Calvinist grimness and wildness, as they thought, the Unitarians now found that the Transcendentalists were reintroducing the very emotionalism and mysticism which they had fought so hard to eliminate.

What happened when the Unitarians fell back on the Calvinists for help against the Transcendentalists, who were to move steadily towards revolutionary ideas in social as well as religious thought, is a fascinating story that can be followed in Perry Miller's fine anthology of the literature of the Transcendalists;[1] but it is not really part of the theme of these lectures. The point which led to me this digression was that the Calvinism—Unitarianism—Transcendentalism sequence in America, especially in New England, evolved in such a way as to avoid any direct attack on the antinomian implications of the Calvinist theory of the elect of the kind we have in Scotland. The poetry of American Puritanism has at its best strong affinities with seventeenth-century English religious poetry, notably that of George Herbert, but much of it has a didactic as well as a devotional tone. Edward Taylor, the late-seventeenth and early-eighteenth-century English-born New England poet, whose manuscripts were not discovered until 1937, wrote a series of poems with the general title *God's Determinations Touching His Elect*. It opens with a simple and direct statement of the power of God the Creator whose basic thought comes partly from the Psalms and partly from the Deutero-Isaiah, but whose homely language is very much his own:

> Infinity, when all things it beheld
> In nothing, and of nothing all did build—

---

[1] *The Transcendentalists: An Anthology*, Cambridge, Mass., 1950.

> Upon what base was fixed the lath wherein
> He turned this globe and riggaled it so trim?
> Who blew the bellows of His furnace fast?
> Or held the mould wherein the world was cast?
> Who laid its corner-stone? Or whose command?
> Where stand the pillars upon which it stands?
> Who laced and filleted the earth so fine
> With rivers like green ribbons smaragdine?
> Who made the sea its selvage, and its locks
> Like a quilt ball within a silver box?
> Who spread its canopy? Or curtains spun?
> Who in this bowling alley bowled the sun?
> Who made it always when it rises set:
> To go at once both down and up to get?
> Who the curtain rods made for this tapestry?
> Who hung the twinkling langhorns in the sky?
> Who? Who did this? Or who is He? Why, know
> It's only Might Almighty this did so.[2]

Burns could not have objected to this.

Even when he talks about the special place of the elect, Taylor is no Holy Willie. These lines are from the section entitled 'The Forwardness of the Elect in the Work of Conversion':

> Those upon whom Almighty doth intend
> His all-eternal glory to expend,
> Lull'd in the lap of sinful nature snug,
> Like pearls in puddles covered o'er with mud,
> Whom, if you search, perhaps some few you'll find
> That to notorious sins were ne'er inclined:
> Some shunning some, some most, some great, some small;
> Some this, that, or the other, some none at all.
> But all, or almost all, you'st easily find
> To all, or almost all, defects inclined:
> To revel with the rabble rout who say,
> 'Let's hiss this piety out of our day.'
> And those whose frame is made of finer twine
> Stand further off from grace than wash from wine.
> Those who suck grace from th' breast are nigh as rare
> As black swans that in milk-white rivers are.
> Grace therefore calls them all, and sweetly woos.

---

[2] *The American Puritans, their Prose and Poetry*, ed. Perry Miller, New York, 1956, p. 303.

Some, won, come in; the rest as yet refuse
And run away. Mercy pursues apace:
Then some cast down their arms, cry 'Quarter, grace!'
Some chased out of breath, drop down with fear,
Perceiving the pursuer drawing near.
The rest, pursued, divide into two ranks,
And this way one, and that the other pranks.[3]

This is Taylor's version of a notion that Francis Thomson was to develop in his own way two centuries later in *The Hound of Heaven*.

What developed in New England in the nineteenth century is what might be called post-Puritan sensibility, of which the poetry of Emily Dickinson is the most striking example. Emily Dickinson's long inheritance of New England Puritanism, with its stern Calvinist logic, furnished her with concepts of suffering, redemption, death, the soul, immortality, eternity, but she used these concepts in her own way. We see too in the language of her poetry the legalism that is found in the Calvinist theological concept of Covenant, sometimes ironically associated with the legalism she knew in her own lawyer father. She did not embrace the great New England philosophy of her day, Transcendentalism, but something of its mystic power, though without its optimistic largeness of romantic acceptance, came together with her post-Puritan heritage. She totally rejected the notion of Original Sin, and indeed lacked the Puritan concept of sin altogether. She could refer to God ironically as 'burglar, banker, father', and she could ask ironic questions about the Calvinist notion of Heaven:

Is Heaven a physician?
They say that he can heal,
But medicine posthumous
Is unavailable.
Is Heaven an exchequer?
They speak of what we owe,
But that negotiation
I'm not a party to.

Yet for Emily Dickinson all significant life marched towards

[3] Ibid. 305-6.

death and immortality, which are associated if not identified
with the ultimate unmoved mover, God.

> The only news I know
> Is bulletins all day
> From immortality;
>
> The only shows I see
> Tomorrow and today,
> Perchance eternity.
>
> The only one I meet
> Is God, the only street
> Existence; this traversed,
>
> If other news there be
> Or admirabler show,
> I'll tell it you.

Emily Dickinson's favourite biblical book was Revelation,
from which she got her symbolic use of words referring to
jewellery and regality, yet she claimed for herself no revelation
of Heaven or God. Her certainties came from within:

> I never saw a moor;
> I never saw the sea.
> Yet I know how heather looks
> And what a billow be.
>
> I never spoke with God,
> Nor visited in Heaven.
> Yet certain am I of the spot
> As if the checks were given.

It is not however the poems in which Emily Dickinson refers
to God that give the most vivid sense of the eternal otherness
that lies in wait for all. In poems about the soul's choice, about
the coming of death, about the journey to immortality, about
moments of fear or glory or vision, she conveys her sense of the
challenge and mystery generated by experience. Nature can be
seen as providing analogues of some ultimate cosmic drama,
but in her most characteristic poems she takes no comfort in
Nature.

> But nature is a stranger yet;
>   The ones that cite her most
> Have never passed her haunted house
>   Nor simplified her ghost

> To pity those that know her not
>   Is helped by the regret
> That those who know her know her less
>   The nearer her they get.

Emily Dickinson's feeling about daffodils is very un-Words-worthian:

> I dared not meet the daffodils
>   For fear their yellow gown
> Would pierce me with a fashion
>   So foreign to my own.

In that strangely powerful poem, 'Because I could not stop for Death', Death is a gentleman caller, a guide to the grave, a conductor to Eternity. Perhaps Death is also God.

> Because I could not stop for Death
> He kindly stopped for me.
> The carriage held but just ourselves
> And immortality.
>
> We slowly drove. He knew no haste,
> And I had put away
> My labour and my leisure too
> For his civility.
>
> We passed the school where children strove
> At recess in the ring,
> We passed the field of gazing grain;
> We passed the setting sun—
>
> Or rather, he passed us.
> The dews drew quivering and chill,
> For only gossamer my gown,
> My tippet only tulle.
>
> We paused before a house that seemed
> A swelling of the ground.
> The roof was scarcely visible,
> The cornice in the ground.
>
> Since then 'tis centuries, and yet
> Feels shorter than the day
> I first surmised the horses' heads
> Were toward Eternity.

The mingling here of the familiar and the strange, of comfort and terror, of the matter-of-fact with the visionary, shows an imagination rooted in daily life and at the same time nourished on lost concepts of religious awe; an imagination, one is tempted to say, that could only have developed in post-Puritan New England with its neatly materialist daily life coexisting with its mutated Calvinist heritage, with Romanticism and Transcendentalism blowing round.

Emily Dickinson's poetry is religious in a highly idiosyncratic way. It is neither devotional nor doctrinal. It does not brood, like so much in Tennyson and Arnold, nor does it work by accumulation and expansiveness like the poetry of her contemporary and fellow-American Walt Whitman. Her aim is not to mirror the totally responsive self, as Whitman's is, nor is it the musing self of the Victorians or the disciplined counterpointing of sensuous and religious response we find in Gerard Manley Hopkins: it is the innocent utterance of one for whom categories of existence are tested wholly and solely by personal experience. Nothing could be less 'dandified' in Whitman's sense, or less religious in Hopkins's. What comes together comes together; the juxtaposition of colloquial and formal speech is the result of how things fell together in her imagination. I am not suggesting that she was an artless primitive; she knew what she was doing, and often she did it too consciously and produced something coy rather than fresh. But if her innocent utterance was deliberate it was none the less innocent, and at its best effectively innocent. A poem such as 'I heard a fly buzz when I died' gains its effect from the pure integrity of the association of images; the rhythm and the rhyme have the function of detaching this awareness from the flux of experience and presenting it as a unit, whole and unspoiled. Half-rhymes are often sufficient for this purpose, for the emphasis is not on the polished perfection of the poem but on its separateness, the way in which it encloses a self-contained and whole experience. Let me try to explain this point by quoting the poem 'The Soul selects her own society':

> The sould selects her own society,
> Then shuts the door;
> To her divine majority
> Present no more.
>
> Unmoved she notes the chariots pausing
> At her low gate;

> Unmoved, an Emperor be kneeling
> Upon her mat.
>
> I've known her from an ample nation
> Choose one,
> Then close the valves of her attention
> Like stone.

Here we have the characteristic combination of domestic, legal, and royal imagery ('shuts the door', 'mat', 'divine majority', 'emperor') presented with a quiet assurance, an absolute *knowledge* that this is so. The soul chooses her own companions then shuts the door to exclude all others, however humble the soul and however high and mighty the suitors, because once fulfilled, once having achieved her divine majority, the soul has no further need of others. The poem is about the self-sufficiency and irrationality of the self within the self. It ends with an image of animal becoming mineral, of a bivalve closing to become a stone on the beach, so that the self-sufficiency is perhaps also death:

> I've known her from an ample nation
> Choose one,
> Then close the valves of her attention
> Like stone.

Those monosyllables shut the poem like a trap. But also like a poem. For this poem is in its way a model of what a poem is: it selects from the flux of experience its own society, its own unit of meaning and pattern of images which tell the truth about that unit, and then stops. Emily Dickinson's poems neither brood nor proclaim, neither point to the centre of the meditating self nor expand to take in a community or a cosmos; they are close-fitting containers for units of experience, the experience being always and only the poet's own, the generalizations presented in such a way that they are not really generalizations at all, only personal knowledge of what is personally lived: 'The soul selects her own society.' Where does she get the air of authority that this statement bears? Is it not the authority of innocence, the authority which comes from feeling no need to test any conviction by anything external at all?

Thus for all her use of religious words—soul, immortallty, eternity, and some times, though not so often, God—Emily

Dickinson is a poet who ignores religion in any institutional or doctrinal sense, who ignores theology, who shows no trace of piety or devotion in any of the senses in which we normally use these words. She is like Blake in her dependence on her own insights, but quite unlike him in her refusal to build up a system of her own to oppose orthodoxy. She has no system; her mind was quite unphilosophical and untheological. Yet she could not be called agnostic. She had a profound sense of the numinous and of the way in which the movement of life in some sense prefigures and leads to something eternally at rest.

For a truly agnostic major American poet we must turn to Wallace Stevens, who was born in 1879 and died in 1955. Steven's lack of any belief in the reality of God and in the efficacy of religious myths in the modern world gave to his view of the role of poetry and of the poetic imagination and of the poem as artefact a very special intensity. 'After one has abandoned a belief in God', he wrote, 'poetry is that essence which takes its place as life's redemption.' This was not Matthew Arnold's position, that the best part of religion is its poetry and that the documents of religion should be interpreted as poetry. Stevens had no wish to preserve a belief in Christianity by moving from a literal to a poetic interpretation of its biblical sources. His stand was much more radical than that. 'In an age of disbelief —I am quoting from him again—'when the gods have come to an end, when we think of them as the aesthetic projections of a time that has passed, men turn to a fundamental glory of their own and from that create a style of bearing themselves in reality.' Since there is nothing 'out there', the function of the imagination, its relation to reality and its role in mediating or concealing or distorting reality is absolutely central. The artist's creativity is the only creativity there is, and the world as we experience it represents the only *donnée*. This is why his poetry is so *responsibly difficult*. It carries enormous responsibility.

In his poem entitled 'The Idea of Order at Key West', Stevens describes a woman singing beside the sea. Like so many of Stevens's poems this is a tightly integrated work, so it is an injustice to quote it only in part, but such partial quotation will give some indication of what Stevens asks his poetry to do. It is both an enquiry into the relation between art and reality and an illustration of that relation.

For she was the maker of the song she sang.
The ever-hooded, tragic-gestured sea
Was merely a place by which she walked to sing.
Whose spirit is this? we said, because we knew
It was the spirit that we sought and knew
That we should ask this often as she sang.

If it was only the dark voice of the sea
That rose, or even colored by many waves;
If it was only the outer voice of sky
And cloud, of the sunken coral water-walled,
However clear, it would have been deep air,
The heaving speech of air, a summer sound
Repeated in a summer without end
And sound alone. But it was more than that,
More even than her voice, and ours, among
The meaningless plungings of water and the wind,
Theatrical distances, bronze shadows heaped
On high horizons, mountainous atmospheres
Of sky and sea.
                         It was her voice that made
The sky acutest at its vanishing.
She measured to the hour its solitude.
She was the single artificer of the world
In which she sang. And when she sang, the sea,
Whatever self it had, became the self
That was her song, for she was the maker. Then we,
As we beheld her striding there alone,
Knew that there never was a world for her
Except the one she sang and, singing, made.

The poet then turns to his companion, Ramon Fernandez, and asks him if he knows why, after singing, the harbour lights and the boats at anchor seem to have 'mastered the night and portioned out the sea'. The woman's song has imposed an order on the environment in which she sang. The poem concludes:

> Oh! Blessed rage for order, pale Ramon,
> The maker's rage to order words of the sea,
> Words of the fragrant portals, dimly-starred,
> And of ourselves and of our origins,
> In ghostlier demarcations, keener sounds.

Art is man's creation, and gives meaning to nature, which is not man's creation but something that he finds around him.

The form of a man-made jar can dominate and give new meaning to the world of nature in which it is set, in a way that 'bird
or bush' could never do alone:

> I placed a jar in Tennessee,
> And round it was, upon a hill.
> It made the slovenly wilderness
> Surround that hill.
>
> The wilderness rose up to it,
> And sprawled around, no longer wild.
> The jar was round upon the ground
> And tall and of a port in air.
>
> It took dominion everywhere.
> The jar was gray and bare.
> It did not give bird or bush,
> Like nothing else in Tennessee.

The poet is the type of man articulating and so creating his
own place in the world:

> The hero's throat in which the words are spoken,
> From which the chant comes close upon the ear,
> Out of the hero's being, the deliverer
>
> Delivering the prisoner by his words,
> So that the skeleton in the moonlight sings,
> Sing of an heroic world beyond the cell,
>
> No, not believing, but to make the cell
> A hero's world in which he is the hero.
> Man must become the hero of his world.
>
> ('Montrachet-le-Jardin')

Of Stevens's many poems taking up the theme of the relation
between the poet, creator of 'supreme fictions', and the world
of nature in which he finds himself, I shall quote from only one
more, 'Landscape with Boat':

> He never supposed
> That he might be truth, himself, or part of it,
> That the things that he rejected might be part
> And the irregular turquoise, part, the perceptible blue
> Grown denser, part, the eye so touched, so played
> Upon by clouds, the ear so magnified
> By thunder, parts, and all these things together,
> Parts, and more things, parts. He never supposed divine

> Things might not look divine, nor that if nothing
> Was divine then all things were, the world itself,
> And that if nothing was the truth, then all
> Things were the truth, the world itself was the truth.
>
> Had he been better able to suppose:
> He might sit on a sofa on a balcony
> Above the Mediterranean, emerald
> Becoming emeralds. He might watch the palms
> Flap green ears in the heat. He might observe
> A yellow wind and follow a steamer's track
> And say, 'The thing I hum appears to be
> The rhythm of this celestial pantomime.'

The 'he' of the poem has not the confidence to trust to his own creative ability, his own fictions, that would make a reality of the perceived world by 'humming' it. As Frank Kermode has put it, for Stevens 'the true hero is the human fictive power applied to reality'.

The concluding lines that I have just quoted illustrate in some degree the special kind of gaudiness of language, a very personal mixture of the everyday and the exotic, of the commonplace and the precious, that is characteristic of much of Stevens's writing. This again is part of his compulsion to use language to startle a form and a meaning out of what the imagination makes of experience. It results in a special kind of bravura, done with a curious combination of enjoyment and sadness. Sometimes it seems that Stevens is impelled to produce puzzles because that is part of the challenge to the poet in a universe that is meaningless without his response to it. The resulting obscurity is wholly unlike that of, say, T.S. Eliot. The earlier Eliot used myth to help restore a lost pattern of meaning, foraging among religious and anthropological sources to find kinds of significance that corresponded to his sense of what the state of culture required him to say; the later Eliot was a religious poet who developed his own meditative modes of expression to evoke kinds of awareness of a religious apprehension of problems of time and history and loss and vision. Nor is Stevens's obscurity in any way akin to that of W.B. Yeats, who, unable to believe in any orthodox religion because, as he said, the possibility had been destroyed for him when he was young by Victorian science, built his own symbolic system. 'I am very religious', Yeats wrote early in his career, 'and deprived by Huxley and Tyndall, whom I detested, of the simple-minded religion of my childhood, I had made a new religion, almost an infallible church of poetic tradition, of a fardel of stories, and of personages, and of emotions, inseparable from their first expression, passed on from generation to generation by poets and painters with some help from philosophers and theologians.' Later, Yeats developed his own private symbolic system which he was able to make persuasive by the way he used it in his poetry.

Stevens is a very different kind of poet from either of these. Here are the first six stanzas of 'The Ordinary Women':

> Then from their poverty they rose,
> From dry catarrhs, and to guitars
> They flitted
> Through the palace walls
>
> They flung monotony behind,
> Turned from their want, and nonchalant,
> They crowded
> The nocturnal halls.
>
> The lacquered loges huddled there
> Mumbled zay-zay and a-zay, a-zay.
> The moonlight
> Fubbed the girandoles.
>
> And the cold dresses that they wore,
> In the vapid haze of the window-bays,
> Were tranquil
> As they leaned and looked
>
> From the window-sills at the alphabets,
> From beta b and gamma g,
> To study
> The canting curlicues
>
> Of heaven and of the heavenly script.
> And there they read of marriage-bed.
> Till-lill-o!
> And they read right long.

I cannot do better than quote Richard Blackmur here:

The loges huddled probably because it was dark or because they didn't like the ordinary women, and mumbled perhaps because of the moonlight, perhaps because of the catarrhs, or even to keep key to the guitars. Moonlight, for Mr. Stevens, is mental, fictive, related to the imagination and meaning of things; naturally it fubbed the girandoles (which is equivalent to cheated the chandeliers, was stronger than the artificial light, if any) . . . . Perhaps and probably but no doubt something else. I am at loss, and quite happy there, to know anything literally about this poem. Internally, inside its own words, I know it quite well by simple perusal. The charm of its rhymes is enough to carry it over any stile. the strange phrase 'fubbed the girandoles', has another charm, like that of the rhyme, and as inexplicable: the approach of language, through the magic of elegance, to nonsense. That the phrase is not nonsense, that on inspection it retrieves itself to sense, is its inner virtue. Somewhere between the realms of ornamental sound and representative statement, the words pause and balance, dissolve and resolve . . . .[4]

One of the interesting things about Stevens's poetic practice is his drive to artifice, his insistence on building with language something concrete and colourful even if not always readily intelligible. This external movement, as it were, distinguishes him sharply from those nineteenth-century romantic poets who sunk into themselves to indulge in solipsistic mood poetry. Stevens never introspects about his own moods. In his short poem 'Disillusionment of Ten O'clock' he first describes the ordinariness of people who wear white night-gowns, not 'green or purple with green rings, or green with yellow rings, or yellow with blue rings', and concludes:

> People are not going
> To dream of baboons and periwinkles.
> Only, here and there, an old sailor,
> Drunk and asleep in his boots,
> Catches tigers
> In red weather.

Adventurous imagination belongs to the old drunken sailor, a conventional image of disreputableness here used most unconventionally. The poet is not describing his own dreams— Stevens never does this—but projects them on to a dramatically suitable character. His poems are constructs, fictions, artefacts, and if an element of rumination ever enters them (as

[4] *Language as Gesture*, by R.P. Blackmur, New York, 1952, p. 225.

in 'Sunday Morning') it is the rumination of an invented
character playing a part in a carefully set scene.

Every age makes its own art, Stevens insisted, creates its own
supreme fiction; older ages did it with religion and constructed
cathedrals out of faith. Different ages and different attitudes
build their art in different ways. Palm leaves may have one
symbolic meaning for the Christian; they have another for the
saxophonist. There is no saying what reverberations of meaning
may be achieved even by exuberant popular art that the stuffy
and respectable despise. Religious ascetics and contorting jazz-
players each in their own way try to impose a significant form
on experienced reality. But of course this is not what Stevens
says. Instead, he writes a poem entitled 'A High-Toned Old
Christian Woman':

> Poetry is the supreme fiction, madame.
> Take the moral law and make a nave of it
> And from the nave build haunted heaven. Thus,
> The conscience is converted into palms,
> Like windy citherns hankering for hymns.
> We agree in principle. That's clear. But take
> The opposing law and make a peristyle,
> And from the peristlye project a masque
> Beyond the planets. Thus, our bawdiness,
> Unpurged by epitaph, indulged at last,
> Is equally converted into palms,
> Squiggling like saxophones. And palm for palm,
> Madame, we are where we began. Allow,
> Therefore, that in the planetary scene
> Your disaffected flagellants, well-stuffed,
> Smacking their muzzy bellies in parade,
> Proud of such novelties of the sublime,
> Such tink and tank and tunk-a-tunk-tunk,
> May, merely may, madame, whip from themselves
> A jovial hullabaloo among the spheres.
> This will make widows wince. But fictive things
> Wink as they will. Wink most when widows wince.

Sometimes, especially in his later poetry, Stevens uses his
poetry not so much to provide an example of the kind of
supreme fiction he believes in, but to express (although always
through the invented personality of another character) a view
of the human situation that makes supreme fictions so neces-

sary. I have not time to discuss his long poem 'Esthétique du Mal', one of Stevens's most remarkable achievements; I quote only some lines from the third section. The speaker is not the poet, but his invented spokesman:

> The fault lies with an over-human god,
> Who by sympathy has made himself a man
> And is not to be distinguished when we cry.
>
> Because we suffer, our oldest parent, peer
> Of the populace of the heart, the reddest lord,
> Who has gone before us in experience.
>
> If only he would not pity us so much,
> Weaken our fate, relieve us of woe both great
> And small, a constant fellow of destiny
>
> A too, too human god, self-pity's kin
> And uncourageous genesis . . . It seems
> As if the health of the world might be enough.
>
> It seems as if the honey of common summer
> Might be enough, as if the golden combs
> Were part of a sustenance itself enough,
>
> As if hell, so modified, had disappeared,
> As if pain, no longer satanic mimicry,
> Could be borne, as if we were sure to find our way.

The myth of a pitying God distracts us from appreciating the realities we have; if we abandoned it, the honey of common summer might be enough, and pain 'no longer satanic mimicry', could be borne. Job, one might say, would have been less agonized if he had not believed in a God who was responsible for it all and who was supposed to be just and loving.

But Stevens's poems are not versified argument; they are for the most part examples of the use of the poetic imagination to construct verbal patterns that both give pleasure in themselves and give meaning to the world we experience. The poet, Stevens wrote, 'creates the world to which we turn incessantly and without knowing it and . . . gives to life the supreme fictions without which we are unable to conceive of it'. So perhaps it is not true that 'the honey of common summer might be enough', unless the poet is there to enable us to see it through his verbal constructions.

All this may sound very abstract, and though in some ways

Stevens is an abstract poet in others he is almost brutally concrete. The gaudy language which he often employs can provide great splashes of colourful meaning to a physical perception or to a leap of imaginatin; it can also provide its own provocative mystery:

> Chieftain Iffucan of Azcan in caftan
> Of tan with henna hackles, halt!

This opening of his short poem 'Bantams in Pine-Wood' is vivid and concrete, verbally amusing, yet mysterious (in spite of its numerous explicators). 'The Emperor of Ice-Cream', again in spite of its explicators, is a teasing mystery poem. Yet these poems are all exciting to read; they give pleasure; even if their meaning is not obvious, they are bulwarks against meaninglessness, which is perhaps all that an agnostic poet can hope to achieve. If the imagination fails—for, like Coleridge yet differently, Stevens believed that 'we receive but what we give'—then, like Coleridge, he has his moods of dejection: Stevens's equivalent of Coleridge's 'Dejection Ode' is, as Frank Kermode has observed, his poem 'The Man Whose Pharynx Was Bad'. It ends:

> The malady of the quotidian . . .
> Perhaps, if winter once could penetrate
> Through all its purples to the final slate,
> Persisting bleakly in an icy haze,
>
> One might in turn become less diffident,
> Out of such mildew plucking neater mould
> And spouting new orations of the cold.
> One might. One might. But time will not relent.

In some ways the most assured poem that Stevens ever wrote, as well as one of the finest and most popular, is 'Sunday Morning', which provides an impressive and moving picture of man without illusions, making his own terms with his time-bound condition in the changing world of nature. It is perhaps the great agnostic poem in the English language.

'Sunday Morning' opens on a note of comfort and relaxation: 'complacencies of the peignoir'. The scene is colourful (note the phrase 'the green freedom of a cockatoo', with the curious abstraction of '*green* freedom', typical of Stevens). A middle-aged, comfortable lady—perhaps on holiday in Florida from

one of the northern states—relaxes in this colourful scene; she
realizes that it is Sunday and dreamily meditates on the Crucifixion ('ancient sacrifice', 'old catastrophe') in terms that make
it clear that she thinks of it as an old, unhappy, far-off event,
which nevertheless disturbs her present comfort. She thinks of
the vast distance in both time and place separting her from
'Silent Palestine' (silent just because it is so distant in time and
space), and the stillness of the present scene encourages her
imagination to travel back to that past.

> Complacencies of the peignoir, and late
> Coffee and oranges in a sunny chair,
> And the green freedom of a cockatoo
> Upon a rug mingle to dissipatè
> The holy hush of ancient sacrifice.
> She dreams a little, and she feels the dark
> Encroachment of that old catastrophe,
> As a calm darkens among water-lights.
> The pungent oranges and bright, green wings
> Seem things in some procession of the dead,
> Winding across wide water, without sound,
> Stilled for the passing of her dreaming feet
> Over the seas, to silent Palestine,
> Dominion of the blood and sephulchre.

She goes in imagination to ancient Palestine and thinks of
the crucifixion. Then she recoils. Why should she involve herself in a death that happened two thousand years ago? And
anyway, what reality has that 'divinity' which one can know
'only in silent shadows and in dreams'? Should she not forget
all that and rejoice in the colour, beauty, variety, of the physical world at the present moment? Are there not *here* 'things to
be cherished as much as there are in thoughts of heaven'?
'Divinity must live within herself'—in her varying moods, her
responses to changing natural scenery, her emotions as they
change in different situations, different seasons. *These* are what
constitute personality; *these* make up the true reality of personal
experience.

> Why should she give her bounty to the dead?
> What is divintity if it can come
> Only in silent shadows and in dreams?
> Shall she not find in comforts of the sun,

In pungent fruit and bright, green wings, or else
In any balm or beauty of the earth,
Things to be cherished like the thought of heaven?
Divinity must live within herself:
Passions of rain, or moods of falling snow;
Grievings in loneliness, or unsubdued
Elations when the forest blooms; gusty
Emotions on wet roads on autumn nights;
All pleasures and all pains, remembering
The bough of summer and the winter branch.
These are the measures destined for her soul.

There follows a stanza evoking man's early mythical invention of God as someone both human and trans-human. But those days are gone: the divine is now brought down to the level of the human. The speaker is content with the beauty and variety of the natural world. Birds, before they migrate, make pre-migration flights around the fields. But what happens when the birds depart? After the present moment has gone, is there an Eternity, a Paradise outside time, where one can rest changelessly for ever? No. None of the haunting old religious prophecies or myths or visions is anything like as real as the physical experience of natural beauty. And that endures, as long as there are individuals to respond to it, remember it, long for it.

She says, 'I am content when wakened birds,
Before they fly, test the reality
Of misty fields, by their sweet questionings;
But when the birds are gone, and their warm fields
Return no more, where, then, is paradise?'
There is not any haunt of prophecy,
Nor any old chimera of the grave,
Neither the golden underground, nor isle
Melodious, where spirits gat them home,
Nor visionary south, nor cloudy palm
Remote on heaven's hill, that has endured
As April's green endures; or will endure
Like her remembrance of awakened birds,
Or her desire for June and evening, tipped
By the consummation of the swallow's wings.

Still, even in present happiness she feels the need of some religious belief in 'some imperishable bliss'. But on the other hand, our appreciation of beauty is sharpened by our knowledge that our own life is limited. (An argument, incidentally, that Milton's Adam might have used to show that the consequences of the Fall were not all bad.) 'Death is the mother of beauty': if we lived for ever, the moment of experienced beauty would be less sharp, less poignant, less real. Although time and change bring forgetfulness of both sorrows and joys, they also bring maturity and new and valuable kinds of emotion.

> She says, 'But in contentment I still feel
> The need of some imperishable bliss.'
> Death is the mother of beauty: hence from her,
> Alone, shall come fulfilment to our dreams
> And our desires. Although she strews the leaves
> Of sure obliteration on our paths,
> The path sick sorrow took, the many paths
> Where triumph rang its brassy phrase, or love
> Whispered a little out of tenderness,
> She makes the willow shiver in the sun
> For maidens who were wont to sit and gaze
> Upon the grass, relinquished to their feet.
> She causes boys to pile new plums and pears
> On disregarded plate. The maidens taste
> And stray impassioned in the littering leaves.

In the religious conception of Paradise, of Eternity, where nothing alters and it is always Spring, there is no movement from unripeness to ripeness. Fruit never falls from the tree, none of the wonderful and moving changes brought by the procession of the seasons can take place. We are wrong, then, to fasten our hopes to this mythical, unalterable Paradise of eternal changelessness. For without change and death there can be no beauty. (Again, there is something here with which the underlying implicit argument of Milton's *Paradise Lost* agrees. Dryden called his play on the Antony and Cleopatra theme, *All for Love: or The World Well Lost*. The underlying theme in Stevens's poem might almost be called *All for Change: or Paradise Well Lost*.)

> Is there no change of death in paradise?
> Does ripe fruit never fall? Or do the boughs
> Hang always heavy in that perfect sky,
> Unchanging, yet so like our perishing earth,

With rivers like our own that seek for seas
They never find, the same receding shores
That never touch with inarticulate pang?
Why set the pear upon those river-banks
Or spice the shores with odors of the plum?
Alas, that they should wear their colors there,
The silken weaving of our afternoons,
And pick the strings of our insipid lutes!
Death is the mother of beauty, mystical,
Within whose burning bosom we devise
Our earthly mothers waiting, sleeplessly.

And so this musing woman rejects the claims of religion. What happened in ancient Palestine occurred in a particular time and place, part of the great procession of events which is life in motion. We must accept this procession of events, this inevitability of change, she concludes. We must accept Time. The wide world of nature, the whole universe, exists in time and space, and as our imagination ranges over it we can sense the sad beauty of a time-bound reality. The sadness is part of the beauty. The bird as it flies 'downward to darkness, on extended wing' becomes a symbol of the brevity of the individual life—but also of its beauty, its satisfaction, its haunting, time-conditioned reality.

She hears, upon that water without sound,
A voice that cries, 'The tomb in Palestine
Is not the porch of spirits lingering.
It is the grave of Jesus, where he lay.'
We live in an old chaos of the sun,
Or old dependency of day and night,
Or island solitude, unsponsored, free,
Of that wide water, inescapable.
Deer walk upon our mountains, and the quail
Whistle about us their spontaneous cries;
Sweet berries ripen in the wilderness;
And, in the isolation of the sky,
At evening, casual flocks of pigeons make
Ambiguous undulations as they sink,
Downward to darkness, on extended wings.

The American poet and critic Randall Jarrell has said of this concluding stanza that 'in these lines man without myth, without God, without anything but the universe which has produced

him, is given an extraordinarily pure and touching grandeur'.[5]
Frank Kermode has called the poem 'the hedonist's "Elegy in a
Country Churchyard"'.[6] But in some ways it is more reminiscent of Keats's two great odes—to a Grecian Urn and 'Autumn'
—with their emphasis on time and change and the relation of
human art to both. That relationship is not explicitly discussed;
it is implicit in the fact that Stevens has written a poem on the
subject. The slow gravity of the verse, the musical eloquence of
the poem's movement together with the touches of surprise and
cunning in the imagery, produce an extraordinarily impressive
effect. This is not one of Stevens's gaudy poems. It does not
exhibit him parading his ability to face experience with a
'supreme fiction'. It operates in a more subdued mode,
although with no less skill, than his more exhibitionist poems.

From one point of view, 'Sunday Morning' illustrates what
Keats called '*Negative Capability*, that is, when a man is capable
of being in uncertainties, mysteries, doubts without any
irritable reaching after fact and reason'. From another, one
might say that far from abandoning any reaching after fact, it
accepts the facts of experience. But not irritably. Unlike so
many of the Victorians, Stevens was not worried by his doubts.
'Sunday Morning' is a poem of calm agnostic acceptance.

---

[5] *Poetry and the Age*, by Randall Jarrell, London, 1966, p. 129.
[6] *Wallace Stevens*, by Frank Kermode, Edinburgh and London, 1960, p. 41.

9 TYPES OF VISION :
EDWIN MUIR AND HUGH MACDIARMID

Edwin Muir was buried on a cold, raw January day in 1959 in the churchyard at Swaffham Prior, the Cambridgeshire village where he spent the last two-and-three-quarter years of his life. After the funeral his widow Willa said to me: 'Edwin believed that the soul was immortal. I don't. No gentle ghost will visit me from the other world.' She spoke in ironic sadness: I am sure she wished she could believe that his gentle spirit *would* revisit her. It is a tribute to their relationship, so movingly described in her autobiography *Belonging*, that they could happily share so much while differing on such a central point of faith. For Edwin Muir in his mature years came to believe profoundly in immortality. 'I do not have the power to prove that man is immortal and that the soul exists', he wrote in his *Autobiography;*

but I know that there must be such a proof, and that compared with it every other demonstration is idle. It is true that human life without immortality would be inconceivable because if man is an animal by direct descent I can see human life only as a nightmare populated by animals wearing top-hats and kid gloves, painting their lips and touching up their cheeks and talking in heated rooms, rubbing their muzzles together in the moment of lust, and going through innumerable clever tricks, learning to make and listen to music, to gaze sentimentally at sunsets, to count, to acquire a sense of humour, to give their lives for some cause or to pray.[1]

Muir did not come quickly or easily to this belief. The cultural shock he suffered in moving from Orkney to Glasgow at the age of fourteen led him, as he himself has eloquently recounted, into a period of horror at the life of industrial Glasgow, from which he sought refuge first in the ironic poses he learned from Heine and then, more strongly and over a longer period, in an aggressive anti-sentimental egotism he learned from Nietzsche. But the Edenic image of his childhood in Orkney continued to haunt him, and the dramatic change

[1] *An Autobiography*, by Edwin Muir, London, 1968, p. 51.

from a pre-industrial to an industrial society produced an obsession with time that was to work fruitfully in his poetry. He explains this himself at the conclusion of the first version of his autobiography which he entitled *The Story and the Fable*:

I was born before the Industrial Revolution, and am now about two hundred years old. But I have skipped a hundred and fifty of them. I was really born in 1737, and till I was fourteen no time-accidents happened to me. Then in 1751 I set out from Orkney for Glasgow. When I arrived I found that it was not 1751, but 1901, and that a hundred and fifty years had been burned up in my two days' journey. But I myself was still in 1751, and remained there for a long time. All my life since I have been trying to overhaul that invisible leeway. No wonder I am obsessed with Time.[2]

It was in Dresden in 1922 that Muir both liberated himself from time and became able to use his concern with time as inspiration for poetry. Again, as he recounts in *The Story and the Fable*:

I realized that I must live over again the years which I had lived wrongly, and that everyone should live his life twice, for the first attempt is always blind. I went over my life in that resting space, like a man who after travelling a long, featureless road suddenly realizes that, at this point or that, he had noticed almost without knowing it, with the corner of his eye, some extraordinary object, some rare treasure, yet in his sleep-walking had gone on, consciously aware only of the blank road flowing back beneath his feet. These objects, like Griseldas, were still patiently waiting at the points where I had first ignored them, and my full gaze could take in now things which an absent glance had once passed over unseeingly, so that life I had wasted was returned to me . . . In turning my head and looking *against* the direction in which Time was hurrying me I won a liberation and a new kind of experience; for now that I no longer marched in step with Time I could see life timelessly, and with that in terms of the imagination . . . .

If one can speak of a turning-point in life, this was my turning-point; since when my past life came alive in me after lying for so long, a dead weight, my actual life came alive too as that new life passed into it; for it was new, though old; indeed, I felt that only now was I truly living it, since only now did I see it as it was, so that at last it could become experience . . . I was thirty-five then, and passing

[2] *The Story and the Fable*, by Edwin Muir, London, 1940, p. 263.

through a stage which, if things had been different, I should have reached ten years earlier. I have felt that handicap ever since. I began to write poetry at thirty-five instead of at twenty-five or twenty.[3]

The poetry that Muir wrote from this point until the end of his life was not devotional. He does not address God or speak of his relation to him. But the great myths of both the Greek and the Christian traditions haunt his memory, and a sense of some archetypal fable underlying human history and human imagination, a conviction that the way time works in the life of man and nature alike is both significant and mysterious, a feeling for the relation between mortality and immortality, the changing and the changeless—these work in his characteristic poetry and continually suggest a universe presided over by God even though God is not mentioned. Many of Muir's poems are religious poems that work by indirection, concerning them-selves not with recognized religious themes but with states of mind, dreams, moments of awareness, sad or hopeful or para-doxical visions of past and future, of cruelty and barrenness and fulfilment and resurrection counterpointed against each other so as to project a questing sensibility that is simultaneously restless and at peace.

At the end of *The Story and the Fable* Muir talks of the impor-tance to him of Proust. 'In *Le Temps Retrouvé* Proust describes how he set out to resuscitate in himself "the Eternal Man" . . . To resuscitate the Eternal Man was an heroic attempt, and Proust was a great writer. Yet I cannot help feeling that that resuscitation was only a beginning. There remains the problem of communion between the Eternal Man in Proust and the Eternal Man in other people, and also their communion with the Eternal Itself. I should have a philosophy to cover these things, but I have not: I think that in the end I rely purely on faith, perhaps too purely.'[4] But of course what he really relied on—or at least what he has left *us* to rely on—is his poetry, which communicates his shifting visions of human fate through the exploration and adaptation of history and myth and perso-nal feeling. 'The major forms of poetry', Muir wrote in *Scott and Scotland*, 'rise from a collision between emotion and intellect on a plane where both meet on equal terms.'[5] And again:

---

[3] Ibid. 234–5.   [4] Ibid. 261–2.

[5] *Scott and Scotland*, by Edwin Muir, London, 1936, p. 20.

'Poetry is not spontaneous in the sense that it is restricted to the
expression of simple and spontaneous feelings, but rather in the
sense that it reconciles the antitheses of feeling and thought into
a harmony, achieving with apparent effortlessness a resolution
of subject-matter which to the ratiocinative mind is known only
as a difficulty to be overcome by intense effort.'[6] This is perhaps to put the matter too schematically, under the influence of
Eliot's famous praise of Donne for uniting thought and emotion. But it is a clue to what he felt he was doing in his own
poetry. And the reference to Proust, who was obsessed with
time as Muir was, if in a different way, shows how central the
topic was to him. He did not, however, find the recapture of
time past readily attainable, and the longing for such a recapture could, in remaining unsatisfied, produce a moving vision:

> I see myself sometimes, an old old man
> Who has walked so long with time as time's true servant,
> That he's grown strange to me—who was once myself—
> Almost as strange as time, and yet familiar
> With old man's staff and legendary cloak,
> For see, it is I, it is I. And I return
> So altered, so adopted, to the house
> Of my own life. There all the doors stand open
> Perpetually, and the rooms ring with sweet voices,
> And there my long life's seasons sound their changes,
> Childhood and youth and manhood all together,
> And welcome waits, and not a room but is
> My own, beloved and longed for. And the voices,
> Sweeter than any sound dreamt of or known,
> Call me, recall me. I draw near at last,
> An old, old man, and scan the ancient walls
> Rounded and softened by the compassionate years,
> The old and heavy and long-leaved trees that watch
> This my inheritance in friendly darkness.
> And yet I cannot enter, for all within
> Rises before me there, rises against me,
> A sweet and terrible labyrinth of longing,
> So that I turn aside and take the road
> That always, early or late, runs on before.
>   ('The Return')

6 Ibid. 40-1.

The notion of return pulses through literature from the Hebrew prophets' appeal to their people to return to the Lord, through Odysseus' *nostos* to Ithaca and Penelope, through combinations of the ideas of returning and turning that recur in both Jewish and Christian religious poetry throughout the centuries (and which Eliot draws on in the opening of 'Ash Wednesday'). The weight of these traditions lies behind this poem to allow this vision of a longed for but unachieved return in time to reach down into something deep in the consciousness—and in the unconscious—of readers whether or not they are aware of these reverberations. This is a mark of Muir's poetry. It is not so much that he has a mythopoeic mind, a mind that creates myths, as that he has, if I may coin a word, a *mythochretic* mind, a mind that knows how to use and draw on myths.

Consider, for example, the wholly original use he makes of the story of Adam and Eve and the Fall in his poem 'Adam's Dream':

> They say the first dream Adam our father had
> After his agelong daydream in the Garden
> When heaven and sun woke in his wakening mind,
> The earth with all its hills and woods and waters,
> The friendly tribes of trees and animals,
> And earth's last wonder Eve (the first great dream
> Which is the ground of every dream since then)—
> They say he dreamt lying on the naked ground,
> The gates shut fast behind him as he lay
> Fallen in Eve's fallen arms, his terror drowned
> In her engulfing terror, in the abyss
> Whence there's no further fall, and comfort is—
> That he was standing on a rocky ledge
> High on the mountainside, bare crag behind,
> In front a plain as far as eye could reach,
> And on the plain a few small figures running
> That were like men and women, yet were so far away
> He could not see their faces. On they ran,
> And fell, and rose again, and ran, and fell,
> And rising were the same yet not the same,
> Identical or interchangeable,
> Different in indifference. As he looked
> Still there were more of them, the plain was filling
> As by an alien arithmetical magic
> Unknown in Eden, a mechanical

Addition without meaning, joining only
Number to number in no mood or order,
Weaving no pattern. For these creatures moved
Towards no fixed mark even when in growing bands
They clashed against each other and clashing fell
In mounds of bodies. For they rose again,
Identical or interchangeable,
And went their way that was not like a way;
Some back and forward, back and forward, some
In a closed circle, wide or narrow, others
In zigzags on the sand. Yet all were busy,
And tense with purpose as they cut the air
Which seemed to press them back. Sometimes they paused
While one stopped one—fortuitous assignations
In the disorder, whereafter two by two
They ran awhile,
Then parted and again were single. Some
Ran straight against the frontier of the plain
Till the horizon drove them back. A few
Stood still and never moved. Then Adam cried
Out of his dream, 'What are you doing there?'
And the crag answered 'Are you doing there?'
'What are you doing there!'—'you doing there?'
The animals had withdrawn and from the caves
And woods stared out in fear or condemnation,
Like outlaws or like judges. All at once
Dreaming or half-remembering, 'This is time',
Thought Adam in his dream, and time was strange
To one lately in Eden. 'I must see',
He cried, 'the faces. Where are the faces? Who
Are you all out there?' Then in his changing dream
He was a little nearer, and he saw
They were about some business strange to him
That had a form and sequence past their knowledge;
And that was why they ran so frenziedly.
Yet all, it seemed, made up a story, illustrated
By these the living, the unknowing, cast
Each singly for his part. But Adam longed
For more, not this mere moving pattern, not
This illustrated storybook of mankind
Always a-making, improvised on nothing.
At that he was among them, and saw each face
Was like his face, so that he would have hailed them
As sons of God but that something restrained him.

And he remembered all, Eden, the Fall,
The Promise, and his place, and took their hands
That were his hands, his and his children's hands,
Cried out and was at peace, and turned again
In love and grief in Eve's encircling arms.

The actual prosody of this poem, as in so many of Muir's, is unadventurous, skilful enough to move the lines along in a way that allows the described vision to make its full impact on the reader but not displaying any conscious virtuosity. It is basically a rather free blank verse; the rhythms rise and fall with the emotions generated; the pauses are placed with great effect, but inconspicuously; the final lines ground the poem in an extraordinary sense of achieved peace. 'Adam's Dream' is quite unparaphrasable. Of course all good poetry is unparaphrasable in the sense that a paraphrase can give no true sense of the poem as it stands. But in many cases a paraphrase can say *something* about the content of the poem. But here I do not think that it can say anything significant. The poem generates as it moves an imagination of a dream—a vision twice removed, one might say—and the distilled effect this achieves is inseparable from the way the vision unfolds. We can say that the poem is about time and history and the relation between innocence and knowledge and the comforts available to men and women after they have come to terms with time and history. But that is a very unsatisfactory description of a poem whose capacity to move—and I find this, as I find 'The Return', deeply moving—lies in the way it enables us to see reality as myth and myth as reality.

In his poem 'One Foot in Eden' Muir recognizes that

Time's handiworks by time are haunted,
And nothing now can separate
The corn and tares compactly grown.

Yet this confused and imperfect time-bound world, this post-lapsarian world, can yield blessings that were not available to pre-lapsarian man. In my second lecture I tried to show that this was an implication that runs through much of Milton's *Paradise Lost*, though it runs counter to the overt argument. Muir makes the point more directly:

Yet still from Eden springs the root
As clean as on the starting day.
Times takes the foliage and the fruit
And burns the archetypal leaf
To shades of terror and of grief
Scattered along the winter way.
But famished field and blackened tree
Bear flowers in Eden never known.
Blosoms of grief and charity
Bloom in these darkened fields alone.
What had Eden ever to say
Of hope and faith and pity and love
Until was buried all its day
And memory found its treasure trove?
Strange blessings never in Paradise
Fall from these beclouded skies.

('One Foot in Eden')

This is a different kind of poetry, making a point rather than communicating a vision, and while it is important as a key to an aspect of Muir's mature thought, and indeed while it is also a pleasing poem in its own right, it does not bring us directly inside the poet's mood and awareness as his more characteristic poetry does. The optimistic implications of 'One Foot in Eden' emerge more memorably at the conclusion of 'The Transfiguration':

But he will come again, it's said, though not
Unwanted and unsummoned; for all things,
Beasts of the field, and woods, and rocks, and seas,
And all mankind from end to end of the earth
Will call him with one voice. In our own time,
Some say, or at a time when time is ripe.
Then he will come, Christ the uncrucified,
His agony unmade, his cross dismantled—
Glad to be so—and the tormented wood
Will cure its hurt and grow into a tree
In a green springing corner of young Eden,
And Judas damned take his long journey backward
From darkness into light and be a child
Beside his mother's knee, and the betrayal
Be quite undone and never more be done.

This is a subdued, chastened, humanized version of the old

Hebrew prophets' vision of the end of the days. The prophets used a very different idiom, but it seems to me at least that this passage, for example, from the fourth chapter of Micah is conveying a vision not unlike Muir's:

> But in the last days it shall come to pass, that the mountain of the house of the Lord shall be established in the top of the mountains, and it shall be exalted above the hills; and the people shall flow unto it. Any many nations shall come, and say, Come, and let us go up to the mountain of the Lord, and to the house of the God of Jacob; and he will teach us of his ways, and we will walk in his paths: for the law shall go forth of Zion, and the word of the Lord from Jerusalem. And he shall judge among many people, and rebuke strong nations afar off; and they shall beat their swords into ploughshares, and their spears into pruning hooks: nation shall not lift up sword against nation, neither shall they learn war any more. But they shall sit every man under his vine and under his fig tree; and none shall make them afraid . . . .

The other great Scottish poet of the first half of this century was born five years after Muir, in 1892, and produced a large and varied body of poetry that in some ways is much more difficult to come to terms with. In 1923, the year after Muir recognized a turning-point of his life in Dresden, C.M. Grieve (he was not yet writing as Hugh MacDiarmid) published an article entitled 'A Russo-Scottish Parallelism' in which he praised a recently published book by Professor J.Y. Simpson entitled *Man and the Attainment of Immortality* and he pointed out the similarity between Professor Simpson's thought and the thought of the Russian poet and philosopher Vladimir Sergeyevich Solovyov. MacDiarmid had been introduced to Solovyov through the pages of the *New Age*, a periodical which greatly influenced both him and Edwin Muir and for which they both wrote. At the conclusion of his article MacDiarmid quoted a long paragraph from Solovyov which ends:

> The kingdom of God, or the perfect moral order, can no more be revealed to a horde of savages than a human being can be born from a mollusc or a sponge. Just as the human spirit in nature requires the most perfect of physical organisms, so the spirit of God in humanity requires for its actual manifestation the most perfect of social organizations, and that is being evolved in the course of history.

MacDiarmid comments (and this is how his essay concludes):

'It is significant that new theological conceptions of so comprehensive a character should be beginning to enter into Scottish
thought at a juncture so rich in promise of national renaissance
in other directions.'[7]

The 'comprehensive character' of the new conceptions involved a combination of the Darwinian notion of evolution
with a variety of theosophical concepts which included ideas
about the expansion of consciousness and the part played in
this process by the wisdom-symbol of agnostic doctrine, Sophia.
Grieve managed to link all this up with his belief in the individuality of Scottish nationhood and the need for Scotland to
find in parallels from Russia (including Dostoyevsky and
modern Russian poets, notably Alexander Blok) sources of
strength with which to assert her own special character against
the cultural forces from England and elsewhere that had been
dominating her. The complex of ideas with which Grieve
worked—or perhaps one might say played—in the early 1920s
did not yield him any single or consistent system: consistency
was never one of his virtues and he liked to quote Whitman's
'Do I contradict myself? Very well then, I contradict myself'.
But they could be called religious, in that they were concerned
with the relation between individual experience and eternal
reality and sometimes quite specifically with the nature and
function of God. In his book *Annals of the Five Senses*, which consisted mostly of prose but included a few poems, published in
the same year as the article from which I have quoted, he has
a poem entitled 'A Moment in Eternity', which describes a
visionary experience after the cessation of some great cosmic
song that he imagines he has heard. The poem concludes:

> Ah, Light,
> That is God's inmost wish,
> His knowledge of Himself,
> Flame of creative judgment,
> God's interrogation of infinity,
> Searching the unsearchable,
> —Silent and steadfast tree
> Housing no birds of song,
> Void to the wind,
> But rooted in God's very self,

---

[7] *Selected Essays of Hugh MacDiarmid*, ed. Duncan Glen, London, 1969, p. 43.

Growing ineffably,
Central in Paradise!

When the song ceased
And I stood still,
Breathing new leaves of life
Upon the eternal air,
Each leaf of all my leaves
Shone with a new delight
Murmuring Your name.

O Thou
Who art the wisdom of the God
Whose ecstasies we are!

One could elaborate on many of the images here, comparing MacDiarmid's use of the image of light to that of Dante and Milton, showing how the 'silent and steadfast tree' links up with 'Ygdrasil', the tree of life in Scandinavian mythology, as well as with the Cross of Christ and with the Scottish thistle (all these connections were to be made later in *A Drunk Man Looks at the Thistle*), and comparing the cosmic song with Milton's concept of the music of the spheres as revealed in his 'At a Solemn Music' and elsewhere. But I would rather go on to show what happens to these and other ideas in MacDiarmid's later poetry. 'A Moment in Eternity' was written before he started writing in Scots (when he was still C.M. Grieve, in fact). In 1925, as Hugh MacDiarmid, he published *Sangschaw*, poems in Scots, which included 'Ballad of the Five Senses'. He has a vision with his five senses, but he wants something more. Here is the second section of the poem:

I was as blithe to be alive
As ony man could be,
And felt as gin the haill braid warl'
Were made yince-yirn for me.

I wot I kept my senses keen,
I wot I used them weel.
As God felt when he made the warl'
I aye socht to feel.

Times are yin sees things as they'd ne'er
Been seen before ava',
As gin a' men had erst been blin',
Or the a'e First Day 'good da'.

Times are yin sees things as they'd ne'er
Been seen afore ava',
I wot I saw things fresh and full,
As few men ever saw.

O I wist it is a bonny warl'
That lies forenenst a' men,
But it's naething but a shaddaw-show
To the warl' that I saw then.

There was nae movement on the earth
But frae my hert it came,
'Let there be licht,' God said, and straucht
My een let oot the same.

Was it a tree? I couldna rest
Till 'neath my hert I kent
A pooer was pent gin it wan loose
Its boughs had heicher sent,

Had gi'en it bark 'gainst bolt and blast
Stranger than granite was,
And leaves sae green, a' ither greens
Were wan shaddaws.

I felt I could haud a' earth's trees
Dancin' upon my bluid,
As they were ba's that at a Fair
Stot in a loupin' flood . . .

Yet sune I kent God or the warl'
Were no' for een to see,
Wi' body and saul I socht to staun'
As in Eternity.

Or bood I ha'e o' a' the warl'
But what my wits could mak',
And for the God made it and me
Nocht but my ain thochts tak'?

Oot o' the way, my senses five,
I ken a' you can tell,
Oot o' the way, my thochts, for noo'
I maun face God mysel'.

This yearning for a transcendent vision unobtainable through the senses seems inconsistent with MacDiarmid's later insistence on the importance of individual things in all their physical reality. But in fact these were alternative ways to an apprehension of ultimate reality, which he continually hungered for. In

'Ballad of the Five Senses' that hunger remained unsatisfied:

> O I wist it is a bonny warl'
> That lies forenenst a' men,
> And that ony man wi' his senses five,
> As weel's the neist may ken.
>
> And I wist that that is a shaddaw show
> To the warl's that can be seen
> By men wha seek as I ha'e socht,
> And keep their senses keen.
>
> But O I'm fain for a gowden sun,
> And fain for a flourishing tree,
> That neither men nor the Gods they'll ken
> In earth or Heaven sall see!

That is how the poem ends. We can put beside it some lines
from the very much later *In Memoriam James Joyce*:

> We must look at the harebell as if
> We had never seen it before.
> Remembrance gives an accumulation of satisfaction
> Yet the desire for change is very strong in us
> And change is itself a recreation.
> To those who take any pleasure
> In flowers, plants, birds, and the rest
> An ecological change is recreative.
> (Come. Climb with me. Even the sheep are different
> And of new importance.
> The course-fleeced, hardy Hardwick,
> The Hampshire Down, artificially fed almost from birth,
> And butcher-fat from the day it is weaned,
> The Lincoln-Longwool, the biggest breed in England,
> With the longest fleece, and the Southdown
> Almost the smallest—and between them thirty other breeds,
> Some white-faced, some black,
> Some with horns and some without,
> Some long-wooled, some short-wooled,
> In England where the men, and women too,
> Are almost as interesting as the sheep.)
> Everything is different, everything changes,
> Except for the white bedstraw which climbs all the way
> Up from the valleys to the tops of the high passes
> The flowers are all different and more precious
> Demanding more search and particularity of vision.

Look! Here and there a pinguicula eloquent of the Alps
Still keeps a purple-blue flower
On the top of its straight and slender stem.
Bog-asphodel, deep-gold, and comely in form,
The queer, almost diabolical, sundew,
And when you leave the bog for the stag moors and the rocks
The parsley fern—a lovelier plant
Than even the proud Osmunda Regalis—
Flourishes in abundance
Showing off oddly contrasted fronds
From the cracks of the lichened stones.
It is pleasant to find the books
Describing it as 'very local'.
Here is a change indeed!
The universal *is* the particular.

This poem is, of course, very different in style from Mac-
Diarmid's earlier poems in Scots, and it appears to be different
too in its basic approach to experience. Earlier he had professed
himself dissatisfied with what the senses can yield: he looks for
the unattainable transcendent vision, associated with death
and eternity and with a kind of apprehension denied to mortal
man. Here he is insisting on the importance of perceiving with
clarity and relish the different shapes and colours of the natural
world, glorying in their *haecceitas* (the word that Hopkins
borrowed from Duns Scotus), their 'thisness', what Hopkins
called their inscape. But 'the universal *is* the particular': the
route to the ultimate vision is by the unrelenting visual noting
of the quiddities in the world about us. The aim has not changed,
only the method. MacDiarmid, for all his intermittent profes-
sions of atheism and materialism, was at heart a visionary and
mystic. His finest poems are concerned with the mystery. The
mystery can be apparent in ordinary earthly things, and indeed
can be apprehended as more uncanny in such a context.

In spite of Eternity, of the mysteries of the universe, of the
challenge of the night sky, it is human experience on earth
(and, as MacDiarmid accepted from Dostoyevsky, human
experience means human suffering) that provides the test of the
meaning of it all. MacDiarmid sometimes seemed to hover
between believing that the noblest destiny of man was to achieve
a kind of Nietzschean disdain for ordinary human feeling and
lose himself in an inhuman abstractness of thought, like the

Ancients in Shaw's *Back to Methusaleh*, and believing that human feeling was the test and justification of everything. It is the latter view that is given marvellously compact expression in 'The Bonnie Broukit Bairn', the first poem in *Sangschaw*:

> Mars is braw in crammasy,
> Venus in a green silk goun,
> The auld mune shak's her gowden feathers,
> Their starry talk's a wheen o' blethers,
> Nane for thee a thochtie sparin',
> Earth, thou bonnie broukit bairn!
> —*But greet, an' in your tears ye'll droun*
> *The haill clanjamfrie!*

This poem is both cosmic and profoundly serious. Mars and Venus wear posh clothes. The moon shakes her golden feathers. The stars are blethering. All are heedless of poor, neglected earth. But earthly tears drown all the splendour of the heavens. The contemptuous, triumphantly vernacular 'the haill clanjamfrie!' ('the whole shebang') puts the universe in its place with respect to the world and its human inhabitants.

The mystery remains, and any human encounter can provide a sense of it. The haunting suggestiveness of that strangely beautiful poem 'The Eemis Stane' (also in *Sangschaw*), not only shows that MacDiarmid could do with Scots, but shows his ability to distil something visionary and disturbing out of the ordinary:

> I' the how-dumb-deid o' the cauld hairst nicht
> The warl' like an eemis stane
> Wags i' the lift;
> An' my eerie memories fa'
> Like a yowdendrift.
>
> Like a yowdendrift so's I couldna read
> The words cut oot i' the stane
> Had the fug o' fame
> An' history's hazelraw
> No' yirdit them.

'How-dumb-deid' was found by MacDiarmid in Jamieson's *Dictionary of the Scottish Language*, where it is given as an Ayshire expression meaning 'the middle of night, when silence reigns'. 'Eemis', says Jamieson, 'is used in relation to an object that is placed insecurely or threatens to fall; as, "That stane stands very eemis," that stone has not a proper bottom.' 'Yowdendrift' MacDiarmid also found in Jamieson, where it is glossed as 'snow driven by the wind'. 'Hazelraw' is given by Jamieson as meaning 'lichen pulmonarius'. MacDiarmid's use of these words, together with more common Scots words such as 'lift' (sky) and 'yirdit' (buried), gives the poem extraordinary compact force and atmospheric power that simply could not have been achieved in standard English. The surface meaning is clear enough: the world shifts in the sky like an unsteady tombstone, and the speaker's memories fall like a snowstorm so that he cannot read the words on the stone, obscured by the lichen of history. There is a vision here, but what exactly is it? Part of the appeal of the poem is the sense of mystery it evokes, but it is not empty mystery. Kenneth Buthlay, in his book on MacDiarmid, interprets the poem like this:

The Earth drifts through space like a stone, a dead star, obscured by the uneasy memories of the speaker, falling like snow driven by the wind, so that he couldn't read the words on the stone, even if the moss of fame (in the old sense of 'rumour', 'popular report') and the lichens of history had not buried them. As I see it, the Earth has become a tombstone marking the demise of its own life-process, of which the only vestiges remaining are the moss and lichens. The speaker is God, with His memories of what He had hoped might come of life on Earth—in interpretation for which there is support in other early poems, most notably 'The Dying Earth'. The words inscribed on the stone are signs of the Logos, which His creature, Man, has failed to comprehend, and finally obliterated in the course of human history.[8]

I am not convinced that the speaker in this poem is God: there seems to be something very humanly personal in the speaker's memories falling like snow blown by the wind and the inability to read the obscured words on the gravestone. But there is certainly a dimension here beyond the personal. The poem is not simply an anecdote about a mood. And in a sense, like so much in MacDiarmid's poetry, it goes beyond the personal. The poem 'The Dying Earth', to which Buthlay refers, goes as follows:

[8] *Hugh MacDiarmid*, by Kenneth Buthlay, Edinburgh, 1982, p. 26.

> Pitmirk the nicht: God's waukrife yet
> An' lichtin'-like his glances flit
> An' sair, sair are the looks he gies
> The auld earth as it dees.
>
> Pitmirk the nicht: an' God's 'good tell
> I' broken thunners to hissel'
> A' that he meent the warl' to be
> An' hoo his plan gaed jee.
>
> He canna steek his weary lids
> But aye anither gey look whids
> Frae pole to pole: an's tears doonfa'
> In lashin' rain owre a'.

This is nothing like as good a poem as 'The Eemis Stane', where, instead of giving an almost sentimental picture of God weeping over the dying earth because his plans for it had all gone wrong, he has found an 'objective correlative' for the sense of mystery with which he contemplates the illegible history of the uncertain planet earth. Perhaps it is God speaking, as Buthlay suggests; but we do not have to accept this to sense the haunting meaning of the poem. As for 'The Dying Earth', it reminds me not so much of other poems by MacDiarmid as of Charles Murray's 'Gin I was God', which says that if the poet were God and contemplated how men had made a hell of his 'braw birlin' Earth'

> I'd cast my coat again, rowe up my sark,
> An', or they'd time to lench a second ark,
> Tak' back my word an' sen' anither spate,
> Droon oot the hale hypothec, dicht the sklate,
> Own my mistak', an', aince I'd cleared the brod,
> Start a'thing ower again, gin I was God.

This is in the tradition of Scottish theological jokes, a tradition that MacDiarmid would have none of. Perhaps that is why he never included 'The Dying Earth' in any collection of his poems.

Catherine Kerrigan, in her study of MacDiarmid's earlier poetry entitled *Whaur Extremes Meet*,[9] refers to the 'haunting sense of man's ambiguous relationship to the natural world' revealed in 'The Eemis Stane' and adds that in those poems which try to explore the relation of finite man to an infinite

---

[9] Edinburgh, 1983, pp. 69, 72.

universe, 'the concept of God is most notable by its absence', commenting that 'this lack of an orthodox representation of the Divine is something which MacDiarmid's poems share with traditional ballad sources, for the Scottish ballad has been singled out as the form least susceptible to the natural merging of pagan and Christian influences found in most mediaeval literature'. It is certainly true that there is no 'orthodox representation of the Divine' in MacDiarmid, but God is not absent, however unusual the contexts in which he appears. The last stanza of the two-stanza poem 'The Frightened Bride' is

> Seil o' yer face! Ye needna seek
> For comfort gin ye show yer plight.
> To Gods an' men, coorse callants baith,
> A fleggit bride's the seilfu' sicht.

True, the word here is 'Gods', in the plural, although spelt with a capital letter (while 'men' is not), but the words 'baith' suggests that the poet is comparing God and man as both 'coorse callants'. In 'Crowdieknowe' the ending is

> *Fegs, God's no blate gin he stirs up*
> *The men o' Crowdieknowe!*

'I Heard Christ Sing' concludes with the lines

> But I wot he did God's will wha made
> Siccar o' Calvary.

Yet another poem from *Sangschaw* is entitled 'God Takes a Rest' and shows the God of evolution tired of his creation and deciding to return to the primeval waters from which life originally emerged:

> For I sall hie me back to the sea
> Frae which I brocht life yince,
> And lie i' the stound o' its whirlpools, free
> Frae a' that's happened since.

These and other poems in *Sangschaw* place God in different contexts, usually highly unorthodox and sometimes deliberately shocking; but there can be no doubt that the idea of God haunted the poet. More interesting, however, than those poems which refer to God by name are those which reveal the poet's deep sense of the mystery of the cosmos and the strangeness of

man's relation to it. These are visionary poems, in a sense
religious poems, if by religious we mean involving an acceptance of irrational mystery at the core of experience and of the
universe. Consider, for example, 'Moonstruck', again a poem
in *Sangschaw*:

> When the warl's couped soon' as a peerie
> That licht-lookin' craw o' a body, the moon,
> Sits on the fower cross-win's
> Peerin' a' roon'.
>
> She's seen me—she's seen me—an' straucht
> Loupit clean on the quick o' my hert.
> The quhither o' gowd's fairly
> Gi'en me a stert.
>
> An' the roarin'o' oceans noo'
> Is peerieweerie to me:
> Thunner's a tinklin' bell: an' Time
> Whuds like a flee.

The slowing down in the last stanza, with the strangely expres-
sive drawn-out word 'peerieweerie' and the four conclusive
monosyllables of the final line—'Whuds like a flee'—shows the
relation between MacDiarmid's use of Scots and his search for
poetic tools to express the inexpressible. These words work in
the poem both onomatopoetically and by virtue of their combination of the colloquial and the strange. MacDiarmid found
'peerieweerie' in Jamieson, where it is defined as an Orkney
word meaning 'very small'. He himself glossed it as 'diminished
to a mere thread of sound' which, one might say, it is made to
mean by its positioning within the stanza: it obviously refers to
the diminishing of the sound of the roaring of oceans, and the
way the word is drawn out, taking up four of the line's seven
syllables (the other three words are all monosyllabic) emphasizes the gradual process of diminution. The whole poem is a
good example of MacDiarmid's ability to combine the almost
contemptuously colloquial ('that licht-lookin' craw o' a body,
the moon') with the visionary and the mysterious. This of course
is only one way in which he exploited the famous (or notorious)
'Caledonian Antisyzygy', that yoking of opposites first diagnosed by Gregory Smith and delightedly accepted by Mac-
Diarmid as both a true diagnosis of a basic element in Scottish

character and literature and a clue to his own work. If we seek
for MacDiarmid's concern with the divine, it will often be
found in his counterpointing of the coarse and the cosmic.

In MacDiarmid's next collection of poems, *Penny Wheep*, he
confronts some of his cosmic preoccupations more directly,
using ideas from Solovyov and others to explore mysteries of
creation and evolution, as in the poem 'Sea-Serpent'. The
Serpent becomes a symbol of the Wisdom of God:

> It fits the universe man can ken
> As a man's soul fits his body;
> And the spirit o' God gaed dirlin' through't
> In stound upon stound o' pride
> Draughtin' his thick-comin' notions o' life
> As fast as they flashed in owre'm
> When there was sea and licht and little beside.

The poem concludes:

> O Thou that we'd fain be ane wi' again
> Frae the weary lapses o' self set free,
> Be to oor lives as life is to Daith,
> And lift and licht us eternally.
> Frae the howe o' the sea to the heich o' the lift,
> To the licht as licht to the darkness is,
> Spring fresh and far frae the spirit o' God
> Like the a'e first thocht that He kent was His.
>
> Loup again in His brain, O Nerve,
> Like a trumpet-stang,
> Lichtnin-clear as when first owre Chaos
> Your shape you flang
> —And swee his mind till the mapamound,
> And meanin' o' ilka man,
> Brenn as then wi' the instant poor
> O' an only plan!

MacDiarmid was to take the snake symbolism much further in
his long and only intermittently successful poem *To Circumjack
Cencrastus*, where, as he wrote to Helen Cruickshank, 'that
snake represents not only an attempt to glimpse the underlying
pattern of human history but identifies it with the evolution of
human thought—the principle of change and the main factor in
the evolutionary development of human consciousness, ''man's

incredible variation'', moving so intricately and swiftly that it is difficult to watch, and impossible to anticipate its next move'. MacDiarmid went on to refer to Solovyov's view that 'man's destiny is through his consciousness to reconcile the lower orders of creation—animals, plants, minerals—to St. Sophia, the Wisdom of God, who is the female hypostasis of the Deity'. He insists that he is dealing with the subject in 'non-mystical and non-religious terms' and that he sees the snake in terms both of the Caledonian Antisyzygy and the Dialectical Process. But one might apply, here as elsewhere in MacDiarmid's work, D.H. Lawrence's dictum, 'never trust the artist, trust the tale'. MacDiarmid's poetry is often not what he says it is, and even in those late poems which profess to be descriptions of the kind of poetry he wants there emerges a poetry that is not quite— some might say not at all—what he is prescribing.

Of MacDiarmid's masterpiece, *A Drunk Man Looks at the Thistle*, I shall say little here, even though this may seem like discussing *Hamlet* without the prince. This is partly because I have discussed it elsewhere, and partly because an adequate analysis of this intricate and powerful poem-sequence would take much longer than the space of a single lecture. I shall confine myself to four quotations. The first illustrates Mac-Diarmid's ability to domicile divine questions in physically real contemporary contexts:

> I tae ha'e heard Eternity drip water
> (Aye water, water!), drap by drap
> On the a'e nerve, like lichtnin', I've become,
> And heard God passin' wi' a bobby's feet
> Ootby in the lang coffin o' the street
> —Seen stang by chitterin' knottit stang loup oot
> Uncrushed by th' echoes o' the thunderin' boot,
> Till a' the dizzy lint-white lines o' torture made
> A monstrous thistle in the space aboot me,
> A symbol o' the puzzle o' man's soul
> —And in my agony been pridefu' I could still
> Tine nae least quiver or twist, watch ilka point
> Like a white-het bodkin ripe my inmaist hert,
> And aye wi' clearer pain that brocht nae anodyne,
> But rose for ever to a fer crescendo
> Like eagles that ootsoar wi' skinklan' wings

The thieveless sun they blin'
            And pridefu' still
That 'yont the sherp wings o' the eagles fleein'
Aboot the dowless pole o' Space,
Like leafs aboot a thistle-shank, my bluid
Could still thraw roses up
            —And up!

A Drunk Man is MacDiarmid's *Divina Commedia*, drunkenness being used as a means of entry to visionary experience and as an appropriate device to counterpoint the everyday realistic and the mystic vision, what I have called the coorse and the cosmic. But the thistle is not only a complex symbol of the tree of life: it stands also for Scotland, and the Scottish dimension of the poem is related to its most mystical element:

And e'en the glory that descends
I kenna whence on *me* depends,
And shapes itsel' to what is left
Whaur I o' me ha'e me bereft.
And still the form is mine, altho'
A force to which I ne'er could grow
Is moving in't as 'twere a sea
That lang syne drooned the last o' me
—That drooned afore the world began
A' that could ever come frae Man.

And as at sicna times am I,
I wad ha'e Scotland to my eye
Until I saw a timeless flame
Tak' Auchtermuchty for a name,
And kent that Ecclefechan stood
As pairt o' an eternal mood.

Ahint the glory comes the nicht
As Maori to London's ruins,
And I'm amused to see the plicht
O' Licht as't in the black tide droons,
Yet even in the brain o' Chaos
For Scotland I wad hain a place,
And let Tighnabruich still
Be pairt and paircel o' its will,
And Culloden, black as Hell,
A knowledge it has o' itsel'.

> Thou, Dostoevski, understood,
> Wha had your ain land in your bluid,
> And into it as in a mould
> The passion o' your bein' rolled,
> Inherited in turn frae Heaven
> Or sources fer abune it even.

The relation between Scottish place-names, eternity, and Dostoyevsky becomes clear when we understand the kind of influence the Russian novelist had on MacDiarmid. He had learned from D.S. Mirsky's book *Modern Russian Literature* of Dostoyevsky's claim that Pushkin was both Russia's national poet and the symbol of the *Vsechelovek*, the Universal Man; he knew Dostoyevsky's recognition that suffering, disease, madness even, were close to the heart of human experience; he knew Dostoyevsky's belief in a deep truth of the people, *narodnaya pravda*, that made conventional orthodoxies seem shallow; and he had his own conviction that the road to the universal was through the particular. All these ideas are woven into *A Drunk Man*, which shows Dostoyevsky's influence not only here but more openly in the four moving stanzas in which he addresses Dostoyevsky directly:

> The wan leafs shak' atour us like the snaw.
> Here is the cavaburd in which Earth's tint.
> There's naebody but Oblivion and us,
> Puir gangrel buddies, waunderin' hameless in't.
>
> The stars are larochs o' auld cottages,
> An a' Time's glen is fu' o blinnin' stew.
> Nae freenly lozen skimmers: and the wund
> Rises and separates even me and you.
>
> I ken nae Russian and you ken nae Scots.
> We canna tell oor voices frae the wund.
> The snaw is seekin' everywhere: oor herts
> At least like roofless ingles it has f'und,
>
> And gethers there in drift on endless drift,
> Oor broken herts that it can never fill;
> And still—its leafs like snaw, its growth like wund—
> The thistle rises and forever will.

The sloganizing implications of this last line are immediately denied by what follows in the poem, a sardonic reflection that

the thistle rises over the buried generations, a monument 'o a'
they were, and a' they hoped and wondered'. But I cannot here
trace the interweaving ideas and changes of mood in *A Drunk
Man* and relate them to its overall pattern. I wish simply to
suggest that the important influence of Dostoyevsky, whose
concept of Russia, that so stirred MacDiarmid, was essentially
religious, is one of many clues to the essentially religious nature
of the poem. The influence, too, of Solovyov and of the mystic
pan-Slavist Russian poet Fyodor Tyutchev with his belief in
the ultimate eloquence of silence, shows how responsive Mac-
Diarmid was to ideas that were deeply at variance with the
materialism (however 'dialectic') that he intermittently professed. Yet the sceptical voice of ordinary experience is never
shut out altogether: it has the last word at the end of this remarkable visionary poem when the poet's wife comments with ironic
matter-of-factness on his eloquent concluding words:

> Yet ha'e I silence left, the croon o' a'.
>
> No' her, wha on the hills langsyne I saw
> Liftin' a foreheid o' perpetual snaw.
>
> No' her, wha in the how-dumb-deid o' nicht
> Kyths, like Eternity in Time's despite.
>
> No' her, withooten shape, wha's name is Daith,
> No' Him, unkennable abies to faith
>
> —God whom, gin e'er He saw a man, 'ud be
> E'en mair dumfooner'd at the sicht than he.
>
> —But Him, whom nocht in man or Deity,
> Or Daith or Dreid or Laneliness can touch,
> *Wha's deed owre often and has seen owre much.*
>
> O I ha'e Silence left,
>
>   —'And weel ye micht,'
> Sae Jean'll say, 'efter sic a nicht!'

It was MacDiarmid's experience during his life on the island
of Whalsey that prompted in him a further movement in his
quasi-mystical quest for an expression of reality. The sheer
objective otherness of stones and rocks on a lonely coast challenged him to enquire into the relation between a human
observer and the stark reality of an unmoved and unmoving
external nature. Is the earth a reflection of God's glory, as a
Psalmist thought? Is there an inherent relationship between the

world of Nature and the mind of man, as Wordsworth proclaimed? How does the physical world of Nature exist and is
its existence related to man's observation of it?

  These are the questions that lie at the heart of MacDiarmid's
other great long poem—written in English this time, or in a sort
of English, not Scots—*On a Raised Beach*. The poem opens with
what Buthlay has called 'a great pile of stony words' massively
challenging in their geological otherness. The word one wants
here is not 'lapidary', because it is not that kind of stone that is
involved, but a word deriving from the Latin *saxum* rather than
lapis, like the Latin *saxosus* for which there is no English equivalent (though Darwin took over the late Latin *saxigenus*, meaning
'sprung from rock', to produce *saxigenous*, which he used in the
sense of 'producing rocks'). I think MacDiarmid would have
been pleased to have the opening of this poem called saxigenous
rather than lapidary. In this extraordinary piling of little-known
words that forces the reader to face with questioning wonder
the meaning of stoniness in the natural world, MacDiarmid
lays down the text, as it were, of which *On a Raised Beach* is a
meditation. He tries to find a way round the indifference of
Nature, to achieve by sheer intensity of vision and power of
expression some kind of *tertium quid* in which man and Nature,
the observer and the observed, can somehow be integrated. It
is possible to interpret the poem in such a way that the poet is
seen as having achieved this; but the terrifying neutrality of the
geological world comes over more strongly.

> We must be humble. We are so easily baffled by appearances
> And do not realise that these stones are one with the stars.
> It makes no difference to them whether they are high or low,
> Mountain peak or ocean floor, palace, or pigsty.
> There are plenty of ruined buildings in the world but no
>   ruined stones.

All the ideas that men have evolved throughout the ages can be
countered by opposing ideas; but the stones remain there.

> It is essential to know the chill of all the objections
> That come creeping into the mind, the battle between opposing
>   ideas
> Which gives the victory to the strongest and most universal
> Over all others, and to wage it to the end
> With increasing freedom, precision, and detachment

A detachment that shocks our instincts and ridicules our desires.
All else in the world cancels out, equal, capable
Of being replaced by other things (even as all the ideas
That madden men now must lose their potency in a few years
And be replaced by others—even as all the religions,
All the material sacrifices and moral restraints,
That in twenty thousand years have brought us no nearer to God
Are irrelevant to the ordered adjustments
Out of the reach of perceptive understanding
Forever taking place on the Earth and in the unthinkable regions
   around it;
This cat's cradle of life; this reality volatile yet determined;
This intense vibration in the stones
That make them seem immobile to us)
But the world cannot dispense with the stones.
They alone are not redundant. Nothing can replace them
Except a new creation of God.

And again:

These stones go through Man, straight to God, if there is one.
What have they not gone through already?
Empires, civilizations, aeons. Only in them
If in anything, can His creation confront Him.

Such a thought is part of what I have called elsewhere Mac-
Diarmid's trans-humanism. In some of his most characteristic
moods he does not see man as using Nature and becoming at
one with it, but Nature as the eternal otherness to which man
must reconcile himself:

What happens to us
Is irrelevant to the world's geology
But what happens to the world's geology
Is not irrelevant to us.
We must reconcile ourselves to the stones,
Not the stones to us.

Yet the stones seem to have a lesson for man, suggesting that
he might by an effort of the will achieve a similarly pure rock-
like identity:

It is a frenzied and chaotic age,
Like a growth of weeds on the site of a demolished building.
How shall we set ourselves against it,

Imperturbable, inscrutable, in the world and yet not in it,
   Silent under the torment it inflicts upon us,
      With a constant centre,
With a single inspiration, foundations firm and invariable;
   By what immense exercise of will,
Inconceivable discipline, courage, and endurance,
     Self-purification and anti-humanity,
       Be ourselves without interruption,
         Adamantine and inexorable?
It will be ever increasingly necessary to find
In the interests of all mankind
Men capable of rejecting all that all other men
   Think, as a stone remains
Essential to the world, inseparable from it,
   And rejects all other life yet.

MacDiarmid's thought moved more and more towards the
notion that some kind of anti-humanity was the mark of the
true genius, and that the transcending of ordinary human concerns through intensity of cold vision was the aim to be sought.
If, as this strange and powerful poem works itself out, the poet
reconciles himself with the stones, it is not only a reconciliation
with some kind of objective sublimity; it is also reconciliation
with death:

I lift a stone; it is the meaning of life I clasp
Which is death, for that is the meaning of death;
How else does any man yet participate
   In the life of a stone,
How else can any man yet become
Sufficiently at one with creation, sufficiently alone,
Till as the stone that covers him he lies dumb
And the stone at the mouth of his grave is not overthrown?
—Each of these stones on this raised beach,
   Every stone in the world,
Covers infinite death . . . .

But the poem does not end on this note; it concludes with a
return to the deliberately difficult vocabulary of the opening
lines to celebrate some kind of cosmic harmony which unites
the poet, the poem, and the natural world. In quoting these last
lines I should explain that 'diallage' is a term in rhetoric indi-
cating the bringing together of different arguments to bear

upon one point; 'auxesis' means 'hyperbole'; 'ébrillade' is
a check given to a horse's bridle by a jerk on the rein; 'enchorial'
refers to the popular writing of the ancient Egyptians (as distinct from 'hieroglyphics', the sacred writing); 'futhorc' is the
Runic alphabet; 'encrinite' is a fossil; 'entrochal' refers to
certain wheel-shaped fossils; and 'epanadiplosis' is a sentence
that begins and ends with the same word. MacDiarmid uses
these unusual words, culled from the dictionary, to indicate the
effort to be made to achieve the final vision through language.
The poem itself is seen as a great rhetorical debate, from which
in the end emerges a resolution that is almost beyond expression:

> Diallage of the world's debate, end of the long auxesis,
> Although no ébrillade of Pegasus can here avail,
> I prefer your enchorial characters—the futhorc of the future—
> To the hieroglyphics of all the other forms of Nature.
> Song, your apprentice encrinite, seems to sweep
> The Heavens with a vast entrochal movement;
> And with the same word that began it, closes
> Earth's vast epanadiplosis.

There are so many other MacDiarmids. There is the gleeful
abuser of those he considers his political and cultural enemies,
the expert in the old Scottish tradition of flyting; there is the
simple propagandist, the versifying journalist; there is the great
plagiarist who chops into lines of verse long articles by others;
there is the poet who in his last years spent so much time writing
verse about 'the kind of poetry I want', the poetry of fact, of
science, of technology, a poetry which recognizes and comes to
terms with all the concepts developed by modern science,
a poetry that takes account of all literatures and all languages,
a poetry that does everything at once while at the same time
recognizing and celebrating the quiddity of everything idiosyncratic and individual, a poetry both concrete and visionary, an
impossible poetry. MacDiarmid was capable of the most appalling McGonagall-like doggerel as well as of those marvellously
wrought Scots lyrics and so much else. What are we to make of
it all? A questing, self-contradictory, multifaceted, un-self-
critical poet, MacDiarmid belongs essentially to the company
of visionary poets which includes Dante, John of the Cross,
and Blake. He would have passionately denied this, in some

moods at least, and perhaps agreed in others. In his discursive
long poem *In Memoriam James Joyce* he talks of

> this notorious conflict
> Between the 'intellectual love' of the universe as it is
> And the moral will that it should be other,
> Concluding that perhaps the only solution
> Lies in the faith, or the mystical perception,
> That the welter of frustration in the parts
> Is instrumental to some loftier perfection
> In the universe as a whole?
>
> Ah! no, no! Intolerable end
> To one who set out to be independent of faith
> And of mystical perception.
> It does not after all seem certain
> That the peace I have found is entirely
> Free from mystical elements.

This quizzical, self-questioning discovery that he has found
a peace that is not without mystical elements is not quite Dante's
'E la sua volontate e nostra pace', and seems even less so when
it is expressed in this discursive kind of conversational verse. In
Dante, the artist, the visionary, and the purveyor of doctrine
are totally assimilated. In MacDiarmid they are very often
separate, and we can turn from this statement *about* his achievement of peace that is perhaps not entirely free from mystical
elements to the vision itself, as expressed in 'Moonstruck' or
'The Eemis Stane' or as emerging from *A Drunk Man Looks at
the Thistle*. These show very clearly that MacDiarmid belongs
with those poets who seek truth through the cosmic vision, a
vision rooted in immediately realized experience yet reaching
out to eternity. That this can also be said of Edwin Muir, a
poet so different in temper and technique, is a testimony to the
rich potential of the visionary tradition in our poetry.

C.S. Lewis used to maintain that there was a species called Old Western Man which began to die out at the time of the Industrial Revolution and was almost extinct by the mid-twentieth century. A primary function of literary study, he argued, was to enable the successors of this species to recapture assumptions underlying the view of the world held by Old Western Man so that they could appreciate the literature based on it. I never heard Professor Lewis argue that the modern student should be persuaded to *share* those assumptions (though he himself did, and argued persuasively in their defence); only that he should learn to know and appreciate them. Of course there were many differences of belief even among members of that almost extinct species, for what characterized Lewis's Old Western Man was not a specific creed but a broad view of the part played by the numinous in human affairs, in general what I suppose could be called a religious view of the universe.

I think we all know what C.S. Lewis meant, and there is a certain truth in his view, although I find it hard to believe that Sappho, Lucretius, Dante, and Montaigne—to pick out only a few examples—belonged to a common species of the kind he had in mind. The question is: assuming that older writers had their thought and imagination rooted in beliefs that we cannot share, how do we appreciate the literature they produce? If we believe that a general numinous view of the universe, in whatever specific set of beliefs it manifested itself, is enough to produce a community of imaginative understanding, then perhaps we can understand how poets like Dante and Spenser and Milton were able to incorporate effortlessly into their profoundly Christian imaginative apparatus much of the mythology of the classical world. But even this is to accept an oversimplified version of cultural history. Great writers can stand in differing relations to the mythology or theology they use: Euripides' handling of Greek mythology was very different from that of Sophocles, and in neither of those dramatists was the question of belief relevant in the way it was for Christian writers of the Christian centuries. The Homeric gods had a different status from that of the Christian God; belief in their central reality and omnipotence was not a proof of virtue or a pre- requisite to salvation. You could with Milton and others regard pagan gods as the later form taken by the fallen angels in their attempt to deceive mankind, but this does not explain how the young Milton could write an Ovidian Latin poem to his former tutor in Hebrew, the Presbyterian divine Thomas Young, then chaplain to the English merchants in Hamburg, which opened like this:

> Curre per immensum subito, mea littera, pontum;
>   I, pete Teutonicos laeve per aequor agros;
> Segnes rumpe moras, et nil, precor, obstet eunti,
>   Et festinantis nil remoretur iter.
> Ipse ego Sicanio fraenantem carcere ventos
>   Aeolon, et virides sollicitabo Deos,
> Caeruleamque suis comitatem Dorida Nymphis,
>   Ut tibi dent placidam per sua regna viam.
> At tu, si poteris, celeres tibi sume iugales,
>   Vecta quibus Colchis fugit ab ore viri;
> Aut queis Triptolemus Scythicas devenit in oras,
>   Gratus Eleusina missus ab urbe puer.

Run over the boundless ocean swiftly, o my letter; go and seek Teutonic lands over the smooth sea. Brook no delay and, I beg you, let nothing prevent your going or hold back the speed of your journey: I myself will offer prayers to Aeolus, who bridles the winds in his Sicanian cave, and to the green gods and to blue-eyed Doris, accom- panied by her Nymphs, that they may give you a quiet journey through their kingdoms. And acquire for yourself if you can the swift team by which the Colchian was borne away when fleeing from the face of her husband or that by which the boy Triptolemus reached the Scythian shores, a welcome messenger from the Eleusinian city.

There are echoes here of Ovid's story (deriving originally from Homer) of Aeolus, son of Hippotas, who kept the winds locked up in a cave on an island; of Ovid's descriptoin of the sea-gods (*virides deos*); of Hesiod's story of the Oceanid Doris, mother of the Nereids (whose father was the sea-god Nereus); of the story of Medea ('the Colchian') as told by Euripides; and of Ovid's story of how Ceres sent Tripolemus in her chariot from Eleusis in Attica to sow the world with wheat, as far as Scythia. And this in a letter from an eighteen-year-old Christian poet to a

Puritan divine who was to play an active part in the pamphlet war against episcopacy! Clearly, Old Western Man had a lot of latitude.

The whole question of Christian attitudes to classical literature and mythology is a fascinating part of the cultural history of the West, into which I cannot now enter. I wish merely to emphasize that there *was* an accommodation which involved acceptance at different levels. One can distinguish the varieties of acceptance found in medieval literature from those found in Renaissance literature: in the former there is almost a folk element in the way in which, say, the Troy story was seen and handled by poets; the orts and fragments of the classical world lay scattered amid the Christian imaginings. But from at least as early as the sixteenth century we find a much more culturally exhibitionist use of non-Christian classical material, which had by now acquired a prestige and was handled by authors with a self-consciousness neither of which is easily found earlier. Poets could be aware in quite a sophisticated way of the symbolic function of non-Christian myth, and when Milton drew on such material in *Paradise Lost* he knew what he was doing. The fruit in the Garden of Eden

> Burnisht with Golden Rind
> Hung amiable, *Hesperian* fables true,
> If true, here only . . . .

It is one thing, however, to find a way of integrating into a Christian poem characters, scenes, and images from pagan classical mythology in order to utilize their symbolic or suggestive or even merely decorative potential. It is something else when one is dealing with the reaction of a reader to a work of the literary imagination rooted in a set of assumptions about the way the world is governed and the forces that govern it that are totally at variance with his own beliefs and attitudes. We know in fact that such a reader can find immense satisfaction in such works, that, shall we say, a modern humanist agnostic can be deeply moved by Dante's *Divina Commedia* or Donne's Divine Sonnets or Hopkins's religious poems. One can go further, and say that someone brought up in a tradition that finds the religious attitudes of some poets not only unacceptable but positively menacing can nevertheless read them with deep appreciation. What is there about imaginative literature and especially about poetry which liberates the reader from his personal beliefs and enables him to enter into the imaginative world of the poet not just with tolerance but with positive joy? The question applies to the Christian's appreciation of Homer and Sophocles and Virgil as much as to the non-Christian's appreciation of Dante and Donne.

One could of course answer the question simply by saying that one appreciates the *art*, the literary skill, the selection and ordering of image and symbol, the structural pattern, and that we get an aesthetic pleasure out of our awareness of these that bears no relation to what might be called the work's ideological content. This seems to me facile. It is true that we appreciate all these elements, but they are intimately bound up with the illumination of experience which the poem communicates. In certain kinds of literary exercise and verbal play we can appreciate an ingenious rhyme-scheme, a complex stanza structure, a clever use of words, and so on, regardless of the total impact of the work on our mind and imagination. But surely nobody says that Dante is a great poet merely because of the skill with which he handles *terza rima* or that Milton's poetic stature derives only from the movement of his blank verse or the sound of his language, or that we enjoy George Herbert's poems just for their ingenious pattern. In a work of poetic art of any significance such factors are elements in a greater whole. But how are they elements in a greater whole and what is that whole?

We can take Matthew Arnold's way out, and distinguish between poetry and history, poetry and fact, accepting for example the Bible as poetry, as emotion-inducing literature which produces in us elevated states of feeling without telling us what is necessarily true in any literal sense, and we can follow this with I.A. Richards's development of the same view by distinguishing between emotive and referential meaning, maintaining that poetry deals only with the former and without presenting us with anything for us to believe builds up in us states of consciousness which are harmonious and therefore psychologically valuable. I don't believe this will do either. Nor will Coleridge's 'willing suspension of disbelief' solve the problem, for that is surely too negative a description of the way in which we accept great poetry: we do more than suspend our disbelief when we read Psalm 23 or Vaughan's Ascension Hymn ('They are all gone into the world of light').

It seems to me that literature differs from music and from abstract visual art in that it does not present us with pure form, to which we respond with aesthetic pleasure, but brings form to bear on a communication which, while not adequately and sometimes not at all paraphrasable in other terms, is nevertheless a communication; it says something—says it memorably, uniquely, movingly, even disturbingly, but it does say something. What it says illuminates experience for us not discursively but intensively and disconcertingly and deeply personally. We may resist the illumination; we may find it distressing (has anyone ever *not* found *Othello* distressing?) or we may find it reassuring or exciting or benedictory or revelatory in some deeply convincing way. How can this happen if we do not share the basic beliefs of the poet whose work we are reading?

Before trying to answer this question let me make some distinctions. A reader of a poem, or indeed of any literary work, written in a tradition with which he is not familiar, will require information about that tradition before he is in a position to read it properly. Students today, largely ignorant of the vast background of biblical and classical knowledge which not only lies behind Milton's *Paradise Lost* but is used as part of the common stock of reference and allusion in the great bulk of our literature until quite recent times, will need to learn the kinds of facts which are, for example, presented in modern annotated editions of Shakespeare or Milton or for that matter Tennyson. There are also symbolic conventions comparable to iconographic traditions in painting that have to be learned about after they have ceased to be part of the accepted cultural background of the age. In other words, readers of works written in a tradition that is no longer living in the culture around them must be prepared to do some homework if they are to understand fully the language in which such works are written and are to be capable of responding to the suggestions, overtones, and resonances that are what give literary expression its characteristic power.

All this, however, is but the preliminary recovery of the text, comparable to learning Homeric Greek if we are to be able to read Homer in the original. We might add to this the

acquisition of knowledge of rhetorical devices at one time so
carefully employed and cunningly wrought but now unrecog-
nizable by most of us because we are unaware of the rhetorical
traditions on which they are based; without such knowledge we
may be unable to respond to effects on which the total impact of
the meaning depends. But having learned all this, where do we
stand? If we do not share the Psalmist's faith or Dante's theology or Herbert's concept of a personal God or Hopkins's sense
of God's presence in Nature, how do we receive the communication which is their poetry?

   I shall try and answer this question indirectly. When I was a
boy, brought up in a orthodox rabbinical Jewish family in Edinburgh, I knew a number of devout old men who would regularly
mumble through the Psalms in Hebrew at high speed—*zog
tillim* was the Yiddish expression—as a pious exercise. It
was almost as though the Psalms consisted of magic formulas
that were to be recited as such, rather than relished as moving
expressions of awe or wonder or anguish or devotion. Again,
when I was a boy we used to sing before the grace after meals
on sabbaths and festivals Psalm 126, to a rather melancholy
tum-ti-tum tune. Psalm 126 is a strange and haunting psalm,
beginning with an expression of trance-like wonder at the ending of the Babylonian captivity, going on to express joy in what
God has done for his people in bringing them back from exile,
then rising to a great plea to God. 'Turn our captivity O Lord
like the streams of the south.' שׁוּבָה is the imperative of the
verb שׁוּב, which can mean turn, return, turn round, convert, repent, recall, restore. What is the Psalmist saying here?
The captivity has already been ended: the very first sentence of
the psalm begins 'When the Lord turned the captivity of Zion'.
What is the meaning, then, of this plea? The psalm concludes:
'They that sow in tears shall reap in joy. Though he goeth on
his way weeping, bearing the store of seed, he shall come back
with joy, bearing his sheaves.' The English version is incapable
of conveying the force of the peculiar Hebrew idiom that uses
two forms of the verb together to give the action described a
special intensity, but even in English we get some impression of
the extraordinary picture of the triumph of hope over grief that
is presented here—indeed, it seems to me a classic expression,

eloquent in its fine economy of utterance, of the will to believe in the future in spite of everything.

הַזֹּרְעִים בְּדִמְעָה בְּרִנָּה יִקְצֹרוּ: הָלֹךְ יֵלֵךְ וּבָכֹה נֹשֵׂא מֶשֶׁךְ־הַזָּרַע בֹּא־יָבֹא בְרִנָּה נֹשֵׂא אֲלֻמֹּתָיו

Yet it is mysterious, for the psalm has opened by describing the mood of incredulous gratitude after the return from captivity ('we were like those that dream'). Why the appeal to God to 'turn' the captivity and what does it mean? Why the contrast between present sorrow and future joy? I do not know; this seems to me a very mysterious and a very wonderful poem about the relationship between despair and hope in human experience and I cannot now read it without being deeply, almost uncannily, moved.

But when we sang it before the grace after meals it was the mere routine expression of religious duty. None of us round the table gave a thought to the psalm's emotion and mystery any more than the pious old men who gabbled through the whole Book of Psalms at high speed recognized for a moment that they were reciting some of the greatest lyrics in the history of world literature. I discovered the haunting beauty of Psalm 126 years after I ceased singing it as a religious exercise. Reading it slowly, submitting myself to its expression, responding to the rise and fall of the emotion, wondering about the paradox at the core of it, I learned to appreciate it as a poem. Did I ask myself as I read it whether I really believed that God had personally brought his people back from their Babylonian exile or even whether I could believe in a personal God of the kind postulated by the Psalmist? I did not, for I did not need to. The communication transcended the specific beliefs that underlay it. I would go further: only when I was in a position to free my reading of the psalm from any question of acquiescence in the Psalmist's system of belief was I able to appreciate the full richness of what it said. Thus it would seem that far from the inability of a reader to share the author's beliefs preventing him from appreciating a poem, such an inability can liberate the reader to see the poem as something more than a document of faith. It might even be argued that the medieval Christian who read the *Divina Commedia* got less out of it than later readers who might not have shared Dante's specific beliefs but who were able to respond to the poetic exploration of the paradoxes of human experience that the poem presents as it moves.

Why should this be so? Perhaps a system of belief as used in a work of literature is—whether the author intended it or not, and generally he did not—a groundwork patterning of ideas about ultimate matters that can be used to sustain a structure of meanings, suggestions, resonances, overtones, that reach out far beyond the limits of that belief to enrich and illuminate our awareness of some aspects of the human condition. I am not saying that we must allegorize Homer's gods or treat Dante's theology as just his tentative way of expressing paradoxes and mysteries. In great literature belief is a kind of *language*, and language is a means of communication, not an element in a creed. Openness to language is the mark of the sensitive reader, and such openness includes readiness to accept any system of beliefs that allows a writer of skill and imagination to use it in treating a work of literary art. Such art, as I have insisted, is, for all its formal qualities, a *communication*, which illuminates an area of experience for the reader in ways quite undefinable outside that particular work of art. The communication authenticates itself by its achievement of an increasingly reverberating meaning, not by the literal truth of any assumption taken for granted by the author while he is writing. We may receive no such reverberations from a poem written by someone with whose beliefs we are in complete agreement, just as we may perceive powerful reverberations in works written by authors in a tradition of belief which we cannot share. Sharing the tradition of belief with the poet may well inhibit an adequately rich reading. Devout evangelicals who read *Paradise Lost* along with the Bible were not the most sensitive readers of Milton's epic and much in it was closed to them. We can appreciate devotion in a devotional poem by Donne or Herbert or Hopkins, but if we read the poet as a simple act of devotion on our part we may be cutting ourselves off from full response to it, as the case of the pious gabbler of the Psalms and my own experience of Psalm 126 illustrate. If I may add a further personal note, my experience as someone brought up in an orthodox Jewish family yet who from childhood has had a passionate love affair with English poetry, so much of it deeply rooted in Christian faith, certainly shows that one *can* appreciate literature based on beliefs one does not share.

None of the points I have just made or the examples I have given and will give destroys the case for the preliminary homework to establish what might be called the emotional grammar of the work under consideration. It is true that in some cases a deep charge of meaning can flow out of a work to a reader who has not done his homework, and I have found this happening in some of the Psalms and in some medieval lyrics, among other poems. But in general we must learn the language and the grammar employed by a given poet if we are to read the poem with any degree of adequacy regardless of our personal beliefs.

The problem with Christian faith is that it demands more than many other systems of belief. One can appreciate Homer and Virgil without being in the least troubled by one's failure to believe in their gods, because belief is not really an issue; the gods are characters in a story and have a similar status to other characters in the story. Christian faith demands more than this; but even so non-Christians can accept this faith as it works through the poem if it works, as I suggested, as a language. Of course there are intrusive moments in some works of literature where the reader simply recoils and is unable to move beyond to the total pattern of meaning because of his hostility to some specific attitude or belief revealed explicitly by the writer. I confess I sometimes feel this in some of Ezra Pound's *Cantos*, when I find the thought so personally offensive that I cannot go further and look for anything else. Perhaps that is a weakness in Pound; perhaps if thoughts were really viable as supports for a rich poetic expressiveness they would not intrude and offend in this way; or perhaps the fact is that there are some issues to which we are so sensitive—perhaps with good reason—that when they are treated in ways repugnant to our own thought and feeling we can go no further with that literary work. I think we must all have had this kind of experience.

There have of course always been objections to works of imaginative literature voiced by those who considered that such literature involved 'feigning', telling lies, making up things that never in fact occurred, or exploiting personal emotion when such emotion should not be exploited but disciplined. The Platonic objection, the objection of some of the early Church fathers, the Puritan objection, were deeply rooted in notions of truth and spiritual health. Generations of critics from Aristotle on have set themselves the task of answering these objections, and I do not propose to rehearse their arguments. I should like simply to point to the achievement of imaginative literature of a great number of kinds and periods of civilization in exploring and illuminating the bafflingly mixed human condition. Man in the green world of nature; finite and fallible man set in a world he never made to cope with that world, with his fellow men, with the conflicting drives of his own nature; man with his hopes and fears and compulsions and yearnings; man with his restless curiosity, his drive towards myth-making, his need for forms and rituals, his difficulty in coming to terms with his own mortality—all this is reflected in the poetry he produces and any myth, any creed, any set of values, which copes with this human situation, which engages with it so as to move and illuminate those who respond to it, which is viable as a mode of rendering reality as it is humanly experienced, can be of service to poetry. The truth of poetry, as distinct from that of philosophy or theology, is self-authenticating. Other truths or alleged truths can be argued about, there can be proofs and disproofs, believers and unbelievers, demonstrations that this theory or that is the reflection of social and economic structure or in some way a projection of self-interest; but poetry operates differently. As it weaves its cumulative meaning through the use of all the resources of language, with image, symbol, cadence, rhythm, pattern, structure, as well as propositional meaning all playing their part in building up the reverberating whole, it gets behind belief to the human dilemmas that belief arose to cope with, even though it may be ostensibly basing itself on a given belief.

It might be argued that some beliefs are not viable for poetry, that they are altogether too narrow or that they too blatantly contradict experience to be available for the poetic imagination. Edwin Muir believed this, rather unfairly perhaps, about the Calvinist version of Christianity. This is how he put the matter in his book on John Knox:

Calvinism . . . was . . . a religion which outraged the imagination, and no doubt helped, therefore, to produce that captivity of the imagination in Scotland which was only broken in the eighteenth century. For this religion laid down that God had elected certain men for His approval from the beginning of time, and it was impossible to believe that His choice showed discrimination. Looking down on the Island of Great Britain in the century which followed Knox's death, the Almighty, it seemed, had rejected Shakespeare, Spenser, and Donne, and chosen Andrew Melville, Donald Cargill and Sandy Peden. And if His choice was restricted to the godly, it was equally strange, for He liked the translators of the Scots version of the Psalms, and rejected Herbert, Vaughan, and Crashaw. Passing over the cacophonous:

> I saw Eternity the other night,
> Like a great ring of pure and endless light,
> All calm, as it was bright,

He listened with rapture to the more truly Calvinistic music of

> But loved be God which doth us safely keep,
> From bloody teeth and their most cruel voice,
> Which as a prey to eat us would rejoice.[1]

This is unfair, and the heavy irony is misdirected. The three lines of bad verse that Muir quotes are not specifically Calvinist; some of the Scots versions of the Psalms were poetically crude, but the belief behind them was that of the original Psalmists, who were capable of great poetry. Alexander Hume, who wrote the beautifully chiselled poem describing a summer's day from dawn to dusk, 'Of the Day Estivall', was a Presbyterian minister and a Calvinist. For that matter, George Herbert was a Calvinist, as Joseph Summers in his book on the poet has quite conclusively shown. One must be careful not to dismiss too easily any specific creed on the grounds that it inhibits the imagination from creating poetry. The poetic imagination is a pretty tough faculty, and can wring the most surprising kinds of significance out of what at first sight may seem very unpromising material. I can think in fact of little that can be less promising as material for poetry than the theology employed by Milton in *Paradise Lost*, but, as I tried to illustrate in my second lecture, the poem goes round behind

[1] *John Knox, Portrait of a Calvinist*, by Edwin Muir, London, 1929, p. 308.

the theology, as it were, to develop unexpected meanings. Those who try to encourage readers to enjoy *Paradise Lost* by attempting to prove that Milton's theology was *right* are in fact directing readers to very limited aspects of the poem and risk alienating from the poem those readrs who cannot accept the arguments put forward. So far as university teaching goes, I would say that the teacher's responsibility is firstly to see that his students are in possession of the relevant knowledge to enable them to read the text properly, and secondly to demonstrate as sensitively as he can the way the poem's meaning reaches out to create its own complex of meaning and emotion that both makes contact with our experience and transcends it.

A test case of the relation between poetry and belief is W.B. Yeats, who erected a strange personal creed from a variety of sources, expounded it in his book *A Vision*, and proceeded to draw on that creed for symbols for his poetry. Scholars such as F.A.C. Wilson have analysed Yeats's creed and its sources in great detail and have explained individual poems and plays as though they are coded messages using the creed as a code-book. But if that is all they were, they would be curiosities rather than great poems. It is of course immensely helpful to know the sources of Yeats's symbolism and the meaning he intended to convey by the use of specific images. It is however the way the images work in the poem that make it a poem, not the fact that that they encipher a message. 'Byzantium' is a poem which draws throughout on the special imagery that Yeats based on his idiosyncratic system, and any serious student of Yeats wants to know what that system was. But the initial inducement to explore the poem further comes from the power and suggestiveness of the language as deployed in the poem as we have it, and that power and that suggestiveness go far beyond any simple decoding that can be provided by the student of Yeats's symbolic system and its sources. I remember when I first read 'Byzantium' I had no idea what it meant, but it moved and indeed possessed me in such a way that I could not leave it alone, and had to come back to it again and again, and to read other of Yeats's poems that threw light on it, until slowly its rich pattern of reverberating meaning began at least to outline itself. The final line

That dolphin-torn, that gong-tormented sea

echoes back into the poem with suggestions of the relation between human passions and the art that freezes them, and with committed reading and rereading we respond more and more to the complex of thought and feeling that the poem builds up. It is true that we can only respond to the poem with full appreciation when we have learned Yeats's language (which a reading of Yeats's other poems as well as his prose works and the works of commentators help to provide), but what drives us to want to learn the language is the certainty that there is something memorable there, a certainty that drives from a reading of the poem before any investigation has been done. Once we understand the system on which Yeats drew in organizing his imagery we can see that 'Byzantium' transcends it, so that the system becomes almost like a scaffolding that can be taken down when the work is finished and that the reader can ignore once he has used it.

Perhaps it is best to stand outside all closed systems of belief if we wish to be able to respond to the way the poet builds up meanings out of the system he believes in. In that way we are free to appreciate fully the way the language works and see the belief itself as part of the language. Perhaps it is the sceptic who is the one capable of the most generous response to poetry of different ages and cultures, the uncommitted open-minded eclectic observer of the varieties of human efforts to explain the contradictions and mysteries revealed by human experience. But the sceptic in this sense cannot be the mere observer. He does not stand outside human race but shares the dilemmas of those he responds to.

This kind of argument assumes a certain uniformity in human nature throughout the ages in spite of vast differences between the cultures of different periods. The critics and philosophers of the eighteenth century were confident that such uniformity existed and praised poets as different as Homer and Shakespeare for their knowledge of 'nature', by which they meant human nature. Later thinkers have been less certain that such uniformity exists and have been at pains to stress differences not only in beliefs and attitudes but in basic understanding of human life and its relation to its natural environment. C.S. Lewis's Old Western Man was, he believed radically different from his modern successor, who could only learn to appreciate Old Western Man's artistic achievements by a combination of scholarship and empathy. But underlying the differences diagnosed by Lewis, which are real and becoming increasingly real with every generation, there must be some points of contact without which all the erudition in the world could not yield the kind of appreciation of earlier literature that we know readers can and do achieve. What do they appreciate it *for*? When Matthew Arnold produced his famous touchstone theory of poetry, citing lines from Homer, Dante, and Shakespeare, responses to which he regarded as proof of their poetic greatness, he was trying to diagnose some profound contact with something at the heart of experience that could be suddenly produced by the way a thought or a situation was expressed.

It is fashionable to reject Arnold's touchstone theory which is often classed with such subjective theories of poetic value as that expressed by A.E. Housman in his lecture *The Name and Nature of Poetry*, where he said that when a line of poetry came into his head when he was shaving he could tell if it was genuine poetry by the way the hair on his skin bristled so that he risked cutting himself with his razor. Such views are rejected partly on the grounds that they ignore the structural element in poetry which makes it impossible to judge it on isolated lines and partly because they are held to be irrationally subjective, not involving any considered evaluation of the poem concerned. While we can accept these criticisms we must, I think, at the same time concede that there are moments in our reading of poetry when we experience that special kind of *frisson* that tells us we are engaging with an expression of some uniquely revelatory insight into some aspect of experience. Such insights can be found in literature of many different ages and many different traditions, and though it may be that we sometimes bring to our reading of such passages preconceptions that were foreign to the poet's cultural world, it is difficult to deny that there is some common human factor involved. If there were not, and if human experience was radically different in different ages, then the appreciation of poetry written in ages other than our own would be impossible. We could reconstruct through scholarship the world of the earlier poet but that would not in itself enable us to engage with it directly as poetry. There are some common factors that link Homer's and Shakespeare's and our world: what the Greeks called ἀνθρώπινον and the Romans translated as *humanum*, what derives from being human, do not differ in essentials. Or so it seems to me. We may be deceiving ourselves into seeing what is not there, but I do not think that we can be doing that all the time.

Where does this leave Old Western Man and our relation to him? Yes, there are great differences between post-industrial Western society and the societies that preceded it. Yes, we have a great deal to learn if we want to understand some of the basic attitudes and preconceptions of our forefathers. But the basic nature of the human predicament remains, and there comes a point at which we can respond with moving recognition to the poetic expression of an aspect of that predicament, from however alien a culture it may have emanated. There are always breaks between phases of culture and I am not sure whether the radical break diagnosed by C.S. Lewis is the most significant one, though I am sure that it is real. Great poetry carries beliefs into its language in such a way that it can achieve a communication transcending the bounds of those beliefs. But we must learn how to read it. In a simple, homogeneous culture where tradition has been transmitted unchanged for countless generations, responses to such manifestations as poetry and music are spontaneous and direct, or at least appear to be so because the training of each generation in its cultural symbols takes place as a matter of course. Our culture is more complicated; it has modulated from phase to phase in ways that leave gaps and discontinuities in spite of continuing factors; and in addition there are signficant differences in the cultural attitude of different classes. To understand the products of our culture we must be prepared to work, to learn, to cultivate empathy. Yet for all this there are sparks that can leap spontaneously across the generations, and it is poetry that often produces them.

Let me conclude with three examples of poems which resound across the centuries to speak movingly even to those who may not share the poet's faith or basic attitudes. The first is from a poem by the great late-medieval Scottish poet William Dunbar on Christ's resurrection and triumph: nothing could

be more specifically and doctrinally Christian than this. But
the impact of the poem, with the rhetorical strength of its
simple yet majestic language and its solemn Latin refrain, *Sur-
rexit Dominus de sepulchro*, 'the Lord had risen from the tomb',
goes below its doctrinal base to make contact with the deepest
human yearnings for comfort, for rituals of reassurance, for the
triumph of good over evil. I quote only the first and last
stanzas:

> Done is a battell on the dragon blak;
> Our campioun Cryst confoindit hes his force:
> The ʒettis of hell ar brokin with a crak,
> The signe triumphall rasit is of the croce,
> The divillis trymmillis with hiddous voce,
> The salulis ar borrowit and to the bliss can go,
> Chryst with his blud our ransonis dois indoce:
> *Surrexit Dominus de sepulchro.* . . .

> The fo is chasit, the battell is done ceis,
> The presone brokin, the jevellouris fleit and flemit;
> The weir is gon, confermit is the peis,
> The fetteris lowsit and the dungeoun temit,
> The ransoun maid, the presoneris redemit;
> The feild is win, ourcumin is the fo,
> Dispulit of the tresur that he ʒemit:
> *Surrexit Dominus de sepulchro.*

I am now going further back in time, to an ode of Horace
whose last stanza has haunted me ever since I first read it as a
schoolboy. It is the fifth ode of Book III, telling the story of
Regulus, the Roman made prisoner of war in Carthage and
released to return to Rome to discuss peace terms on condition
that should satisfactory terms not be reached he would return
to Carthage to face his fate there: the story went that he volun-
tarily returned to torture and death. Now the kind of patriotic
self-sacrifice celebrated by this poem is not something I consider edifying or indeed very real, and the ode's opening assertion of the kingship of Jove and the divine quality of Augustus
hardly strikes sympathetic chords in me. Yet the concluding
stanzas of the poem, describing Regulus pushing aside those
who would hinder his departure and setting out from Rome to
Carthage, where he knew he would meet torture and death, as
though he were a lawyer going off into the country after the

conclusion of a tedious case in court, produces exactly the effect
of Arnold's touchstones or of Housman's beard-bristling lines.
It has something to do with the quiet specification of place.
Regulus moves away, like a tired lawyer leaving court for the
Venafran fields or Lacedaemonian Tarentum:

> quam si clientum longa negotia
> diudicata lite relinqueret
> tendens Venefranos in agros
> aut Lacaedomium Tarentum.

The poem dies away in the naming of these places, which
somehow suggest the rhythms of ordinary life lying behind
and below this example of heroic self-sacrifice. This gentle
anchoring of the poem in the quotidian through the simple act
of naming, with the language flowing in the gently rocking
rhythms of the Alcaic metre, I find hauntingly memorable. I
never consciously memorized the lines, but they have stayed in
my memory for over fifty years. When I walked down the Via
Appia Antica in Rome for the first time in the early 1960s,
these lines came suddenly into my head with most moving
force.

My last example comes from even further back. It is a poem
—and it *is* a poem, though not generally thought of as one—
which represents the old Hebrew priestly blessing. It invokes
God with total confidence and authority. Its incantatory rhythms create a sense of communicating assurance of well-being
and peace. It is, in a way, what we all want— a totally certain
invocation, by someone whose communally agreed role it is to
utter it, of divine good for us. When my father addressed a boy
celebrating his bar mitzvah in the synagogue he always ended
with these resonant Hebrew words of blessing:

> יְבָרֶכְךָ יְיָ וְיִשְׁמְרֶךָ
>
> יָאֵר יְיָ פָּנָיו אֵלֶיךָ וִיחֻנֶּךָ
>
> יִשָּׂא יְיָ פָּנָיו אֵלֶיךָ וְיָשֵׂם לְךָ שָׁלוֹם:

May the Lord bless you and keep you.
May the Lord make his face to shine upon you and be
   gracious unto you.
May the Lord turn his face to you and grant you peace.

The power and beauty of these benedictory words transcend
any question of belief in a personal God. The cadence of the
repetitions, the incantatory effect, the sense of transmitting a
force for good through an intermediary, the simple finality of
that resting of the last word shalom, peace—this is poetry,
spoken poetry, that goes behind and beyond questions of belief
to express the universal yearning for reassurance and for some
kind of personal relationship with the giver of that reassurance.
Matthew Arnold said that more and more people would turn to
poetry 'to interpret life for us, to console us, to sustain us',[2] I
doubt if his prophecy has been fulfilled to the degree that he
anticipated. But poetry *can* have these functions, and this
ancient priestly blessing can still console and sustain even those
who do not share the faith of those who first framed it. The
poetry of Old Western Man—and for that matter of Old
Middle-Eastern Man—can still speak to us across the ages.

---

[2] *The Study of Poetry*, 1880.

INDEX